ULTIMATE
DOG

ULTIMATE
DOG

DAVID TAYLOR

BVMS, FRCVS

COMMISSIONED PHOTOGRAPHY BY

DAVE KING • JANE BURTON

LONDON, NEW YORK, MELBOURNE,
MUNICH, DELHI

Original edition (1990)
Project Editors: Sharon Lucas, Maria Pal
Project Art Editor: Gillian Shaw
Editor: Richard Williams
Designer: Sally Ann Hibbard
Managing Editor: Vicky Davenport
Managing Art Editor: Colin Walton

This edition
FOR DORLING KINDERSLEY
Senior Editor: Simon Tuite
Senior Art Editor: Joanne Doran
Managing Editor: Deirdre Headon
Managing Art Editor: Lee Griffiths
DTP Designer: Louise Waller
Production Manager: Lauren Britton
Production Controller: Kevin Ward
Picture Researcher: Diana Morris
Picture Library: Claire Bowers

FOR SANDS PUBLISHING SOLUTIONS
Project Editors: David & Sylvia Tombesi-Walton
Project Art Editor: Simon Murrell

Produced for Dorling Kindersley by
Sands Publishing Solutions
4 Jenner Way, Eccles, Aylesford, Kent ME20 7SQ

2 4 6 8 10 9 7 5 3 1

First published in Great Britain in 1990
by Dorling Kindersley Limited,
80 Strand, London, WC2R 0RL

Penguin Group

Reprinted 1993 (twice), 1994 (twice),
1995, 1996, 1997
This revised edition 2005

Illustrations copyright © 1990, 2005
Dorling Kindersley Limited, London
Text copyright © 1990, 2005 David Taylor

A CIP catalogue record for this book is available
from the British Library.

ISBN 1-7513-3394-8

Colour reproduction by Colourscan, Singapore
Printed and bound in China by Toppan Printing Co. Ltd

Discover more at
www.dk.com

Contents

The Essential Dog

The most popular pet worldwide is the domestic dog, or *Canis familiaris*. The relationship between dog and man is that of two more-or-less carnivorous mammals that have worked, played, and endured together for 10,000 years.

Man has employed dogs in a variety of ways – as guards, guides, hunters, and rodent controllers, as well as providers of hair and meat. Today, around six million pet dogs are kept in Britain and at least 50 million in the US. There are about 400 breeds. Their sizes and shapes vary enormously, but all dogs are essentially the same animal. They range from something as tiny as the Yorkshire Terrier from Lancashire, England, that weighed just 113 g (4 oz) at two years of age, to an Old English Mastiff named Zorba who, in 1989, tipped the scales at 155 kg (343 lb). They are resilient, adaptable creatures, and evolution has not altered them much.

The number of breeds means there will always be one just right for you. Whatever you choose, if treated with care and intelligence, a dog will repay your kindness in companionship and affection. It may even become your best friend.

LONG-LASTING FRIENDSHIP Of all his domestic animals, man has had the closest and most enduring relationship with the dog. As St Bernard wrote in the 12th century, "Who loves me will love my dog also".

Origins and Domestication

About 60 million years ago, a small mammal rather like a weasel or polecat clambered through the primeval forests. Its name was *Miacis* and it was the ancestor of the group of animals that we call canids: the dog, jackal, wolf, and fox family.

Unlike modern dogs, which walk on their toes, *Miacis* was flat-footed. It had a carnivore's teeth and a smallish brain but was more intelligent than its contemporaries, the creodonts, another group of primitive meat-eaters. The creodonts were more common than *Miacis*, but they became extinct around 20 million years ago.

CANINE ANCESTORS

By around 35 million years ago, *Miacis* had given rise to a variety of early canids. We know of over 40 types – some like bears, some like hyenas, and some like cats. Some, however, were like dogs: *Cynodictis*, for example, resembled a primitive Cardigan Welsh Corgi. These dog-like canids were the only ones to survive the evolutionary process, and some of them provided the basis for the domestic dog.

Dogs as we know them first came on the scene in Eurasia between 12,000 and 14,000 years ago. It was originally thought that their ancestor was a form of jackal or jackal–wolf cross, but scientists now believe that it was the smaller southern strain of the grey wolf (*Canis lupus pallipes*) still found in India. During the period in question, the grey wolf was found throughout Europe, Asia, and North America.

Other possible dog ancestors include the woolly wolf of northern India and Tibet and the desert wolf of the Middle East. It is certain that all domestic dogs sprang from one of these sources (or possibly more than one, in parallel development) and that they are not genetically connected with any other species. Very recent research on canine DNA suggests that all dogs derive from just a few wolves tamed in China around 13,000 years ago.

ANCIENT DOG BREEDS

THE WOLF Wolves of different types were common all over the world in ancient times, and the grey wolf is probably the ancestor of all modern dogs.

SHARED HERITAGE The Mexican Hairless Dog found in South America has much in common with the Chinese Crested Dog of mainland Asia, and they may be related.

RARE BREED The African Wild Dog is an endangered species, having been hunted to extinction by man because of its success as a predator.

THE EARLIEST TYPES OF DOG

Five distinct types of dog have been identified from fossil remains dating from the beginning of the Bronze Age, *c* 4500 BC:

- Mastiffs
- wolf-like dogs
- Greyhounds
- Pointers
- sheepdogs

These basic types proliferated by selective breeding and natural genetic mutation to produce the hundreds of breeds we know today.

CANIS FAMILIARIS INOSTRANZEVI Mastiff-type dogs from Tibet were domesticated in the Stone Age and later used in battle by the Babylonians, Assyrians, Persians, and Greeks.

EARLY DOG The Siberian Husky is a northern Spitz-type breed descended from the wolf-like dog, which was one of the earliest dog types.

SYRIAN DOG The Saluki shares common ancestry with the Greyhound and originated in the area now known as Syria at least 4,000 years ago.

WILD ROOTS The Basenji comes from Africa and is an oddity among domestic dogs, having a similar reproductive cycle to wild dogs and no bark.

BACK TO THE WILD The Dingo was brought to Australia as a domesticated dog by the first immigrants thousands of years ago and has since returned to the wild.

DOG DIVERSIFICATION

Because of their intelligence, versatility, and use of social co-operation within the pack, wild dogs spread quickly all over the world. The Dingo, however, which many believe was the basic type of *Canis* from which the modern dog evolved, was already domesticated when it was introduced to Australia thousands of years ago by the first immigrants. Wild dogs were probably domesticated in different ways in different parts of the world; some while scavenging for food around human settlements, others when early man hunted dogs for food and took litters of puppies back to the homestead for fattening up.

From bones and fossils found around the world and dated back to about 6,500 years ago, we can say that at that period there were five different types of dogs: Mastiffs, wolf-like dogs, Greyhounds, Pointer-type dogs, and sheepdogs. Since then, thousands of breeds have been developed by both artificial and natural selection. But over the centuries many have been lost, and only about 400 remain today.

When the Europeans first arrived in North and South America in the 15th and 16th centuries, for example, they found at least 20 distinct dog breeds: now the Mexican Hairless, Eskimo Dog, and Peruvian and Chilean Wild Dogs are among the few surviving natives. Other ancient breeds include the Basenji, native to Africa, and, from the Middle East, the equally venerable Saluki and the Afghan.

CANIS FAMILIARIS PALUSTRIS
This wolf-like dog is similar to Spitz-type dogs such as the Elkhound (above), Siberian Husky, Keeshond, and Eskimo Dog.

CANIS FAMILIARIS LEINERI
The Greyhound is one of the oldest types, identified from drawings on Mesopotamian pottery dating back 8,000 years.

CANIS FAMILIARIS INTERMEDIUS
These Pointer-type dogs were probably developed from Greyhounds for the purpose of hunting small game.

CANIS FAMILIARIS METRIS OPTIMAE
Sheepdogs have been used to guard flocks from predators for thousands of years, and they probably originated in Europe.

Design and Anatomy

The dog is essentially an animal of the chase: enduring, patient, intelligent, and fleet of foot. Above all, it is a sociable beast, with none of the aloof, lordly, go-it-alone attitude of cats.

This sociability is seen in the behaviour of packs of wild dogs, which not only co-operate in setting up group ambushes, but also make sure that unattached adults contribute to the community by acting as baby-sitters while parents go hunting.

The dog family is not highly specialized biologically. In fact, its broad adaptability and multipurpose form have been major factors in its survival worldwide. However, it is important to consider some of the dog's systems that contribute to its ability to survive and that are generally common to all canines, from Dingo to Dachshund.

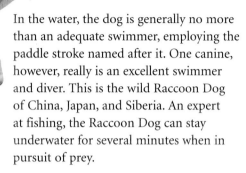

LOCOMOTION

It is a well-known fact that the cheetah is the world's fastest land mammal, achieving speeds of possibly up to 129 km/h (80 mph) over short distances. The fleetest members of the dog family are not in the same league, although wolves can achieve speeds of around 56 km/h (35 mph), and Salukis and Greyhounds bred specially for racing can even approach 70 km/h (43 mph). But hunting in the animal world is often carried out over long distances. Here is where the stamina of the dog family pays dividends. African Wild Dogs will pace one another, some loping behind for a while as others race ahead. When the leaders tire, the lopers move to the front and keep up the relentless pace of the vanguard. After a long chase this species may actually run down and kill lions.

In the water, the dog is generally no more than an adequate swimmer, employing the paddle stroke named after it. One canine, however, really is an excellent swimmer and diver. This is the wild Raccoon Dog of China, Japan, and Siberia. An expert at fishing, the Raccoon Dog can stay underwater for several minutes when in pursuit of prey.

SENSES

A dog has the same senses as a human, but they differ markedly in power. This is because of the different needs of our respective ancestors.

Smell

Dogs have a marvellous sense of smell. Although it varies from breed to breed, and among individuals in any one breed, a dog's olfactory ability is outstanding and far superior to our own – in fact about one million times better. Only eels are notably better smellers than dogs, while butterflies have a sense of smell approximately equal in sensitivity, but can use it at much longer distances. Dogs are

GRACE AND POWER
When a dog leaps, the spring comes from the powerful hindquarters, and the tail is used to balance the dog while it is in the air.

THE JOYS OF RUNNING
(left) Dogs are essentially long-distance runners. They can sprint in short bursts, but they owe their success as hunters to their easy, loping gait and their great stamina.

AGILITY CHAMPIONS (right)
Despite the powerful build of the average dog, they are surprisingly agile creatures that can jump many times their own height.

used in France and Italy to find the truffle fungus, which grows up to 30 cm (12 in) underground, and in Holland and Denmark to detect gas leaks. Dogs are more sensitive than the most advanced of odour-measuring machines and are used all over the world to search for explosives, drugs, and people. How do they do it?

Smells consist of molecules of particular chemicals floating in the air. When these molecules land on the special olfactory membrane inside a nose, nerve impulses convey the "smell information" to a particular part of the brain. This olfactory centre is highly developed in the dog and far larger than in man. The olfactory area in the adult human nose is about 3 sq cm (½ sq in), whereas in the average canine nose it covers almost 130 sq cm (20 sq in), being arranged in folds to filter smells from the incoming air. To accommodate such a structure, dogs have developed long noses (with some exceptions among the recent "artificial" breeds). There are also far more sensory cells in the dog's olfactory membrane than there are in the human's. We have five million sensory cells. A Dachshund has 125 million, a Fox Terrier 147 million, and a German Shepherd 220 million.

A wet nose helps in smelling: it dissolves molecules floating in the air, bringing them into contact with the olfactory membrane, and clears old smells away. Pigment helps too, but how this works is not clear. The pigment is not in the sensory cells but nearby: a dog's nasal membranes are dark, and the black pigment in the nose pad may also play a part in improving the dog's sense of smell. Tracker dogs take advantage of the fact that the sweat of every individual human being is as unique to him or her as fingerprints are. A dog can recognize the "scent image" of a person and make deductions from the evaporation of various ingredients of the smell with time. This allows it to run along a trail for a few metres, register the change in the image, and thus even determine which way the person was going.

Taste

The dog's sense of taste is relatively poorly developed, compared with man's. This is probably because, unlike man's ancestors, vegetarian primates that can select from a range of foods in front of them, dogs are carnivores that spot their prey at a distance, and have to eat what they can catch.

SOFT LANDINGS
The strong muscles of the shoulders take most of the strain on landing, and the pads of the forefeet ensure a good grip.

DOGGY PADDLE (left) All dogs are natural swimmers, although some, such as the Labrador, are especially good at it.

WORKING DOGS (right) The sight of dogs being used as draught animals to pull carts is now rare. Spitz-type dogs are well adapted for this work, however, and in cold regions they continue to pull sleds as they have done for centuries.

DOGS' EYES

Field of vision 200°

Field of binocular vision

Field of vision 270°

Boston Terrier

Greyhound

WIDE FIELD OF VISION The dog's eyes are set further towards the sides of its head, which gives it a wider field of vision than man. The field of vision ranges from 200 degrees in flat-nosed breeds to 270 degrees in long-nosed breeds, compared to 100 degrees in man. Dogs are not as good as man at focusing on objects at close range or at judging distance, however, because of their smaller field of binocular vision.

Vision

A dog's sight is well adapted to hunting small, fast-moving animals. Most species do not hunt primarily by sight, however, and often miss creatures that stand still. Dogs are not sensitive to colour and see mainly in black, white, and shades of grey.

Hearing

This is something else at which dogs are excellent. Although some breeds have better hearing than others, most dogs are equipped with large external ears that are served by 17 muscles, and they can prick and swivel these sound receivers to focus on the source of any noise. They can register sounds of 35,000 vibrations per second (compared to 20,000 per second in man and 25,000 per second in the cat), which means that they can detect noises well beyond the range of the human ear. They are also sensitive enough to tell the difference between, for example, two metronomes, one ticking at 100 beats per minute and the other at 96. Dogs can also shut off their inner ear so as to filter from the general din those sounds on which they want to concentrate. (This gift makes them ideal guests at cocktail parties!)

POINTS OF THE DOG The height of a dog is measured from the withers to the ground. The length is measured from point of shoulder to point of buttock. The stop is the depression beneath the eyes where the nasal bones meet the skull. Many countries now frown on the practices of docking tails and cropping ears, and in some it is even illegal.

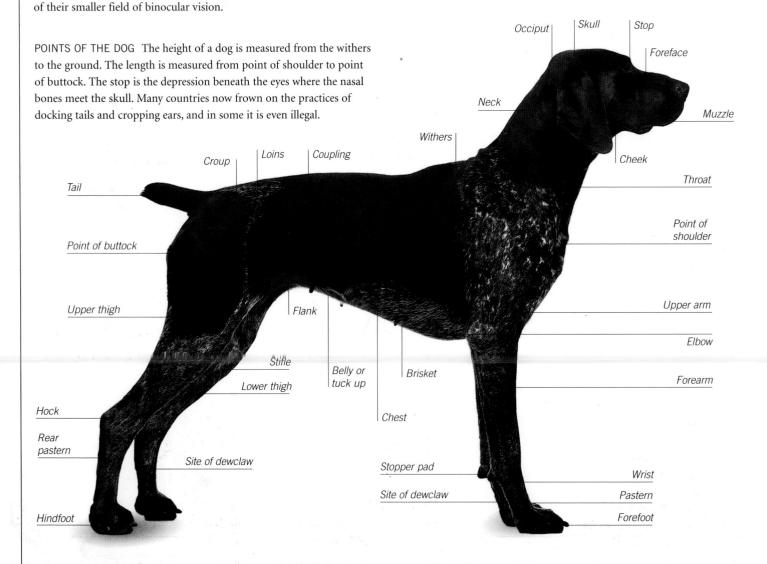

Occiput | Skull | Stop

Foreface

Neck

Muzzle

Withers

Cheek

Croup | Loins | Coupling

Throat

Tail

Point of shoulder

Point of buttock

Upper arm

Upper thigh

Flank

Elbow

Stifle

Belly or tuck up

Brisket

Forearm

Lower thigh

Hock

Chest

Rear pastern

Site of dewclaw

Stopper pad

Wrist

Site of dewclaw

Pastern

Hindfoot

Forefoot

Other abilities

Like cats, dogs are very sensitive to vibrations and will give warning of earth tremors some considerable time, and occasionally even days, before humans are aware of any movement. The curious thing is that dogs react like this only to the imminence of true earthquakes; somehow they can tell the difference between advance tremors of the real thing and the 150,000 other harmless vibrations of the earth's crust that occur each year and do not alarm them.

The dog is equipped with one efficient weapons system – its teeth. Its powerful jaw muscles provide a hefty bite if needed. A 20-kg (44-lb) mongrel has been found to exert a bite of 165-kg (363-lb) pressure. The average human adult can gnaw no harder than 20–29 kg (45–65 lb), and the strongest of men under special training can only manage 73 kg (160 lb). Finally, what about extrasensory perception in dogs? Repeated testing under apparently stringent conditions has produced evidence to suggest that certain canines possess psychic/telepathic abilities: what is usually referred to in humans as a "sixth sense". This is how your dog knows you're going for a walk before you've even decided yourself!

DOGS' EARS

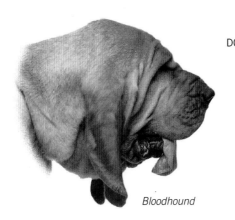

Bloodhound

German Shepherd

EAR VARIETIES Dogs vary in the sensitivity of their hearing: those with erect ears, such as the German Shepherd, can swivel them to improve reception and determine the direction of a sound; those with long, floppy ears, like the Bloodhound for example, do not have this ability. The purpose of long ears remains unclear: they may have been bred into dogs used to hunt in thick undergrowth to prevent foreign bodies falling into the ear canal. Another suggestion is that they help to channel scents to the nose as they brush along the ground.

COAT COLOURS The following specialist terms are used in the canine world to describe the colours and markings of dogs' coats.

BLUE MERLE Marbled mixture of black, blue, and grey hairs.

PARTICOLOUR (OR PIED) Marked in patches of two colours.

SADDLE Marking on the back in the shape or position of a saddle.

WHEATEN The colour of ripening wheat, pale yellow to fawn.

TRICOLOUR A coat in three colours – black, white, and tan, for example.

ROAN Fine mixture of coloured and white hairs.

SABLE Black-tipped hairs on a background of grey, fawn, tan, gold, or silver.

BRINDLE Streaked effect caused by black hairs on a light-coloured background.

GRIZZLE Mixture of bluish-grey, red, and black.

Behaviour and Intelligence

Dogs stand higher in the IQ league than cats, budgerigars, or ponies. They are excellent learners with good powers of association.

As social animals, they are adept at interpreting subtle signals conveyed by other individuals – canine or human. Together, these traits enable the dog to "understand" people and to establish friendships with them.

SCENT AND VISUAL SIGNALLING
Signalling plays an important part in a dog's life. Many messages involve smell: dogs mark territory by frequent urination and by scratching the ground to leave scent from sweat glands in the paws.

They also roll in pungent substances, such as manure, in order to enhance (to a dog's nose, at least) their body odour.

Visual signalling by body language is highly developed too. A varied repertoire of body postures, facial expressions, and tail signals transmits information that other dogs, animals, and humans can interpret. There is also a wide range of sounds that includes aggressive growls and snarls, whines, howls, "yips" (from hounds while hunting), and a variety of barks.

THE IMPORTANCE OF PLAY
Puppies love to play, and their play is more than just *joie de vivre*. Its purpose can be traced back to their wild relatives. Not only is it a substitute for hunting, prompted by the instinct of the pack-hunter, but it also

FROM BEGGING TO BITING "Play-mouthing" is a feature of dog behaviour that probably derives from food-begging.

provides valuable physical exercise for the growing animal. The puppy learns about the world as it investigates with its senses, and meanwhile it develops the social skills so important to such a gregarious species. Even more than kittens, which inherit a self-reliant, rather solitary way of life,

THE BODY LANGUAGE OF DOGS

SUBMISSION Faced with a dominant adult, this puppy is lying down exposing its belly, in a posture of extreme submissiveness.

DOMINANCE The standing dog is showing aggressive dominance, with tail raised, the hair bristling on its back, and teeth bared in a snarl.

EXTREME DOMINANCE During play, this dog is practising the position of extreme dominance by placing its paws on its rival's back.

AVOIDING CONFLICT In this confrontation the Border Collie is averting its gaze in order not to arouse the aggression of the dominant Poodle.

SCENT-MARKING

Dog 1 makes his mark on a grass stem…

Dog 2 sniffs and marks the same stem…

and Dog 3 sniffs the stem before marking.

puppies need lots of contact with their peers and human friends in order to grow into well-adjusted adults. Puppies deprived of contact with other dogs during the crucial period from three to ten weeks, when they are at their most playful, will not develop correct social responses. What is lost during this period cannot be instilled later.

Such individuals become neurotic and tend to be antisocial and unable to form normal relationships with other dogs.

For adult dogs, play is mainly fun and exercise, although in their wild cousins it may also remind each animal of its position in the social pecking order. This helps to reduce the risk of serious fighting.

PLAYING OR FIGHTING? Playful wrestling can turn in an instant into something more serious with growls and snarls as one of the puppies tries to assert dominance over the other.

LOOKING FOR FUN The bowing stance is an unmistakable invitation to play.

ANTISOCIAL BEHAVIOUR

With such a complex and intelligent species, things can go wrong, and dogs sometimes present behavioural, psychological problems. These can range from the "problem puppy" that will not house-train, to serious biters, barkers, leg-mounters, and dogs with specific phobias.

Very rarely is a dog truly psychotic – behaving totally irrationally. In almost every case, its behaviour can be explained by an examination of the fundamental nature of *Canis familiaris*. The fact that the dog is descended from social hunting animals, and an individual has had a deficient upbringing, usually explains everything.

A good owner must study and understand their dog's character. If antisocial behaviour arises, consult the vet, and then perhaps an animal behaviourist or "dog psychologist".

BACK-SCRATCHING The enjoyable abandon with which this Great Dane is rolling suggests that it is scratching its back. Dogs use a more workman-like technique to cover themselves in muck.

GETTING TO KNOW YOU Scent-signalling is very important to dogs. It is therefore natural for them to sniff each other whenever they meet.

Breeds

Although it is generally believed that the wolf is the ancestor of all dogs, we do not know many details of the ancient family tree. Certainly it seems that man's first association with the wolf-dog that was to become his companion and collaborator changed its body form in fundamental ways, partly perhaps through primitive selective breeding, and also because life close to man altered the wolf-dog's lifestyle in ways that were gradually reflected in its anatomy.

By the Bronze Age there were at least five clearly differentiated types of dog, two of them originating from the large wolves of the sub-Arctic regions. One was the ancestor of the Spitz breeds, the other of the mastiffs. Three further types – sheepdogs, pointers, and Greyhounds – are thought to have descended from the small wolves of India and the Middle East, and an early intermediate form may be represented today by the Australian Dingo and the Pariah Dog of Asia.

Dog breeds have been gathered into a system of groups since the late 1800s for the convenience of judging at shows. There are seven groups in most countries, and the English-speaking world uses the same terminology, but with the odd variation. The groups that are known as Utility, Gundogs, and Pastoral in Britain are known respectively in the US and Canada as Non-Sporting, Sporting, and Herding.

MODERN ANCIENT ANIMAL Although there are more than 200 distinct breeds of domesticated dog in the world today, most modern breeds were established no more than about 100 years ago.

Hounds

Athleticism and a wonderful sense of smell are the two great features of this group, and a hound may possess one or both of them. Hounds were the earliest hunting dogs used by man, providing the speed that Homo sapiens lacked when pursuing food. So it is not surprising that, over the centuries, hounds have featured in more writings than any other kind of dog.

SIGHT HOUNDS

As with other aspects of the remarkable history of the domestic dog, it all began in the Middle East, where sleek and leggy animals that had long, flexible, muscular trunks, were selected for the chase of game in open desert country. We have proof of this from excavated pottery shards dated to the Assyria and Persia of 6000 BC, which are decorated with greyhound-like dogs that are in pursuit of gazelle. Sight hounds or "gaze-hounds" of this kind were swift, silent sprinters that relied mainly on good eyesight in the chase.

SCENT HOUNDS

Several centuries later, hounds that tracked game by ground scents were developed in Europe. Typically, scent hounds had, like their present-day counterparts, strong, sturdy legs, long heads, pendulous ears, and muzzles with a remarkable sense of smell – up to one million times better than a human being's. Today, there are also specialist scent hounds that have long bodies and short legs.

EUROPEAN BREEDS

Before 1066 there was at least one hound type, the St Hubert, in France, and it seems likely that William the Conqueror imported examples of this dog into Britain, introducing blood-lines that still persist in modern breeds. From the St Hubert, the Bloodhound, the now-extinct Talbot, and the old English Staghound were derived.

BREED DEVELOPMENT

During the Middle Ages, landed gentry was responsible for the development of hound breeds. Long before fox-hunting became popular, they hunted deer and hare, using a large hound for the deer and, as their name indicates, harriers, along with Beagles, for the hare. Other hounds of the same period included the Northern, a heavy, solid type, and the Southern, a lighter and faster hound. Other, now extinct, hounds, were the Devon Staghound and the Welsh Hound.

OTHER DISTINCTIVE BREEDS

Some scent hounds were trained to kill their quarry, whereas others, like the Elkhound, kept the prey cornered and then summoned the huntsman by "giving tongue" or baying. The long-bodied, short-legged hounds, such as the Dachshund, also have a long history, as ancient Egyptian wall carvings bear witness. Although the breed is nowadays rarely used for underground hunting, it was popular in the 15th and 16th centuries in England, Germany, and Italy for the pursuit of foxes, rabbits, and badgers. Today, the Dachshund and Beagle are the two most popular hound breeds in the US.

GREYHOUND (Top right) The Greyhound, Afghan, and Saluki are the modern descendants of the sight hounds used for hunting game 8,000 years ago. They are the canine equivalents of human 100-metre champions: generally tall individuals with a long stride.

AFGHAN HOUND (Below right) A classic example of a sight hound, the Afghan Hound hunts by combining its sharp eyesight with great fleetness of foot. Having especially flexible hip-joints, it is able to cross broken, boulder-littered country without slackening its speed, hurdling or swerving with consummate ease.

FOXHOUND (Left) Foxhounds were probably developed through crossing one of the old English hounds of the Bloodhound type with a Greyhound to give speed. In general, though, scent hounds display great stamina in wearing down their quarry, rather than by using high speed.

Afghan Hound

This chic, majestic breed should not be judged merely by its elegant appearance. As well as stunning good looks, the Afghan Hound possesses remarkable agility and a hardy constitution, enabling it to cope with the most rugged terrain.

HISTORY

Sometimes also known as the Kabul Dog, this ancient breed was depicted in 4,000-year-old Afghan paint drawings and on a Greek tapestry dating back to the 6th century BC. Originating probably in the Middle East, the Afghan spread along the trade routes to Afghanistan and was used for the hunting of antelope, gazelle, wolves, and snow leopards. The first Afghans to reach Britain arrived in 1886, but the breed was not introduced into the US until 1926.

TEMPERAMENT

Afghan Hounds have an independent, lively, amicable, yet sensitive temperament. Though tough, they will pine if they are deprived of attention. At one time, the breed had a reputation for being untrustworthy, but that has now been replaced by a character that, while still spirited, is said to be more amenable to training and discipline.

BODY *Tall, with a trunk of moderate length, a level, muscular back, and a deep chest.*

COAT *Very long and silky, except along the back and face, where it is short and close. All colours are acceptable.*

ALL MOD CONS The Afghan delights in the comforts of the modern home.

SIZE
Ideal height: dogs 68–74 cm (27–29 in); bitches 63–69 cm (25–27 in).

AFGHAN REQUIREMENTS Elegant and athletic, the Afghan requires considerable grooming and exercise to keep it in peak physical and mental shape.

TAIL Not too short, set low, but carried high when the dog moves. Ringed at the end and sparingly feathered.

WARM, PROTECTIVE COAT The Afghan evolved its long coat as protection against the bitter cold of the high mountains in Afghanistan and the Middle East.

EARS Long, covered with silky hair, set low, and carried close to the head.

FACIAL CHARACTERISTICS

EYES Golden or, preferably, dark, with an oriental slant.

LEGS The long and powerful hindlegs are well angled; forelegs are straight.

FEET Large and strong, covered with thick hair. Toes are arched.

HEAD Long, but not too narrow, with strong jaws. Nose should be black or, in pale dogs, liver-coloured.

Basenji

This is a truly remarkable dog – it trots like a horse, keeps itself clean by fastidious licking, and "yodels" rather than barks! It derives its name from the Bantu word *Basenji*, meaning native (of the bush), and is also sometimes known as the Congo Dog. In Africa, it is used as a tracker and watchdog.

HISTORY

The ancestors of the breed were probably around at the time of the Ancient Egyptians, for carvings of dogs resembling the Basenji have been found in many pharaohs' tombs. Basenjis were discovered by Westerners a little over 100 years ago in Central Africa, where they were being used as pack hunting dogs. They arrived in Britain at the beginning of the 20th century, but quickly succumbed to distemper, a disease to which they had no natural immunity. They were first bred in Britain in 1937 and in the US in 1941.

TEMPERAMENT

Basenjis are cheerful, perky, and mischievous creatures. Although sometimes aloof with strangers, they are generally very good with people. If they have to live with other dogs, their pack-dog instincts will probably dominate family life for a while, so be well prepared for considerable scrapping and bickering until leadership is firmly established!

HEAD Of medium length and narrowing evenly from the eyes. Nose pad is preferably black.

ADAPTABLE DOG Although full of energy and curiosity, the Basenji is quite content to laze around the house.

COAT Loose skin carrying short, fine hair. Colours are black, tan, white, black and white, chestnut and white, and black, tan, and white. White is preferable on the feet, chest, and tail-tip.

LEGS Strong, muscular, and shapely.

FEET Small and narrow, with prominently arched toes.

SIZE
Ideal height:
dogs 43 cm (17 in);
bitches 40 cm (16 in).

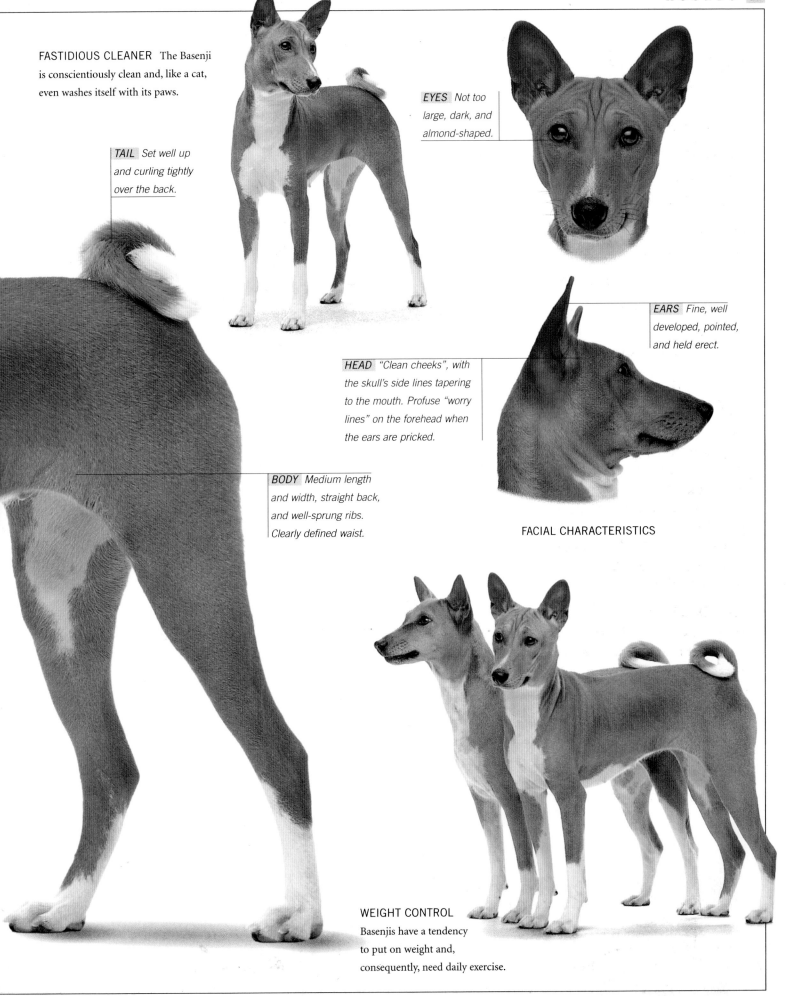

FASTIDIOUS CLEANER The Basenji is conscientiously clean and, like a cat, even washes itself with its paws.

TAIL Set well up and curling tightly over the back.

EYES Not too large, dark, and almond-shaped.

HEAD "Clean cheeks", with the skull's side lines tapering to the mouth. Profuse "worry lines" on the forehead when the ears are pricked.

EARS Fine, well developed, pointed, and held erect.

BODY Medium length and width, straight back, and well-sprung ribs. Clearly defined waist.

FACIAL CHARACTERISTICS

WEIGHT CONTROL
Basenjis have a tendency to put on weight and, consequently, need daily exercise.

Basset Griffon Vendéen

Long popular in France, particularly in the Vendée, in the west of the country, the Basset Griffon Vendéen now comes in two sizes, the larger Grand, and the smaller Petit. Both are extremely energetic, sparkling, affectionate animals that deserve a wider following than they have at present.

HISTORY

Ancient Gallic hunting hounds formed the root stock from which the Basset Griffon Vendéen was developed, and by the mid-19th century the breed was, in essence, a rough-coated (griffon) form of the Basset Hound (see pp.26–7). The Grand was originally used for hunting wolves, and it is still employed in wild-boar hunts. It is one of the biggest of the French bassets, a group that includes the Basset Artésien Normand, the Basset Bleu de Gascogne, and the Basset Fauve de Bretagne. The Petit is simply a miniature version of the Grand, produced by selective breeding.

TEMPERAMENT

The Basset Griffon Vendéen is cheerful, sociable, loyal, and excellent with children. Both the Grand and the Petit must have plenty of exercise to burn off their abundant energy and are, therefore, not usually suitable for the confined life of a town apartment.

HEAD Domed, but not too broad, with a distinct stop, a long muzzle, and a black nose. Eyebrows are pronounced but not overhanging, and a well-developed beard and moustache of long hair cover the lips.

ITALIAN SPINONE One of the most distinguished, and oldest, members of the Griffon family, the Italian Spinone is skilled as a hunter's companion on open tracts of land as well as in water. It is regarded by many as one of the best pointing breeds of all.

FEET Large and compact, with short, strong nails and solid pads.

EYES *Large and dark, showing no white of the eye, nor any red lining of the lower eyelid.*

FACIAL CHARACTERISTICS

EARS *Set low and long; they are fine and supple, oval-shaped at the tips, and covered with long hair.*

BODY *Low-slung, compact, and well balanced.*

TAIL *Set high, tapering smoothly, well covered with hair, and carried like a sabre.*

LEGS *Thick-boned with straight forelegs and strong, muscular hindquarters. Elbows should be held close to the body, rather than turned out.*

COAT *Long and rough, never silky or woolly, with a dense undercoat. For showing purposes, the coat is not trimmed. Colour is white, with any combination of lemon, orange, tricolour, or grizzle markings.*

SIZE
Average height: 39–43 cm (15½–17 in).

GRAND BASSET GRIFFON VENDÉEN A breed that still earns its living through the chase of the boar, the Basset Griffon Vendéen is not only one of the more well-established European breeds, it is also one that is slowly gaining recognition elsewhere.

Basset Hound

Rather placid and with a tendency towards laziness, the Basset is nevertheless a most useful hunting dog. It is surprisingly agile and energetic, and can follow hares, rabbits, and pheasants by scent through the thickest undergrowth. One of the most famous Basset Hounds is Fred Basset, the popular cartoon character.

HISTORY

This breed originated in the late 16th century in France, the name "Basset" coming from the French word *bas*, meaning low. The general features of the Basset's head and its acute sense of smell suggest that the breed was produced from a dwarf mutation of the Bloodhound *(see pp.32–3)*. The Basset was not introduced into Britain until the second half of the 19th century, and one appeared at the Wolverhampton Dog Show in 1875. The Basset Hound Club was formed in 1883. Queen Alexandra, wife of Edward VII, was a Basset enthusiast and regular exhibitor, and one of her dogs won at Crufts in 1909.

TEMPERAMENT

Though they look rather lugubrious, Bassets are lively, sociable, and good-natured characters. They need lots of exercise, and relish country walks where they can investigate hedgerows and thickets to their hearts' content. Kept as sedentary house-dogs, Bassets tend to become overweight and, as a consequence, can be arthritic in later life.

LEGS *Stocky, short, and sturdy, with loose, wrinkled skin.*

SIZE
Ideal height: 33–38 cm (13–15 in).

FEET *Padded, broad, heavy, and well knuckled.*

HEAD *Dome-shaped, prominently peaked, tapering slightly to the muzzle. Nose is black, or brown in light-coloured dogs. The long upper lip should hang well down over the lower lip.*

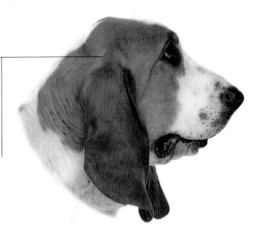

EYES *Dark to mid-brown, with heavy eyebrows. The pink of the lower eyelid is just visible.*

EARS *Long and velvety, set below the eye.*

FACIAL CHARACTERISTICS

BASSET VOICE The Basset has a deep, bell-like bark; the sound of a pack giving voice is a stirring, memorable experience.

BODY *Broad, long, and barrel-shaped.*

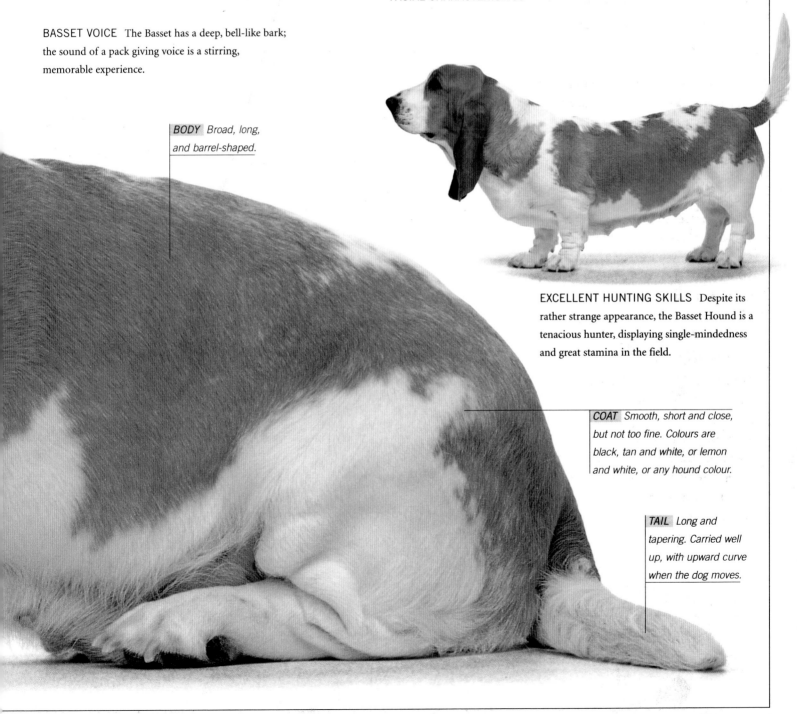

EXCELLENT HUNTING SKILLS Despite its rather strange appearance, the Basset Hound is a tenacious hunter, displaying single-mindedness and great stamina in the field.

COAT *Smooth, short and close, but not too fine. Colours are black, tan and white, or lemon and white, or any hound colour.*

TAIL *Long and tapering. Carried well up, with upward curve when the dog moves.*

Beagle

The French word *begueule*, meaning "gape throat", probably gave the Beagle its name, referring perhaps to the noisy clamour of the dogs when gathered into a pack. Equally content at the hunt or on the hearth-rug, the Beagle makes an energetic and faithful companion.

HISTORY

These smallest of hounds perhaps go as far back as the ancient Greeks. Certainly the Norman French used Beagles for pursuing hare and brought them to England in 1066. They were slightly smaller animals then and were sometimes carried in saddlebags or even the pockets of mounted men. A mini-variety, the Pocket Beagle, was developed from such portable animals but now no longer exists. One of several dogs associated with royalty, Beagles have been owned by Elizabeth I, William III, and George IV, who hunted his pack on the Sussex downs near Brighton. US president Lyndon B Johnson also had a pair, called Him and Her, though the most famous Beagle of all must surely be Snoopy of the *Peanuts* cartoons. The Beagle Club was established in the UK in 1895, and a few years later Beagles were exported to the US.

TEMPERAMENT

Beagles are good-natured, active, happy dogs, but they can be wilful and need firm handling.

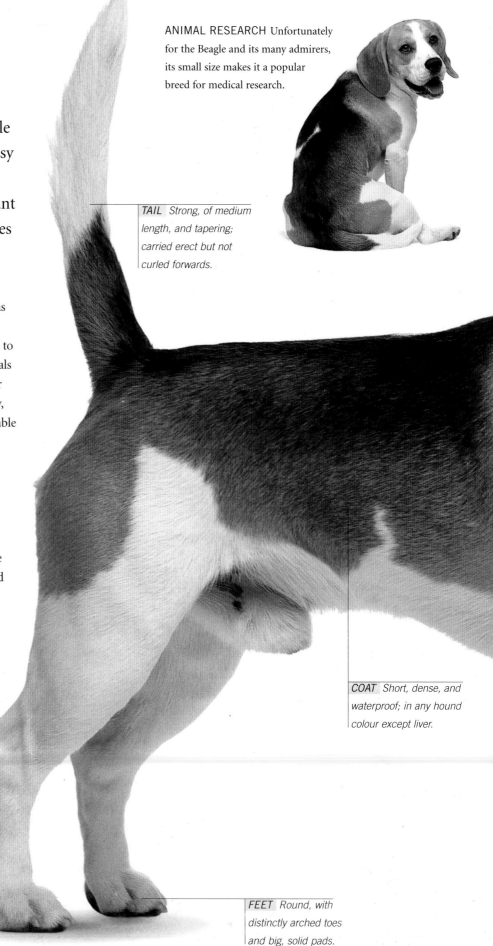

ANIMAL RESEARCH Unfortunately for the Beagle and its many admirers, its small size makes it a popular breed for medical research.

TAIL *Strong, of medium length, and tapering; carried erect but not curled forwards.*

COAT *Short, dense, and waterproof; in any hound colour except liver.*

SIZE *Minimum height 33 cm (13 in); maximum height 40 cm (16 in).*

FEET *Round, with distinctly arched toes and big, solid pads.*

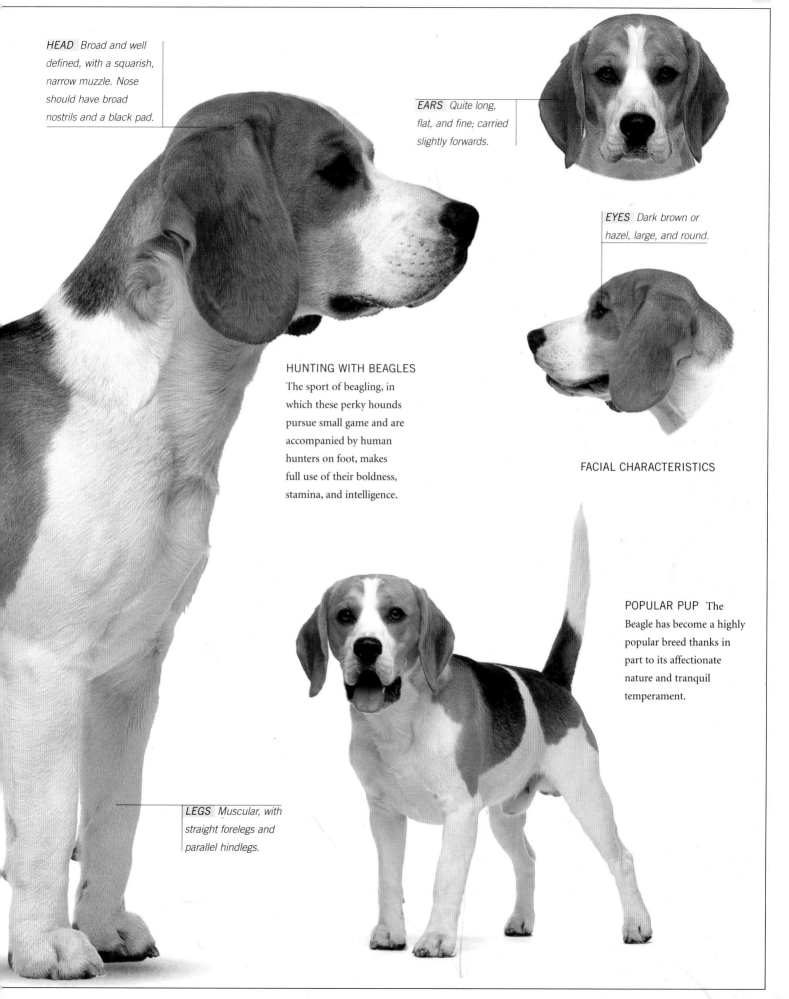

HEAD Broad and well defined, with a squarish, narrow muzzle. Nose should have broad nostrils and a black pad.

EARS Quite long, flat, and fine; carried slightly forwards.

EYES Dark brown or hazel, large, and round.

HUNTING WITH BEAGLES

The sport of beagling, in which these perky hounds pursue small game and are accompanied by human hunters on foot, makes full use of their boldness, stamina, and intelligence.

FACIAL CHARACTERISTICS

POPULAR PUP The Beagle has become a highly popular breed thanks in part to its affectionate nature and tranquil temperament.

LEGS Muscular, with straight forelegs and parallel hindlegs.

Black-and-Tan Coonhound

Coonhounds, highly specialized hunters of raccoons, are American breeds and include the Redbone Coonhound, the Bluelick Coonhound, and, commonest of all, the Black-and-Tan Coonhound. Like all coonhounds, the Black-and-Tan pursues a raccoon by scent, "trees" its quarry, and then tells the hunter trailing far behind what has happened by altering the tone of its voice and baying distinctively. Tough and strong, able to work in the most rugged conditions in all seasons and all weather, this brave dog is also able to track deer, bear, and puma purely by scent.

HISTORY

The breed may well have its origins in the Talbot Hound of the 12th century. Certainly its forebears include the Bloodhound *(see pp.32–3)*, Foxhound *(see pp.42–3)*, Irish Kerry Beagle, and, in the 18th century, the Virginia Foxhound.

TEMPERAMENT.

Even-tempered, alert, friendly, and obedient, this dog is essentially a powerful working dog that demands plenty of exercise. It is no dog for the inner-city apartment.

COAT *Short and dense; tends to cast all year round so needs regular thorough grooming. Colour is jet-black with rich tan markings.*

HEAD *Cleanly modelled with a large, black nose and well-opened nostrils.*

SHORT ATTENTION SPAN Of all the raccoon-hunting Coonhounds, the Black-and-Tan seems to be the one most easily distracted by other potential quarry, and it has a tendency to charge joyously after any squirrel or rabbit that it comes across.

FEET *Compact with well-arched toes and thick pads.*

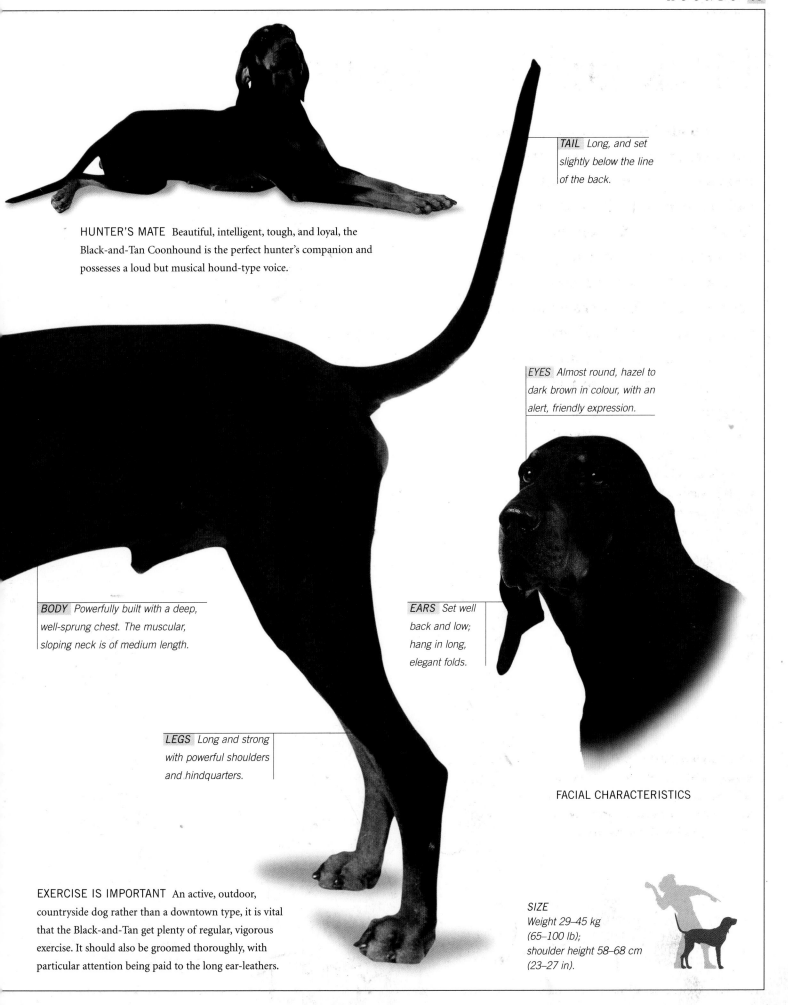

TAIL *Long, and set slightly below the line of the back.*

HUNTER'S MATE Beautiful, intelligent, tough, and loyal, the Black-and-Tan Coonhound is the perfect hunter's companion and possesses a loud but musical hound-type voice.

EYES *Almost round, hazel to dark brown in colour, with an alert, friendly expression.*

BODY *Powerfully built with a deep, well-sprung chest. The muscular, sloping neck is of medium length.*

EARS *Set well back and low; hang in long, elegant folds.*

LEGS *Long and strong with powerful shoulders and hindquarters.*

FACIAL CHARACTERISTICS

EXERCISE IS IMPORTANT An active, outdoor, countryside dog rather than a downtown type, it is vital that the Black-and-Tan get plenty of regular, vigorous exercise. It should also be groomed thoroughly, with particular attention being paid to the long ear-leathers.

SIZE
Weight 29–45 kg (65–100 lb); shoulder height 58–68 cm (23–27 in).

Bloodhound

This famous tracking hound of real and fictional criminology is pleasant, polite, and rather reserved. It probably derives its name from its amazing sense of smell in locating wounded (bleeding) game, or perhaps from belonging to a breed closely associated with the "blue blood" of the aristocracy.

HISTORY

As well as being among the purest of breeds, this lugubrious-looking creature is one of the oldest of hounds. Its origins can be traced back to 8th-century Belgium, in the Ardennes Forest, where St Hubert, the patron saint of hunting, kept a large pack of hounds (later to be known as St Huberts). They became a favourite breed of the French kings, and William the Conqueror brought them to England in 1066. Over the centuries, selective breeding in England refined the St Hubert into the Bloodhound as we know it today.

TEMPERAMENT

The Bloodhound is shy, gentle, and rather solemn. Once it has its nose down, it will be unable to pay attention to anything else, including the voice of its owner!

COAT Short, dense hair on the body, with softer, finer hair on the head and ears. Colours should be black and tan, liver and tan, or red. Some white on the chest, feet and tail-tip is permissible.

LEGS Strong and sturdy, with rounded bones and muscular thighs.

CHILDREN'S FAVOURITES

Bloodhounds can make affectionate pets and are popular with children, but they will need plenty of space and exercise.

TAIL Long, thick, and tapering. Set low.

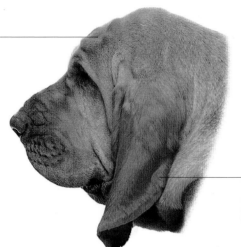

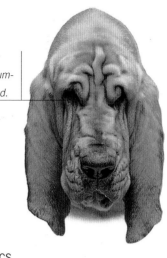

HEAD Big, long, and narrow, with slight tapering to the muzzle and wrinkles on the forehead and the side of the face. Large, open nostrils. The upper teeth overlap the lower teeth ("scissor bite").

EYES Dark brown or hazel in colour, medium-sized, and oval-shaped.

EARS Very long, with a thin and silky texture. Set low.

FACIAL CHARACTERISTICS

BODY A broad, muscular back, deep chest, and powerful, solid loins.

GREAT SENSE OF SCENT This breed is renowned for its inexhaustible enthusiasm for sniffing. Having found its quarry, the Bloodhound is unlikely to do it any harm, and will probably try to make friends instead!

DOUBLE CHIN The Bloodhound's dewlap, the loose, wrinkled fold of skin that hangs beneath its throat, is particularly pronounced.

FEET Round and strong, with well-developed knuckles.

SIZE
Ideal height: dogs 63–69 cm (25–27 in); bitches 58–63 cm (23–25 in).

Borzoi

The Russian word for swift, *borzoi*, gave this slender and athletic dog its name. The tsars and aristocracy of pre-Revolutionary Russia used them in the ceremonial wolf-hunt. Also known as the Russian Wolfhound, the Borzoi is a speedy and impetuous chaser by nature, and in many cases needs obedience training to curb its instincts.

HISTORY

The Borzoi probably originated in the Middle East as a shorthaired "gaze-hound" that hunted by sight. Taken to the northern lands, it was crossed with a long-legged Russian collie-type to give added hardiness and a long coat for the cold climate. It has many royal connections: as a traditional royal gift, Borzois were presented first to Queen Victoria in 1842, and then to Queen Alexandra (wife of Edward VII) by the tsars. Queen Alexandra's dogs were kept at the king's Sandringham estate in Norfolk and bred with local collies to produce a new, refined Rough-Coated Collie, white in colour, and with a long, elegant muzzle. Borzois were first exported to the US in 1889.

TEMPERAMENT

Though they are often reserved and sometimes stubborn, Borzois are generally tranquil and affectionate with their friends.

COAT Long, silky, and curly or wavy on the body; short and smooth on head, ears, and forelegs. Chest and forelegs are well feathered. Any colour, though usually white with darker markings.

DEMANDING DOG The Borzoi requires much attention in the form of grooming, exercise, and the management of a fairly complex personality.

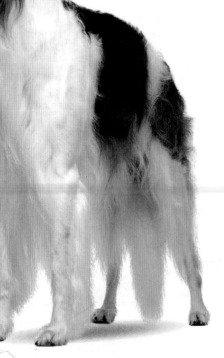

*SIZE
Minimum height:
dogs 73 cm (29 in);
bitches 68 cm (27 in).*

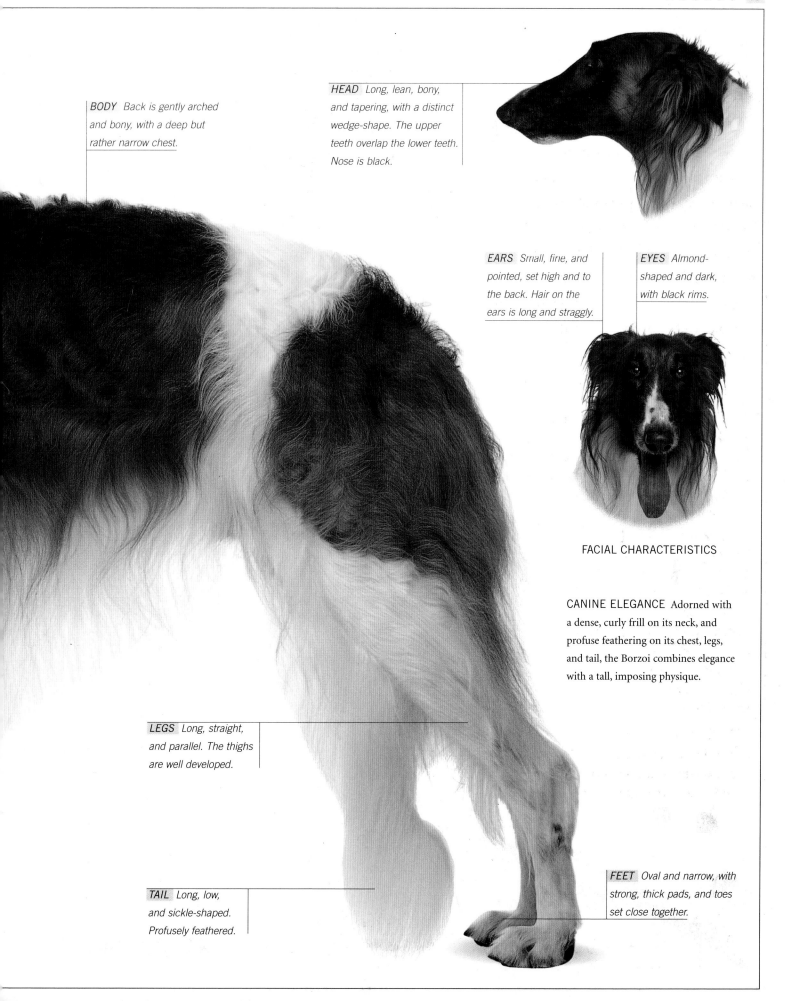

HEAD Long, lean, bony, and tapering, with a distinct wedge-shape. The upper teeth overlap the lower teeth. Nose is black.

BODY Back is gently arched and bony, with a deep but rather narrow chest.

EARS Small, fine, and pointed, set high and to the back. Hair on the ears is long and straggly.

EYES Almond-shaped and dark, with black rims.

FACIAL CHARACTERISTICS

CANINE ELEGANCE Adorned with a dense, curly frill on its neck, and profuse feathering on its chest, legs, and tail, the Borzoi combines elegance with a tall, imposing physique.

LEGS Long, straight, and parallel. The thighs are well developed.

TAIL Long, low, and sickle-shaped. Profusely feathered.

FEET Oval and narrow, with strong, thick pads, and toes set close together.

Dachshunds

Rather maligned as a "sausage dog", the Dachshund is actually a spirited and plucky creature, bred for hunting, which will display immense tenacity and stamina when in pursuit of its prey. In German, *Dachshund* means "badger dog" (not badger hound), and although it has a good nose, it seems to be more of a natural terrier than a hound, happy to go underground to confront rabbits, foxes, and, predictably, badgers.

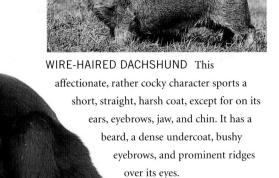

WIRE-HAIRED DACHSHUND This affectionate, rather cocky character sports a short, straight, harsh coat, except for on its ears, eyebrows, jaw, and chin. It has a beard, a dense undercoat, bushy eyebrows, and prominent ridges over its eyes.

HISTORY

Dogs with long bodies and little legs are depicted on the walls of Ancient Egyptian temples, and stone and clay models of Dachshund-like dogs have been found in Mexico, Greece, Peru, and China. Some believe the breed to be purely Teutonic, for remains resembling the Dachshund have been excavated in several Roman settlements in Germany. There are six separate Dachshund breeds: smooth-haired, long-haired, and wire-haired, in standard and miniature sizes. The basic features of all six are the same, and they differ only in size and coat-type. The early miniatures, the Kaninchenteckels, were created by crossing terriers and Pinschers with the smallest and lightest Dachshunds.

TEMPERAMENT

All Dachshunds are lively and intelligent, but can sometimes be a little fussy.

BODY Long and muscular, and sufficiently clear of the ground to allow unhindered movement.

EXPERT HUNTERS

Dachshunds have a brilliant sense of smell and have been known to track a wounded wild boar for up to two days.

COLOUR All colours. White should only be a small patch on the chest, or as even markings in dapples.

FEET Full front feet, with smaller hindfeet.

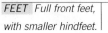

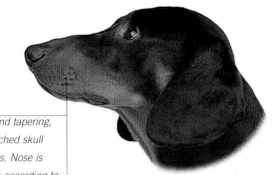

HEAD *Long and tapering, with slightly arched skull and strong jaws. Nose is black or brown according to the coat colour.*

EYES *Medium-sized and dark. In dapples, one or both eyes can be partly or wholly light blue.*

EARS *Mobile, fairly long, broad, and set high.*

FACIAL CHARACTERISTICS

HEALTH ISSUES All Dachshunds are prone to "slipped disc" problems of the back, a tendency aggravated by their predisposition to overeat and become obese as they grow older. Although they do not need large amounts of exercise, regular romps and a controlled diet are essential for their healthy maintenance.

COAT *Smooth-haired: short, dense coat, with loose, supple skin. Coarse hair on the underside of the tail.*

LEGS *Muscular forelegs. When viewed from behind, the hindlegs are parallel.*

ALARM DOG Dachshunds make good watchdogs by dint of their alertness and a loud bark that belies their small size. They can make devoted and most affectionate pets.

COAT *Longhaired: soft, flat, and straight, or very slightly waved. Abundant feathering behind the legs.*

TAIL *Slightly curved, continuing the line of the spine.*

SIZE
Ideal weight: standard 9–12 kg (20–26 lb); miniature 4.5 kg (10 lb).

Elkhound

Cold winds, snow, and ice do not deter this most dogged of dogs, for it is Scandinavian through and through. The Elkhound can be trained to pull sledges, but it also makes a first-class household pet. A member of the Spitz family of dogs, it has remained essentially unchanged over thousands of years.

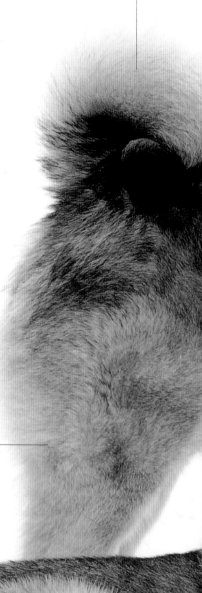

TAIL Thick and hairy, set high, and curled forwards.

HISTORY

In Norway, ancient fossil skeletons of dogs have been found that are identical to the living Elkhound. It worked with Nordic hunters a thousand years before the time of Christ, and later accompanied the Viking raiders across the sea. Its traditional quarry ranged from rabbits and deer to lynx, bear, and elk. It arrived in Britain shortly after World War I, and was recognized by the American Kennel Club in 1935. Although it is not used as a hunting dog outside its native land, this Nordic creature is still used to catch prey in some parts of Scandinavia.

TEMPERAMENT

It is an independent, civilized, and courageous breed. Elkhounds are particularly determined dogs, for after cornering their prey they must stand their ground, and yet also avoid the deadly swipes of a bear's paw or the powerful spear-thrusts of an elk's antlers.

VOCAL COMMUNICATION This breed has a wide range of communication noises, from sighs, yelps, and yaps, to a variety of meaningful barks. On the hunt, the Elkhound informs its master that it has sighted its quarry by uttering a particular cry.

BODY Shortish, compact, and powerful.

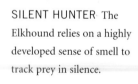

SILENT HUNTER The Elkhound relies on a highly developed sense of smell to track prey in silence.

SIZE Ideal height: dogs 52 cm (20½ in); bitches 49.5 cm (19½ in).

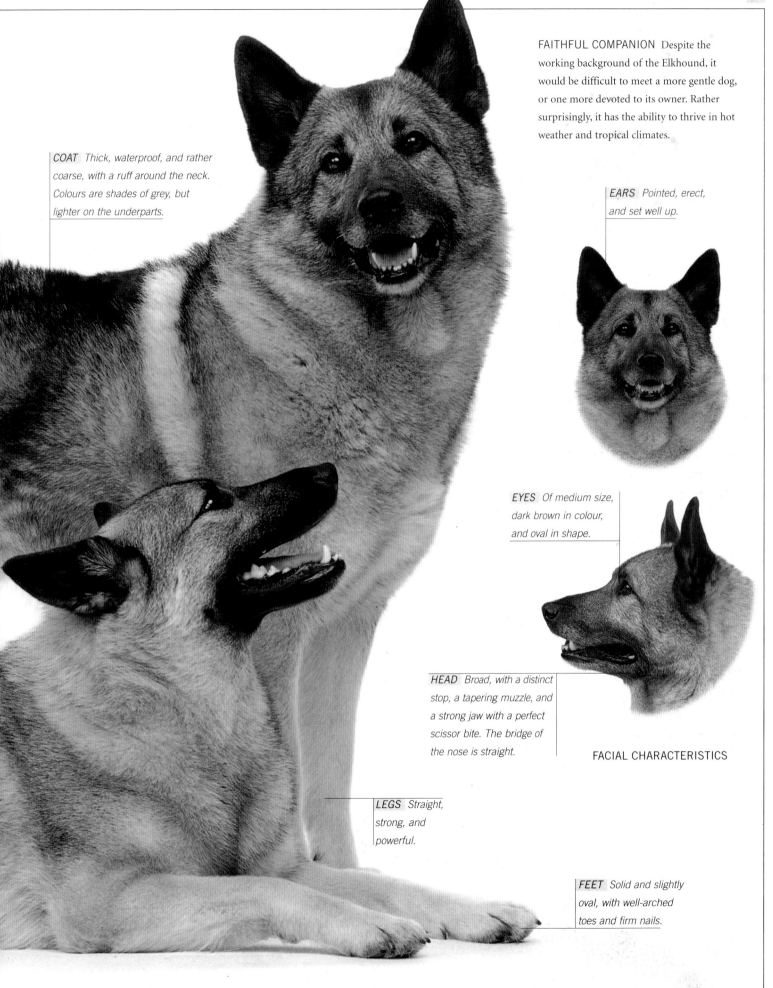

FAITHFUL COMPANION Despite the working background of the Elkhound, it would be difficult to meet a more gentle dog, or one more devoted to its owner. Rather surprisingly, it has the ability to thrive in hot weather and tropical climates.

COAT Thick, waterproof, and rather coarse, with a ruff around the neck. Colours are shades of grey, but lighter on the underparts.

EARS Pointed, erect, and set well up.

EYES Of medium size, dark brown in colour, and oval in shape.

HEAD Broad, with a distinct stop, a tapering muzzle, and a strong jaw with a perfect scissor bite. The bridge of the nose is straight.

FACIAL CHARACTERISTICS

LEGS Straight, strong, and powerful.

FEET Solid and slightly oval, with well-arched toes and firm nails.

Finnish Spitz

By far the most popular dog in its home country of Finland, the Finnish Spitz (or Suomenpystykorva, as it is called in Finnish) was used up to the beginning of the 20th century to pursue and corner brown bears as well as many types of game. Nowadays, the Finnish Spitz is mainly a flusher of woodland grouse, indicating the whereabouts of the bird by barking loudly and rapidly.

HISTORY

The forebears of this ancient breed probably accompanied the mysterious Finno-Ugrian people who crossed over from the southern shores of the Gulf of Finland to establish the first settlements around AD 100. Over the centuries there was much crossbreeding with other Scandinavian dogs, and by the mid-19th century the breed had seriously deteriorated. Then the Finns took steps to locate any remaining pure-bred Spitz in the north of the country, established breeding programmes, and, in 1892, laid down a breed standard. Thus was the modern Finnish Spitz saved from oblivion. As well as in Finland, it is extremely popular in Sweden and increasingly common in Britain and the United States.

TEMPERAMENT

Intelligent, vivacious, brave and friendly, the Finnish Spitz makes a most loyal and protective companion. It can be rather demanding, attention-seeking, and rather off-hand with strangers but, with patience, it quickly becomes a first-rate family pet, good with children and other animals.

BODY *The body of this small-medium dog is squarish with a deep chest.*

BIRD DOG As a working dog, the Finnish Spitz is nowadays principally a bird dog, often used for flushing wood grouse with a rousing bark.

COAT COLOURS The coat of the Finnish Spitz should be bright red or golden brown on the back, lighter inside the ears, on the cheeks, throat, chest, belly, inside of legs, back of the thighs, and on the tail. The undercoat is lighter in colour.

TAIL Plumed; curls up over the back and down the side.

HEAD Of average size, with a slightly arched forehead and a narrow muzzle. Nose is black.

EYES Almond-shaped, dark, and alert.

EARS Small and pointed; set high, and always erect.

FACIAL CHARACTERISTICS

COAT Fairly long double coat. Rigid or semi-rigid on the body, stiffer on the neck and back, long and coarse on the shoulders, long and dense on the back of the thighs and tail, short and close on the head and the front of the legs. Undercoat is soft and short.

LEGS Powerful hindlegs.

FEET Small and round, with black pads and dense insulating hair on the sides.

SIZE
Weight 14–16 kg (31–35 lb); shoulder height 38–51 cm (15–20 in).

Foxhound

When describing the Foxhound, who could be more poetic than Shakespeare? In *A Midsummer Night's Dream* he writes: "My hounds are bred out of the Spartan kind, So flewed, so sanded; and their heads are hung with ears that sweep away the morning dew; crook-kneed, and dew-lapped like Thessalian bulls; slow in pursuit, but matched in mouth like bells."

AMERICAN FOXHOUND The American Foxhound is lighter, has a narrower chest, and carries longer ears than its English cousin. In the US the breed is used as a hunter but is also seen in the show ring.

HISTORY

The Foxhound's history can he traced back to the 13th century, when organized fox-hunting first became established in England. It seems likely that its lineage includes the now-extinct St Hubert (also ancestor of the Bloodhound, *see pp.32–3*), and Talbot Hound, together with terrier, Bulldog *(see pp.120–21)* and Greyhound *(see pp.44–5)* blood. In the 1770s, George Washington played a significant part in the creation of the distinct American Foxhound, by introducing French hounds into his pack of English Foxhounds. Later crossings with selected Irish and English hounds gradually refined the breed to produce the faster American type.

TEMPERAMENT

Foxhounds are lively, friendly, and happy-go-lucky dogs, but they can be wilful and disobedient. Obedience training and firm handling are required, and they are not recommended as family pets, least of all for city dwellers.

BODY Deep chest, long shoulders, and a very muscular, level back that runs smoothly into the loins.

FEET Compact, round, and cat-like. Pads are well developed, and toes are distinctly arched with strong nails.

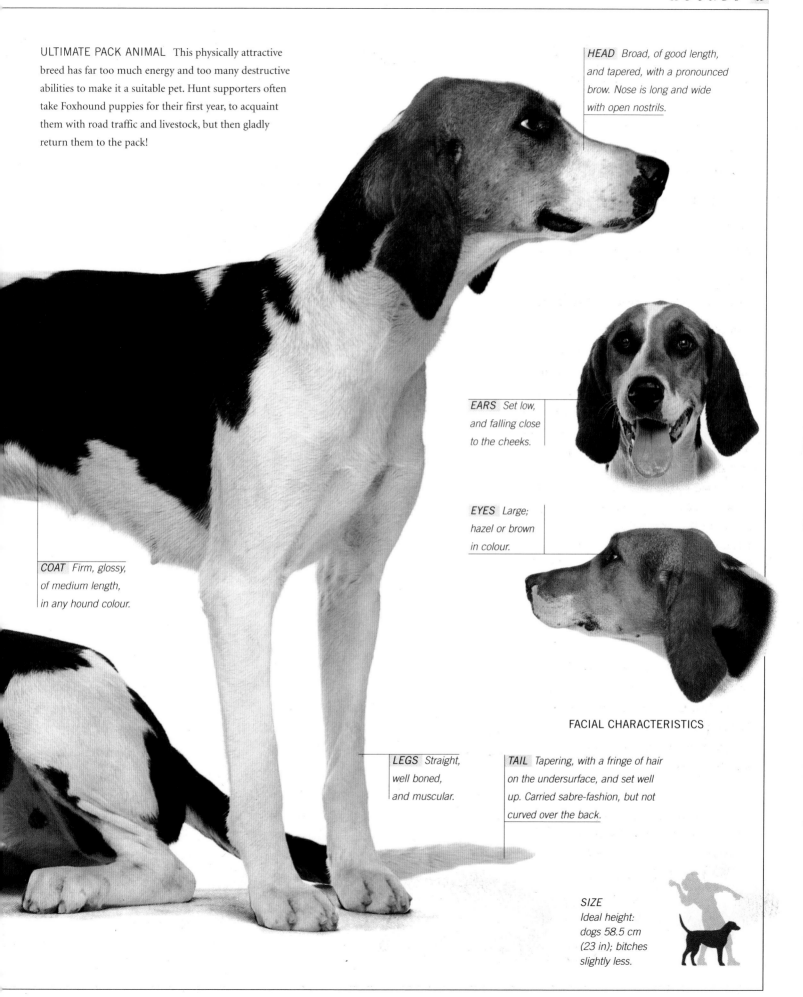

ULTIMATE PACK ANIMAL This physically attractive breed has far too much energy and too many destructive abilities to make it a suitable pet. Hunt supporters often take Foxhound puppies for their first year, to acquaint them with road traffic and livestock, but then gladly return them to the pack!

HEAD Broad, of good length, and tapered, with a pronounced brow. Nose is long and wide with open nostrils.

EARS Set low, and falling close to the cheeks.

EYES Large; hazel or brown in colour.

COAT Firm, glossy, of medium length, in any hound colour.

FACIAL CHARACTERISTICS

LEGS Straight, well boned, and muscular.

TAIL Tapering, with a fringe of hair on the undersurface, and set well up. Carried sabre-fashion, but not curved over the back.

SIZE
Ideal height:
dogs 58.5 cm
(23 in); bitches
slightly less.

Greyhounds

A most ancient breed, Greyhounds are archetypes of the dogs that were trained to hunt by sight, the "gaze-hounds". The name "greyhound" has nothing to do with colour, but comes from the old Saxon word *grei*, meaning fine, or beautiful.

HISTORY

The breed probably has Middle Eastern origins, and it seems likely that it came to Europe with the first Phoenician trading ships. The Greyhound and its miniature version, the Italian Greyhound, became very popular in Europe in the Middle Ages and were a favourite of royalty. Indeed, they are the most common heraldic dog, to be found in the coats of arms of Charles V of France and Henry VIII of England. Because of their excellent powers of acceleration (they can reach speeds of 65 km/h, or 40 mph), Greyhounds were extremely successful hunters of small game, such as hare. These old adversaries still face each other in the sport of greyhound racing, but today the hare is mechanical rather than flesh and blood!

TEMPERAMENT

Greyhounds are sensitive, loving, well-behaved dogs. They are particularly good with children.

SEGUGIO ITALIANO This hunting dog arose from crosses of Egyptian hounds and the mastiffs of classical Rome and Greece. Popular in the Renaissance, the breed was revived at the beginning of the 20th century.

HEAD Long but quite broad between the ears, with a flat skull and a slight stop. Well-sculpted, powerful jaw.

BODY Broad, square back, and well-sprung ribs. Chest is deep, providing adequate room for the heart, and the loins are arched and powerful.

LEGS Long and strong, with muscular, powerful thighs.

FEET Fairly long, compact, well knuckled, and rather hare-like, with strong pads.

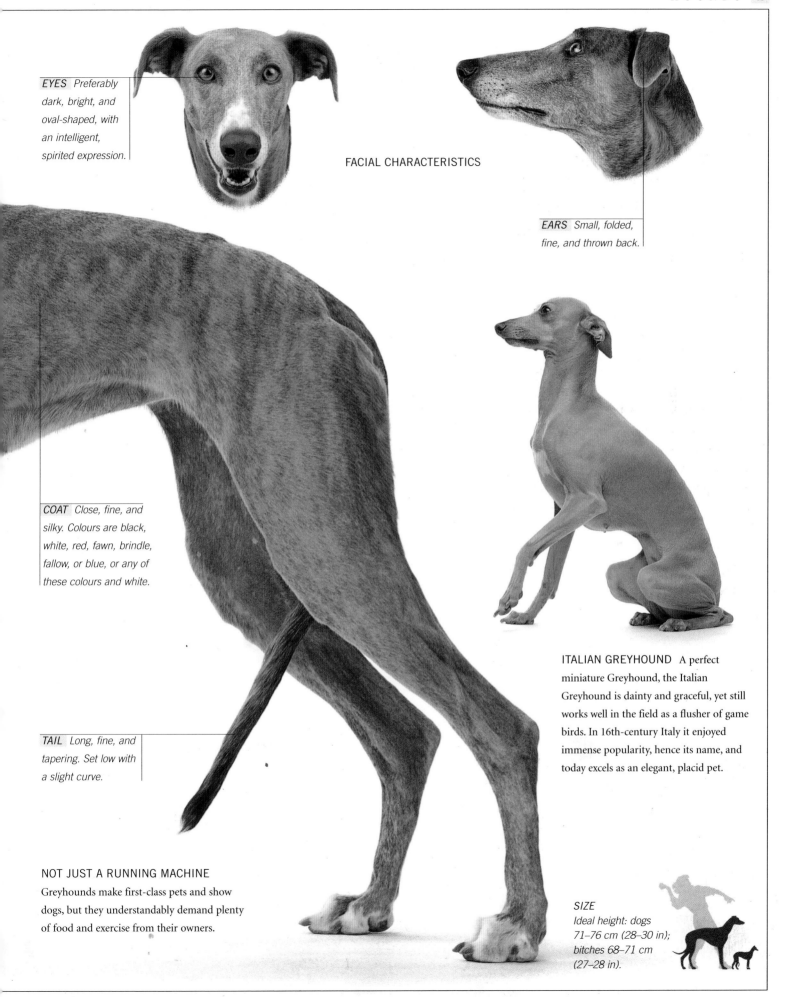

EYES *Preferably dark, bright, and oval-shaped, with an intelligent, spirited expression.*

FACIAL CHARACTERISTICS

EARS *Small, folded, fine, and thrown back.*

COAT *Close, fine, and silky. Colours are black, white, red, fawn, brindle, fallow, or blue, or any of these colours and white.*

TAIL *Long, fine, and tapering. Set low with a slight curve.*

ITALIAN GREYHOUND A perfect miniature Greyhound, the Italian Greyhound is dainty and graceful, yet still works well in the field as a flusher of game birds. In 16th-century Italy it enjoyed immense popularity, hence its name, and today excels as an elegant, placid pet.

NOT JUST A RUNNING MACHINE
Greyhounds make first-class pets and show dogs, but they understandably demand plenty of food and exercise from their owners.

SIZE
Ideal height: dogs 71–76 cm (28–30 in); bitches 68–71 cm (27–28 in).

Irish Wolfhound

This sturdy creature – frequently mentioned in legends, songs, and stories because of its gentleness and courage – almost became extinct in the 19th century, but after input from other breeds, particularly the Scottish Deerhound, its future was secured.

HISTORY

The Irish Wolfhound's ancestor was the Cu, a massive shaggy-coated dog used for the pursuit of wolves, elk, and wild boar. Irish Wolfhounds were often given as royal presents and eventually became such popular gifts that Oliver Cromwell had to stop their export from Britain. With the last wolf in Scotland being killed in the early 18th century, and the species disappearing from Ireland in 1766, the great dog that had hunted it likewise went into decline. The breed was revived in the second half of the 19th century, principally by a British army officer, Captain George Graham.

TEMPERAMENT

The Irish Wolfhound is reliable, sweet-tempered, intelligent, and can be trusted with children.

BODY *Fairly long back, deep chest, and arched loins.*

COAT *Rough and wiry. Colours are grey, steel grey, brindle, red, black, pure white, fawn, and wheaten.*

IRISH PRIDE This breed is the national dog of Ireland, and is also known as the Wolfdog, the Irish Greyhound, and the Great Dog of Ireland.

TAIL *Long, moderately thick, and slightly curved.*

SIZE
*Minimum height:
dogs 79 cm (31 in);
bitches 71 cm (28 in).*

EARS Velvety, small, and lying flat. They should be dark in colour.

EYES Dark and oval-shaped, with black eyelids.

FACIAL CHARACTERISTICS

IMPOSING DOG These muscular, commanding creatures will need lots of space in which to gambol, but, surprisingly, they require no more exercise than the smaller breeds. Today's breeders are aiming to produce Wolfhounds of even greater size, and in the future it is hoped that an "extra large" breed averaging 81–86 cm (32–34 in) will be firmly established.

HEAD Long but not too broad, with a slightly tapering muzzle. Frontal bones on the forehead are slightly raised. Black nose and lips.

LEGS Forelegs are straight and strong; hindlegs long and muscular.

FEET Big and round, with a pronounced arching of the toes.

Rhodesian Ridgeback

Rather surprisingly, the native land of this shapely hound is South Africa, not Rhodesia (now Zimbabwe). "Ridgeback" refers to its unique feature – the distinctive, dagger-shaped line of hair running along its back, growing in the opposite direction to the rest of its coat.

HISTORY

In the 16th and 17th centuries, European settlers took breeds such as Bloodhounds *(see pp.32–3)*, mastiffs, and various terriers to South Africa. These dogs interbred with the local stock, such as the half-wild African Hottentot Hunting Dog, to create the breed that we know today. Ridgebacks make excellent hunting dogs, for they have great stamina, can go without water for more than 24 hours, and are able to cope with the extreme temperature changes of the African bush. Used in packs, they hunt leopard, buffalo, and antelope, and can pursue lion with such success that the breed is now also known as the Rhodesian Lion Dog.

TEMPERAMENT

The Rhodesian Ridgeback is a sharp-witted, friendly character and makes a popular family pet. Although a formidable fighter when roused, essentially it has a quiet temperament and rarely barks.

HEAD Long, well jawed, with a flat skull and a long, deep muzzle. Nose is black or brown, depending on the eye colour.

RHODESIAN RIDGEBACK The "dog with a snake on its back" is a fierce, indomitable hunter and, usually working in a pack of three, will even attack a pride of five lions.

BODY Deep chested, powerful, and distinctly muscular.

MULTIPURPOSE HOUND This Rhodesian Ridgeback is a hunter, a guardian, and a friend. He requires ample space and relishes vigorous exercise.

COAT Short, dense, sleek, and glossy. Colours are light wheaten to red wheaten.

SIZE
Desirable height:
dogs 63–67 cm
(25–27 in);
bitches 61–66 cm
(24–26 in).

EYES Amber or dark brown, with black rims.

EARS Medium length, placed high, and carried close to the head.

FACIAL CHARACTERISTICS

TAIL Fairly long, tapering and strong at the root. When active, carried with an upward curve.

LEGS Strong, with well-defined muscles.

FEET Of medium size, with toes that are distinctly arched.

Saluki

This svelte and graceful dog is extremely fast and agile; the Bedouin of southern Arabia still use Salukis and falcons to capture prey such as gazelles and bustards. The Saluki hunts by sight, not by scent, and, with its blistering turn of speed, can run down virtually any game.

HISTORY

The Saluki's ancient origins lie in the Middle East, and it was named after the Arabian city of Saluk, now vanished beneath the sands. Used by various nomadic desert peoples, Salukis spread from the Caspian Sea to the Sahara Desert. Saluki-like dogs are depicted on Persian pottery dating from 4200 BC. The pharaohs reputedly hunted with hawks on their wrists and Salukis on leads, and mummified Saluki remains have been found in Egyptian tombs. Mediaeval Muslim huntsmen called the breed "the sacred gift of Allah". This religious connection made it permissible for Muslims to eat the game run down by the dog, which would otherwise be considered unclean. The Saluki is also known as the Gazelle Hound, Arabian Hound, or Persian Greyhound, and, as its appearance suggests, it is probably quite closely related to another ancient breed, the Afghan Hound (see pp.20–21).

TEMPERAMENT

The Saluki is an even-tempered, loyal, and sensitive dog, with an aristocratic air. It may require obedience training to keep its deep-rooted hunting instincts under control.

COAT Soft, smooth, and delicate. Colours include white, cream, fawn, golden red, grizzle, black and tan, tricolour (white, black, and tan), and various combinations of these colours.

BODY Fine, shapely, and muscular, with a broad back, and deep, rather narrow chest.

FEATHERED SALUKI There are two varieties of Saluki: the feathered and the smooth-haired. The feathered Saluki displays light, silky feathering on the backs of its legs and thighs.

LEGS Long and fine, with well-muscled thighs.

FEET Quite long; toes are distinctly arched, with plenty of feathering.

HEAD Long, narrow head, with a fairly wide gap between the ears. Nose is black or liver in colour. Upper teeth closely overlap the lower teeth.

EYES Large, oval-shaped, and hazel to dark brown in colour.

EARS Long, covered with feathered, silky hair, and hanging down close to the face.

FACIAL CHARACTERISTICS

CANINE GIFT There is an ancient tradition among Muslim peoples that the Saluki is never sold but only presented as a gift or as a tribute to a superior.

TAIL Long, gently curved, and feathered with long hair on the underside. Set low.

SIZE
Ideal height:
dogs 58–71 cm
(23–28 in);
bitches slightly less.

Whippet

As finely sculpted, elegant, and graceful as its ancestor the Greyhound *(see pp.44–5)*, the Whippet also contains terrier blood, particularly that of the Bedlington *(see pp.88–9)* and Manchester Terriers *(see pp.104–5).* Although it enjoys the excitement of the racing track, it is just as happy with a comfortable home life and makes an excellent, reliable pet.

HISTORY

In Victorian times, miners in the coalfields of north-east England crossed local terriers with small Greyhounds to use for "snap racing" (rabbit or hare coursing in an enclosed space). On cruelty grounds, this sport was made illegal in Great Britain, and the early Whippets quickly switched to "rag racing". This legal sport had Whippets racing towards their owners at top speed in response to a wave of a piece of cloth. As a consequence, Whippets became affectionately known as "rag dogs", and this form of racing is still a popular Sunday activity in the north of England.

TEMPERAMENT

This is the nicest dog you could hope to meet – gentle, loving, and loyal. It is perfectly happy to live in a town house or apartment, but it does need plenty of daily exercise.

BODY *Deep chested with a broad, muscular back, and strong, powerful loins. It forms a sleek and graceful outline.*

WHIPPET Although the Whippet looks frail, it is surprisingly powerful for such a small creature, and it possesses remarkable acceleration.

SHAKING DOG The Whippet's habit of shivering does not necessarily indicate that it is frightened or cold, though it will require some protection against poor weather and should not be exposed to draughts.

EYES Dark in colour, bright, alert, and oval-shaped; fairly wide gap between them.

HEAD Long and fine, with a flat top to the skull. Nose has a slight stop. The strong jaw has a perfect scissor bite.

COAT Very fine, short, and close set. It can be any colour or mix of colours; this Whippet's coat colour is grey brindle.

EARS Small, fine, and rose-shaped.

FACIAL CHARACTERISTICS

LEGS Hindlegs are wide, well muscled at the thighs, and set well under the body; forelegs are straight and not too wide.

TAIL Long and tapering, with a gentle curve.

FEET Well-spaced toes with thick pads.

SIZE
Dogs 47–51 cm
(18½–20 in) tall;
bitches 44–47 cm
(17½–18½ in).

Gundogs

The Gundog group, called Sporting Dogs in the US, comprises a wide variety of breeds, all of which were developed to act as hunters' assistants in some fashion – mainly by finding and retrieving game. They hunt principally by picking up scents carried in the air. Between 1990 and 2002, gundogs won Best in Show at Crufts on five occasions.

SPANIELS

The largest subdivision of gundogs is the spaniel tribe. These intelligent, medium-sized dogs stand not too high off the ground. They have a well-developed muzzle, a keen nose, and ears protected by long flaps – all sensible features for animals that must work in rough country. The word "spaniel" probably comes from the old French *espaignol*, meaning "Spanish dog", and some of the first users of spaniels, the Irish, are thought to have obtained their stock from the Iberian Peninsula.

SPANIEL BREEDS

Spaniels can be divided into those breeds that hunt and retrieve, those that retrieve only, and finally toy spaniels, which do not hunt and are nowadays considered toy dogs. Most of the sporting spaniels range over the ground ahead of the hunter but still stay relatively close to the gun, usually at a distance of 20–65 m (22–70 yd) so that the charge from the shotgun can reach and kill the game that the dogs flush out. For such a dog to chase flushed game would be very bad manners indeed. If the game is killed, the spaniel is sent after it to bring it back. They can also be trained to retrieve waterfowl from a shooting blind (a concealed enclosure), the Springer Spaniel being especially adept at such work.

POINTERS AND SETTERS

The second subdivision of gundogs includes the pointers and setters, in general bigger dogs than spaniels and with longer legs. The athletic-looking pointers plainly show their close relationship to true hounds.

Unlike the spaniels, these dogs move far ahead of the hunter, often out of sight. When they scent game, pointers do not immediately disturb the birds into flying, but stand rigidly with muzzle stretched (pointed) towards the quarry, usually with one forefoot raised. They remain in this position until the hunter flushes and shoots the birds. Like pointers, setters freeze when they find their target, but then "set" (drop to the ground). Setters were in use by the 16th century, but pointers are relatively recent breeds whose rise parallels the development of sporting guns.

RETRIEVERS

The third gundog group, the retrievers, are hunting specialists. Friendly, strong, well-built dogs, they are expert "finders and returners" of game, and were often used in conjunction with "flushing" spaniels. The method was for spaniels to quarter the ground and "spring" the game, while the retrievers stayed close beside the guns. When the game was shot, the retrievers were sent out to bring it back.

ENGLISH SETTER (Top right) Once they have found their prey, well-trained setters and pointers will remain as mobile as a statue, if necessary for as long as an hour or more, awaiting the hunter's next command.

WEIMARANER (Below right) Outside of the three main groups there are a few other gundogs, such as the Weimaraner, which is an all-rounder capable of tackling both large and small game.

CHESAPEAKE BAY RETRIEVER (Left) An intelligent, brave, and willing dog, the Chesapeake Bay Retriever is a natural hunter. It has an excellent nose, a passion for water work in all weathers, and a remarkable memory, being able unfailingly to recall the the positions of multiple fallen game.

Pointers

These are among the oldest sporting dogs, and they have been used for centuries to "point" game out to the hunter. The various types have different skills and specialities, but the common characteristic is the classic pointing stance, with tail and foreleg raised and the head extended towards the quarry.

HISTORY

The earliest pointers were used to help in netting birds, particularly quail and partridge. In the early 18th century, shooting game birds with shot pellets came into fashion, and the Spanish Pointer was introduced into England. This was a slow, heavy dog that kept its nose to the ground; to improve its speed and air-scenting abilities it was bred with the Greyhound (see pp.44–5) and English Foxhound (see pp.42–3). The result was the English Pointer, which has since been introduced all over the world and is now known simply as the Pointer. Another type of pointer was developed in Germany in the 17th century by crossing German hound stock with Spanish Pointers and Bloodhounds (see pp.32–3). This was a more substantial dog than the modern German Shorthaired Pointer, which appeared in the 19th century when English Pointer blood was added to the breed.

TEMPERAMENT

Pointers are generally kind and even-tempered, loyal, and obedient. They are also very energetic and always eager to work.

GERMAN WIRE-HAIRED POINTER Developed at the beginning of the 20th century, the German Wire-haired Pointer combines the assets of an all-round gundog with the weather-resistant wiry coat of the terriers.

HUNTING EXPERT The German Shorthaired Pointer is not only an expert at hunting all sorts of game, it also makes an excellent guard and house-dog.

BODY Deep chest, with short, level back, and powerful loins. Neck is long, muscular, and slightly arched.

LEGS Forelegs are straight, strong, and lean; hindlegs are muscular.

SIZE
Dogs 58–64 cm (23–25 in) tall; bitches 53–58 cm (21–23 in).

HEAD Elegant, with broad, slightly rounded skull, and long muzzle. Nose is black or brown, according to coat colour, with wide nostrils.

EARS Broad, set high, and hanging down close to head.

FACIAL CHARACTERISTICS

EYES Medium in size, with soft and intelligent expression.

TAIL Set high, thick at base, and tapering. Customarily docked by two fifths to half of its length. Carried horizontally when on the move.

COAT Short, coarse hairs giving a dense, flat coat. Colours are black or liver, with or without white spots and/or flecks.

GERMAN SHORTHAIRED POINTER This hardy athlete is among the most versatile of gundogs, tracking and pointing a wide variety of game, and retrieving on land or from water. Since its introduction in the 1920s, it has become very popular in the US.

POINTER Also known as the English Pointer, this is a medium-sized, elegant gundog renowned for its speed, intelligence, and enthusiasm. Working best on land, it has legendary tracking and pointing skills but is not usually expected to retrieve game.

FEET Compact and round to oval in shape, with arched toes. Hard pads and strong nails.

Bracco Italiano

Arguably the oldest of European hunting breeds, the Bracco Italiano – or Italian Hound – is an athletic, open-air-loving animal whose character clearly reflects its rugged past.

HISTORY

Records show that the Bracco Italiano dates back to at least the 5th century BC. Developed at that time from the crossing of mastiffs that had originated in Mesopotamia (modern Iraq) with lighter, fleet-footed Egyptian coursing hounds, it is the breed from which, probably via the Spanish Pointer, all modern European pointers have sprung *(see pp.56–7)*. It worked first with mediaeval net hunters and falconers, and later became the supreme gundog.

TEMPERAMENT

Sensible almost to the point of over-seriousness, the Bracco is well mannered but still very friendly. Not a "townie" by nature, it demands wide-open spaces, lots of exercise, and, principally because of its long, crinkly ears, plenty of loving attention from its owners.

HEAD Long and lean with a distinct, shapely cranium and well-formed jowls. Nose can be straight or hooked slightly.

BODY Deep, well-sprung chest, a broad, muscular back, and strong, sloping shoulders.

COAT Short with a smart sheen, in colours of pure white, roan, or white marked or flecked with orange or brown.

LEGS Long, muscular, and well balanced.

FEET Well formed, with distinctly arched toes.

BRAQUE FRANÇAIS The Braque Français, or French Pointer, was developed in the 17th century, possibly using the Bracco Italiano and the Spanish Pointer. A tough, energetic, and talented hunter, the breed has two varieties: the "de Gascogne", and the smaller "des Pyrénées". Often called the Braque Charles X, it was numerous in France up until the 19th century but later gave ground to other pointing and setting breeds.

SIZE
Height 55–67 cm (21–26 in).

FACIAL CHARACTERISTICS

EYES Should be neither too deep nor too prominent. Yellow, orange, or brown in colour.

EARS Set back, well developed, and pendulous; wrinkled and particularly sensitive to the touch.

TAIL Thick and customarily docked.

POPULAR HOUND Although European pointers have in recent times outdistanced the Bracco Italiano in popularity, the breed is still firmly lodged in more than a few hearts.

DOG OF KINGS A breed that has always kept illustrious company, the Bracco is mentioned by Pliny and Dante and was a feature of the French courts of Louis XII and Francis I.

WIRE-HAIRED POINTING GRIFFON Often called the Korthals Griffon after the Dutch sportsman who, through selective breeding at the end of the 19th century, recreated the ancient Griffon hound, this is an all-weather, dedicated pointer and retriever of game. It carries the blood of setters, spaniels, Otterhounds, and German Pointers, as well as that of the old Griffon.

Golden Retriever

Hardy and hard-working, the Golden Retriever was developed for wildfowl hunting, which explains why these dogs are always ready for a swim whatever the weather. They are now popular family dogs, as well as continuing to be a favourite with sportsmen.

SHEER PERFECTION The Golden Retriever's ancestry makes it the perfect dog for working or playing in very wet, cold conditions.

HISTORY

The exact origins of the Golden Retriever are still hotly disputed, but the breed can certainly be attributed to the efforts of Lord Tweedmouth in the mid-19th century. Possibly starting with a mysterious dog called a Russian Tracker, he then introduced some Flat-coated Retriever (see opposite), Bloodhound (see pp.32–3), and Water Spaniel genes. The result was a dog with a natural retrieving instinct and an acute sense of smell for tracking. It was recognized as a distinct breed by the UK Kennel Club in 1913.

TEMPERAMENT

This is a gentle-natured, confident dog, with a well-developed sense of loyalty. Extremely patient with children, the Golden Retriever is an ideal family dog, provided it is given ample exercise.

COAT Dense undercoat, with flat or wavy outer coat. Abundant feathering. Colours are solid gold or solid cream. There may be a few white hairs, but only on the chest. Neck is strong, muscular, and of a good length.

GLOBAL APPRECIATION The Golden Retriever has been steadily increasing in popularity since its show debut in 1908. It is now a well-established favourite all over the world.

HEAD Broad skull, with a definite stop, leading to a powerful muzzle. Nose should be black. Strong jaws, with a perfect scissor bite.

EYES Set wide apart, dark brown in colour, with dark rims.

FACIAL CHARACTERISTICS

EARS Medium-sized, set on a level with eyes.

TAIL Carried level with back without curling at the end or arching over the back.

BODY Well-balanced; deep-chested with a level back and muscular loins.

FLAT-COATED RETRIEVER Despite not being as popular today as in the early decades of the 20th century, the Flat-coated Retriever is still a much-loved gundog and show dog, and it makes a very good, if energetic, pet.

LEGS Hindlegs are straight, strong, and muscular; forelegs are straight.

SIZE
Dogs 56–61 cm (22–24 in) tall; bitches 51–56 cm (20–22 in).

FEET Round, compact, cat-like in appearance, with generous foot pads.

Labrador Retriever

The most popular retriever of all, the Labrador has become renowned for its versatility. Widely used as police dogs and guide dogs for the blind, Labradors are also excellent gundogs, in and out of water, and make reliable family pets.

HISTORY

This breed originated not in Labrador but on the coast of Newfoundland, where they were trained to bring in fishing nets through icy waters. In the 19th century, Newfoundland's fishermen came to the English West Country to sell fish, and some were persuaded to sell their dogs too. The breed was immediately successful as a gundog and was recognized by the English Kennel Club in 1903. It was the Earl of Malmesbury who first called them Labradors in 1887.

TEMPERAMENT

The Labrador is gentle, loyal, even-tempered, intelligent, and exceptionally reliable with children. It is always eager to please, but will guard against intruders. The breed is much better suited to country life than to that of the town.

HEAD Broad skull, with pronounced stop. Nose should be large and well developed. Jaws are powerful, and the upper teeth closely overlap the lower teeth.

COAT Short, straight, dense coat, hard to the touch, and exceptionally waterproof. Colours are solid black, yellow, or liver chocolate.

CHESAPEAKE BAY RETRIEVER This breed has a dense oily coat, webbed feet, and yellow or amber eyes. It was developed in the US in the early 19th century from two dogs, Canton and Sailor, thought to be Newfoundlands *(see pp.160–61)* that had been shipwrecked off Maryland. They were then crossed with the Flat-coated *(see p.61)* and Curly Coated Retriever *(see opposite)*, and also with the Otterhound.

SIZE
Dogs 56–57 cm (22–22½ in) tall; bitches 54–56 cm (21–22 in).

FEET Compact and round with well-arched toes and generous pads. Nails to match coat.

EARS *Set far back, not too heavy, hanging close to the head.*

EYES *Medium-sized, brown or hazel, with intelligent expression.*

FACIAL CHARACTERISTICS

A KEEN NOSE Equipped with an excellent nose, Labradors were used in both World Wars to detect mines, and as police dogs their present-day duties include sniffing out drugs.

BODY *Well-built, with a deep, broad chest, a level back, and wide loins.*

CURLY COATED RETRIEVER Distinctive in its tightly curled black or brown coat, the Curly Coated Retriever was widely used in the 19th century to retrieve waterfowl and other game in all weathers. Its relations probably include the Labrador and the Water Spaniel.

DISTINGUISHED OWNERS Famous owners of Labrador Retrievers have included Bing Crosby and François Mitterand.

LEGS *Hindquarters are powerful; forelegs are straight from the elbow.*

TAIL *Distinctive "otter tail", covered with dense fur; medium length, thick at the root, and tapering.*

Setters

Setter-type dogs have long been used for hunting, and they are also among the most graceful and natural of field dogs. The Irish, English, and Gordon Setters are similar in shape and style, but they have widely varying coat colours.

HISTORY

Derived from a variety of spaniels, setters, and pointers, the Irish Setter was initially a red-and-white dog, with shorter legs than today's breed. In the 19th century, following intensive selective breeding efforts, the lustrous, pure chestnut-red setter emerged, to win both prizes and hearts. Around the same time, the good-natured and handsome English Setter was being lovingly developed, principally by Sir Edward Laverack; it is consequently also known as the Laverack Setter. The Gordon Setter was carefully bred by the Dukes of Gordon on their Scottish estate and owes its black and tan coloration to a collie ancestor.

TEMPERAMENT

Setters are generally affectionate, high-spirited, and full of vitality. Some are difficult to train, probably as a result of their independent spirit, but given firm handling and plenty of exercise, these dogs can be a joy to own.

IRISH SETTER The Irish Setter finally had its name settled by the Ulster Irish Setter Club in 1876. Known long ago in its native Ireland as the Red Spaniel, today the breed is also called the Red Setter. The Irish Setter won Best in Show at Crufts three times in the 1990s (in 1993, 1995, and 1999).

PRESIDENTIAL DOG
Former US President Harry S Truman owned an Irish Setter named Mike.

GORDON SETTER The largest and strongest of the setters, this breed possesses excellent stamina and the useful ability to work for long periods without drinking. It has a calmer temperament than the other setters, and hunts slowly and methodically.

HEAD Long and lean, with a deep, square-ended muzzle. The top of the skull and the top of the muzzle are parallel and of equal length. Nose should be dark brown or black, with wide nostrils.

EYES Almond-shaped, set level; hazel or dark brown in colour.

FACIAL CHARACTERISTICS

EARS Medium-sized, set low and well back, and hanging close to the head.

BODY Deep, rather narrow chest; straight back and arched loins.

TAIL Medium-length, set low, and tapering. Carried level or below the line of the back.

ENGLISH SETTER This dog is a dependable hunter over all terrain, but its long coat tends to attract seeds and burrs.

COAT Medium-length, straight, silky hair, with feathering on the belly, tail, and backs of legs. Colour is deep chestnut.

LEGS Hindlegs are long and muscular; forelegs straight and sinewy.

FEET Rather small feet with arched toes. Feathered fur between the toes.

SIZE
Dogs 61–66 cm (24–26 in) tall; bitches slightly less.

Cocker Spaniel

This excellent gundog flushes out woodcock, pheasant, or partridge and retrieves them from both land and water. But today the Cocker Spaniel is perhaps better known as a show dog. Extremely popular in Britain and also the US, it has won more championships at Crufts than any other breed.

HISTORY

"Spaniel" is probably a corruption of the Old French for "Spanish dog", *espaignol*. The spaniel family can, as the name suggests, be traced back to 14th-century Spain. By the 1600s many types of spaniel were being used as gundogs in western Europe, and by the 18th century two members of the family had made their mark in Britain: the larger Springer Spaniel *(see pp.72–3)* and the Cocker Spaniel. The breed that we know today was firmly established in the late 19th century, and by the 1930s it had become the most popular dog in Britain.

TEMPERAMENT

A very active, playful, and intelligent animal, the Cocker Spaniel can be rather wilful at times. Its enthusiastic nature is demonstrated by its tail, which wags furiously most of the time, especially when the dog is on the move or working in the field.

HEAD Skull and muzzle of equal length, with definite stop between; cheekbones are not very prominent. Nostrils are well developed.

BODY Broad, deep chest, well-sprung ribs, and wide, short loins.

FEET Cat-like and compact, with robust pads. Nails match coat colour.

SIZE
Dogs 39–41 cm (15½–16 in) tall; bitches 38–39 cm (15–15½ in).

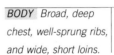

MULTIPLE OPTIONS Cockers come in 17 colours, particolours, and tricolours. One of the most popular is the Black-and-White.

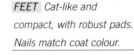

CLUMBER SPANIEL

The heavy-set Clumber was developed in France and has traces of Basset Hound in its ancestry. It is renowned for its stealth and silence when working in the field.

EARS *Long, set low, level with eyes, and covered with straight, silky hair.*

COAT *A flat-lying coat of silky hair, in various colours, with feathering on the legs and belly.*

EYES *Large, dark brown or dark hazel, with a friendly, intelligent expression.*

FACIAL CHARACTERISTICS

TAIL *Set low and customarily docked.*

LEGS *Very muscular hindlegs; well-boned, straight, short forelegs.*

GROOMING AND EXERCISE This breed makes a faithful companion but will need lots of attention in return! Regular brushing is required, as well as trimming of hair on the feet and ears. Plenty of exercise is essential to avoid obesity.

American Cocker Spaniel

Although now primarily a show dog and pet, the American Cocker Spaniel has a sporting background, which is clearly reflected in its intelligent and energetic nature. The name Cocker is probably short for "woodcocker", a reference to the dog's skills as a flusher of woodcock.

HISTORY

English Cocker Spaniels *(see pp.66–7)* were introduced into America in the 1880s, and before long a distinctly new breed had been developed to suit the special needs of US sportsmen. By the 1930s, the two types were significantly different, and by the 1940s they were officially recognized as two separate breeds. After World War II they became one of the most popular dogs in America, and were soon introduced back into Europe.

TEMPERAMENT

Bold, lively, intelligent, and keen to work, the American Cocker Spaniel is equally suited to life as a gundog or a household pet.

HEAD Rounded skull, with broad, deep muzzle. Nose and nostrils are black or brown and well developed. Upper teeth closely overlap lower teeth in a scissor bite.

COAT Dense, silky, flat, or wavy coat of good length. Prominent feathering. Many colours acceptable, including black, brown, red, cream, black and tan, brown and tan, particolours, and tricolours.

BODY Short, compact body, with a deep chest, and gently sloping back. Neck is long, muscular, and slightly arched.

FEET Compact and round with strong pads.

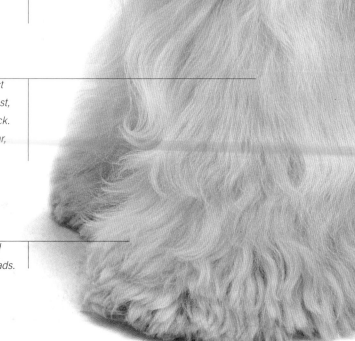

BLACK AMERICAN COCKER SPANIEL The American Cocker Spaniel has a smaller body and longer legs than its English cousin.

EYES Round and full, dark hazel to black in colour, and looking directly forward.

FACIAL CHARACTERISTICS

EARS Long, well haired, and set low.

TAIL Customarily docked by three fifths of its length. Carried in line with, or just above, the back.

AMERICAN COCKER SPANIEL This is a strong, athletic dog that needs lots of exercise and regular grooming.

LEGS Hindlegs strong and parallel; forelegs straight and muscular.

SIZE
Dogs 36–39 cm (14–15 in) tall; bitches 34–36 cm (13–14 in).

Brittany Spaniel

This superb all-round gundog is the smallest and best known of the French spaniels. It is highly popular among hunters in France, the United States, Canada, and the English-speaking world in general. Whereas spaniels generally flush game birds for the guns, and pointers and setters then locate the fallen quarry, the Brittany can do both, and indeed some believe it possesses setter blood in its ancestry. In addition, this intelligent and hard-working dog is oblivious to bad weather and will quite happily plunge into an icy pond to retrieve pheasant, partridge, or woodcock. The Brittany Spaniel is never flagging and unfailingly obedient.

HISTORY

The French Chien d'Oysel ("bird dog") of the 14th century was probably an early ancestor of the Brittany. Some of Rembrandt's paintings in the 17th century show a tailless dog very similar to the Brittany but with a more narrow face than we see in the modern breed. During the 19th century, English Setter *(see p.65)* and possibly pointer *(see pp.56–7)* blood produced a bigger dog with a more sensitive nose, and interbreeding with a small French spaniel, the Épagneul Fougères, may well have helped in neatening the dog's lines.

TEMPERAMENT

The Brittany Spaniel is affable, intelligent, co-operative, and willing, but rather wary of strangers.

BODY A short, straight back and muscular, sloping shoulders.

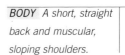

STYLISH POINTER A versatile, hardy, and sensitive hunting dog, the Brittany points game in the field in a very stylish manner and can then be relied upon to retrieve as efficiently as any spaniel.

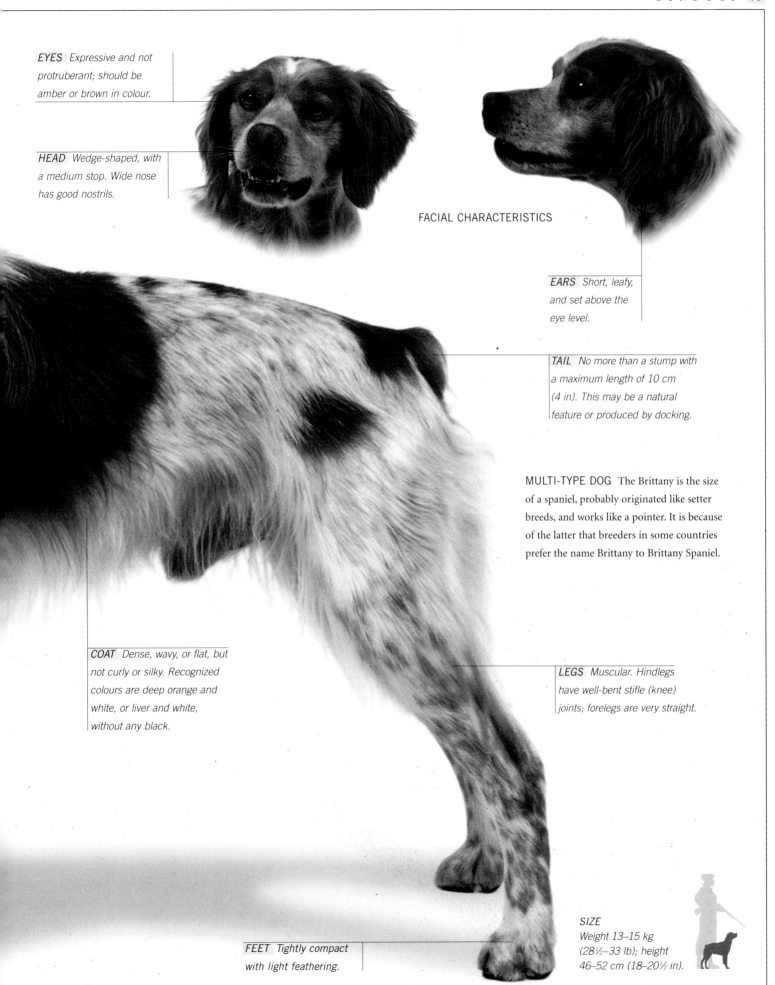

EYES Expressive and not protruberant; should be amber or brown in colour.

HEAD Wedge-shaped, with a medium stop. Wide nose has good nostrils.

FACIAL CHARACTERISTICS

EARS Short, leafy, and set above the eye level.

TAIL No more than a stump with a maximum length of 10 cm (4 in). This may be a natural feature or produced by docking.

MULTI-TYPE DOG The Brittany is the size of a spaniel, probably originated like setter breeds, and works like a pointer. It is because of the latter that breeders in some countries prefer the name Brittany to Brittany Spaniel.

COAT Dense, wavy, or flat, but not curly or silky. Recognized colours are deep orange and white, or liver and white, without any black.

LEGS Muscular. Hindlegs have well-bent stifle (knee) joints; forelegs are very straight.

SIZE
Weight 13–15 kg (28½–33 lb); height 46–52 cm (18–20½ in).

FEET Tightly compact with light feathering.

English Springer Spaniel

The very versatile English Springer excels as one of the most robust hunting spaniels, makes a reliable watchdog, and – with its affectionate, patient, and obedient character – fits in perfectly as a family pet, but one that demands abundant exercise. It occupies a central position in the history of spaniel development as the oldest of the spaniel family, and also having probably been the forebear of most spaniel breeds and some other gundogs. Its name derives from its characteristic springing forwards to flush out game for the hunter. In the field it is enthusiastic and active, good on land or in water, oblivious to the weather, and equally skilled at searching for quarry by means of its super-sensitive nose, flushing birds from cover, pointing, and retrieving.

A DOG WITHOUT EQUAL As a sporting dog, the English Springer – originally known as the Springing Spaniel – has no equal, being stronger, faster, and having more stamina than most other spaniels.

HISTORY

This type of dog has been around in England since at least the Middle Ages. Selective breeding to develop the Springer characteristics began in the early 19th century, and by the 1850s the breed as we know it today was well established. It was recognized in Britain in 1902 and introduced into the United States and Canada in 1907.

TEMPERAMENT

A most friendly dog, eager to please, quick to learn, obedient, and biddable. It can be rather reserved in the presence of strangers.

SPRINGER COLOURS English Springer Spaniels can be found in liver and white, black and white (with or without tan markings), blue, or liver roan.

TAIL Well feathered and carried low, with a lot of wagging activity! Often docked, but, increasingly, undocked tails (as shown here) are becoming the preferred style.

LEGS Hindlegs are muscular with broad thighs and wide-set, rounded hips; forelegs are straight and well feathered.

WELSH SPRINGER SPANIEL Closely related to the English Springer is the smaller, rich-red-and-white Welsh Springer Spaniel. It is an ancient breed; a painting by van Dyck in 1680 shows a dog that looks very much like a Welsh Springer.

FEET Round or slightly oval, compact, and well-arched with thick pads and plenty of feathering between the toes.

DUTCH PARTRIDGE HOUND A fine, versatile hunting dog, this is a breed that has existed in the Netherlands, virtually unchanged, since at least the 17th century. It is part spaniel and part setter, and it may have played an important role in the development of other major breeds of gundog. It makes an excellent pet.

COAT Flat or wavy, of medium length, and not too thick – but dense enough to be proof against water, weather, and thorns.

BODY Medium-sized, well-proportioned, neat, and compact.

HEAD Of medium length with a broad, high face and a moderate stop divided by a shallow groove. Black or liver-coloured nose with well-developed nostrils.

EYES Medium sized, set quite well apart, and fairly deep in their sockets. An alert, gentle expression.

EARS Long and wide, hanging close to the cheeks, and set on a level with the line of the eye, not too far back.

FACIAL CHARACTERISTICS

SIZE
Weight: dogs 20–25 kg (44–55 lb), bitches 18–23 kg (40–51 lb); height: dogs 48–56 cm (19–22 in), bitches 46–51 cm (18–20 in).

American Water Spaniel

This dog, a rugged, hard-working game-bird flusher and retriever, was originally developed in the American Midwest as a talented all-rounder, equally at home on dry land or carried by skiffs and canoes on water. One of only a few breeds originating in the United States, it is still rather uncommon there and virtually unknown overseas. Typically, the American Water Spaniel accompanies hunters exploring the chilly wetland waters of Michigan, Wisconsin, and Minnesota. The American Water Spaniel is the state dog of Wisconsin.

COAT Dense and waterproof; closely curled or waved, with a substantial undercoat. Liver, brown, or dark chocolate in colour, sometimes with a little white on the chest and toes.

HISTORY
Reliable records of the breed date back only to the mid-19th century. It is likely that the Curly Coated Retriever *(see p.63)* and Irish Water Spaniel are among its forebears. Recognition of the breed came in 1940.

TEMPERAMENT
Very friendly and intelligent, eager to please, and active.

TAIL Gently S-curved, lively, and of moderate length.

LEGS Moderate in length, strong, and feathered, with waterproofing hair.

HUNTER, GUARD, FRIEND Not only is the American Water Spaniel one of the toughest "waterproof" all-round hunting dogs, it also makes an alert and efficient guard dog and an excellent companion animal in the home.

UNCOMMON BREED Surprisingly, considering its fine character and attributes, the American Water Spaniel is still a relatively rare breed, virtually unknown outside the United States. Even there, it is mainly to be found around the Great Lakes region.

HEAD *Fairly defined and of moderate length, with a broad skull.*

EYES *Medium in size, set well apart, and light yellowish-brown to brown, hazel, or dark in colour.*

BODY *Wiry, lean, and light. Muscular and solidly built.*

EARS *Long and set slightly above the eye line, with close curls.*

FACIAL CHARACTERISTICS

FEET *Webbed and well padded, with the toes compactly grouped.*

SIZE
Weight 11–20 kg (25–45 lb); height 38–45 cm (15–18 in).

Nova Scotia Duck-Tolling Retriever

This Canadian breed, also known as Little River Duck Dog, looks a bit like a small Golden Retriever *(see pp.60–61)*. The Toller tolls (lures) wild ducks to within range of the guns by playing a game of "fetch the stick" with a hunter. The stick is thrown in the water several times and, as the game goes on, the activity of the dog attracts the curiosity of the birds, who paddle towards their nemesis to get a better look. As soon as they are within range, the hunter fires and the dog retrieves the fallen ducks. This artful ability to lure ducks is inbred, not trained. Tollers will happily retrieve thrown sticks for hours.

HISTORY

Tollers developed in Canada in the 19th century from so-called Red Decoy Dogs brought from England to Nova Scotia. They have retriever and working-spaniel blood in their veins. The Canadian Kennel Club recognized them in the 1950s, and full international recognition by the FCI came in 1985. They are a popular gundog breed in North America, and there is a good number of Toller breed clubs in the United States.

TEMPERAMENT

Intelligent, caring, playful, and patient, Tollers make superb companion and family dogs. They get on very well with children and other pets but are slightly aloof with strangers.

FEET *Round, strongly webbed, and medium in size.*

GREAT FAMILY DOG The delightful Toller is incredibly lively, energetic, and eager to play, which, along with its gentle friendly character, makes it ideal for children.

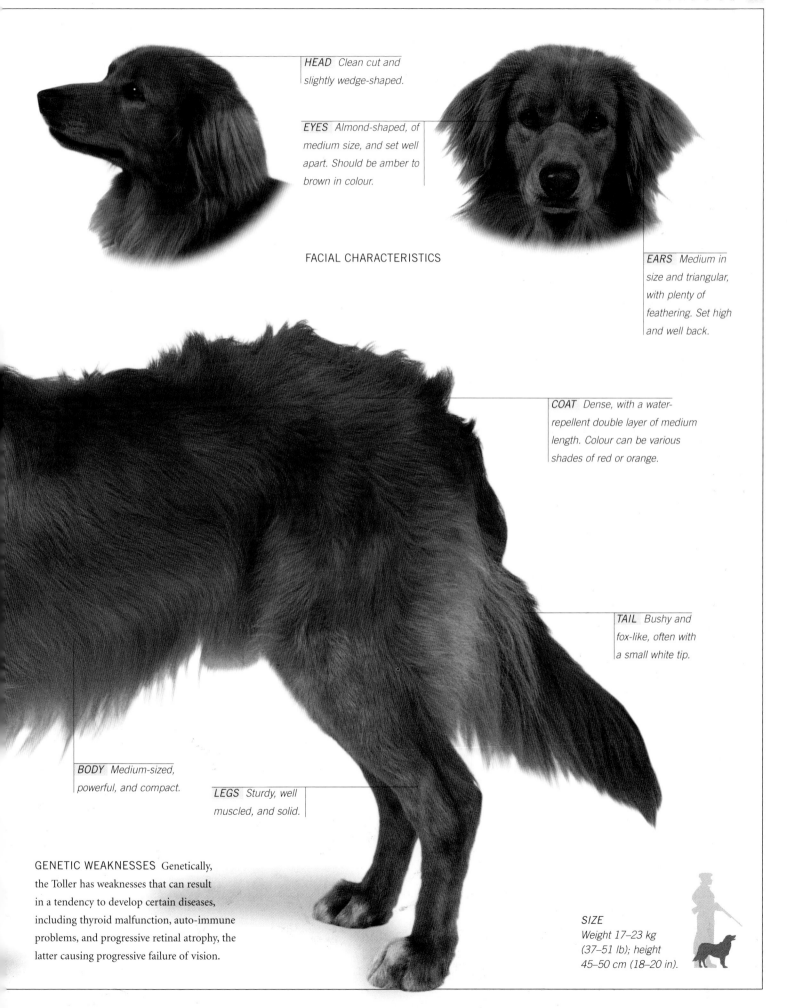

HEAD *Clean cut and slightly wedge-shaped.*

EYES *Almond-shaped, of medium size, and set well apart. Should be amber to brown in colour.*

FACIAL CHARACTERISTICS

EARS *Medium in size and triangular, with plenty of feathering. Set high and well back.*

COAT *Dense, with a water-repellent double layer of medium length. Colour can be various shades of red or orange.*

TAIL *Bushy and fox-like, often with a small white tip.*

BODY *Medium-sized, powerful, and compact.*

LEGS *Sturdy, well muscled, and solid.*

GENETIC WEAKNESSES Genetically, the Toller has weaknesses that can result in a tendency to develop certain diseases, including thyroid malfunction, auto-immune problems, and progressive retinal atrophy, the latter causing progressive failure of vision.

SIZE
Weight 17–23 kg (37–51 lb); height 45–50 cm (18–20 in).

Hungarian Vizsla

This elegant breed is a natural gundog with outstanding field skills. Vizslas are still bred primarily for tracking, pointing, and retrieving game, but they can also be kept as family pets if their owners are prepared for plenty of exercise!

HISTORY

The history of Hungary's national dog dates back to the Middle Ages, and its ancestors are said to have accompanied the Magyar hordes as they swept across Europe into Hungary around 1000 AD. The Vizsla probably developed into the sturdy dog that we know today on the game-rich Hungarian plains. The breed was almost wiped out by the disruption of two World Wars, but in the 1940s a few Vizslas were imported into Austria, where they were very carefully bred, and eventually spread to other parts of the world. Former owners of Hungarian Vizslas include Pope Pius XII and Zsa Zsa Gabor.

TEMPERAMENT

The Vizsla is an extremely active dog with a gentle, intelligent, obedient, and very affectionate character. It is easily trained and has great reserves of stamina.

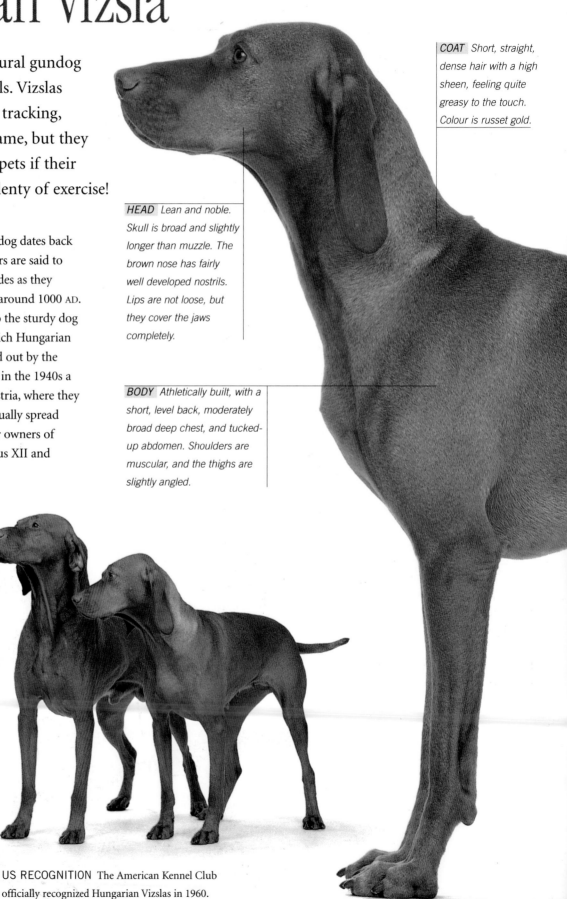

COAT Short, straight, dense hair with a high sheen, feeling quite greasy to the touch. Colour is russet gold.

HEAD Lean and noble. Skull is broad and slightly longer than muzzle. The brown nose has fairly well developed nostrils. Lips are not loose, but they cover the jaws completely.

BODY Athletically built, with a short, level back, moderately broad deep chest, and tucked-up abdomen. Shoulders are muscular, and the thighs are slightly angled.

US RECOGNITION The American Kennel Club officially recognized Hungarian Vizslas in 1960.

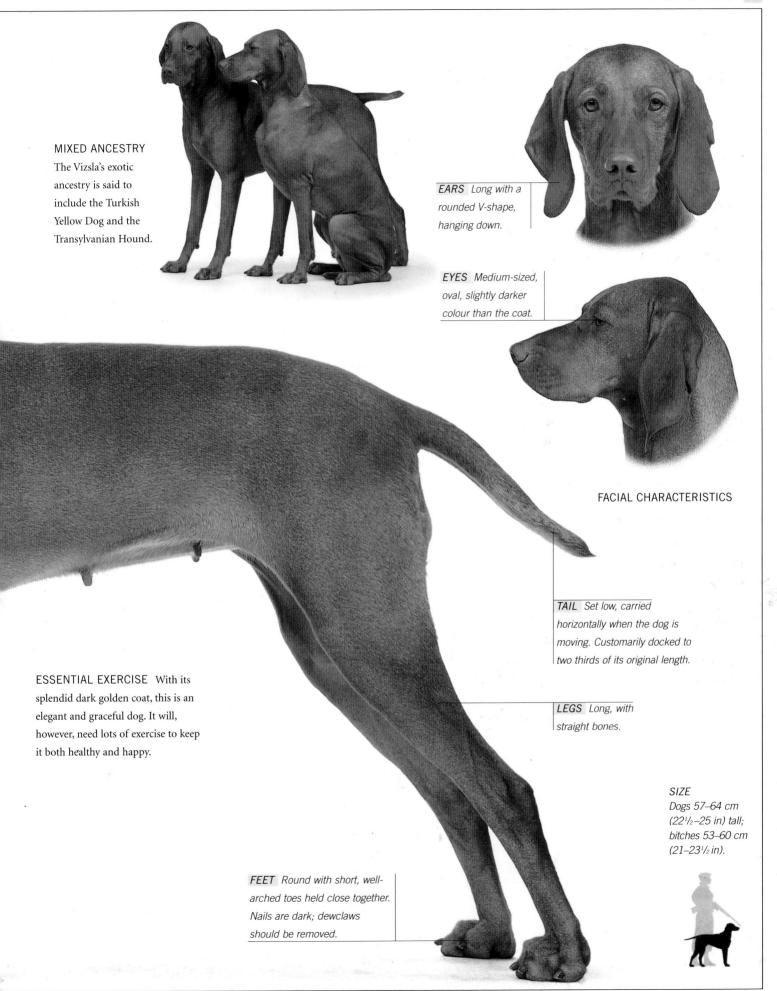

MIXED ANCESTRY
The Vizsla's exotic ancestry is said to include the Turkish Yellow Dog and the Transylvanian Hound.

EARS Long with a rounded V-shape, hanging down.

EYES Medium-sized, oval, slightly darker colour than the coat.

FACIAL CHARACTERISTICS

TAIL Set low, carried horizontally when the dog is moving. Customarily docked to two thirds of its original length.

ESSENTIAL EXERCISE With its splendid dark golden coat, this is an elegant and graceful dog. It will, however, need lots of exercise to keep it both healthy and happy.

LEGS Long, with straight bones.

SIZE
Dogs 57–64 cm (22½–25 in) tall; bitches 53–60 cm (21–23½ in).

FEET Round with short, well-arched toes held close together. Nails are dark; dewclaws should be removed.

Weimaraner

This large grey dog is renowned for its all-round hunting skills. It was first used to hunt big game such as wolves, bears, and boars, but later the breed was adapted for the tracking and retrieving of game birds.

HISTORY

Large grey hunting dogs have been used in Germany since the 17th century, but the Weimaraner only emerged as a distinct breed early in the 19th century. It was developed by the nobility of the grand duchy of Weimar, probably by crossing Bloodhounds *(see pp.32–3)* with a variety of hunting dogs. Its excellent nose is undoubtedly a result of these origins. As big game died out in Germany with the encroachment of civilization, the Weimaraner was adapted into a pointing dog for use with game birds. Although no longer the exclusive preserve of the gentry, the breeding of Weimaraners was still tightly controlled and was not permitted at all outside Germany until the 1930s. The breed has since gained a significant following in both the US and Britain.

TEMPERAMENT

Originally bred as a gentleman's personal sporting dog and companion, the Weimaraner is active, strong-willed, intelligent, and fearless, and it needs plenty of exercise and firm control.

VARIANT TYPE Most Weimaraners are shorthaired, but there is a longhaired variety that has a coat 2.5–5 cm (1–2 in) long, with feathering on the tail, ears, and the backs of the legs. With this type, only the tip of the tail is docked.

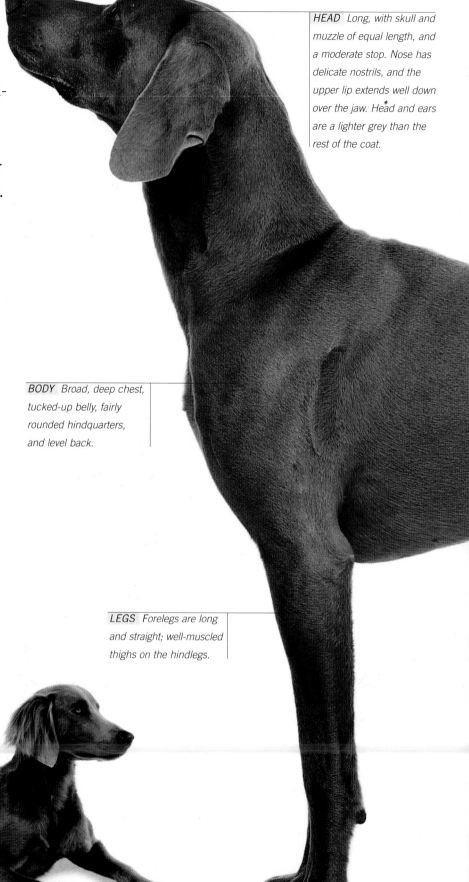

HEAD Long, with skull and muzzle of equal length, and a moderate stop. Nose has delicate nostrils, and the upper lip extends well down over the jaw. Head and ears are a lighter grey than the rest of the coat.

BODY Broad, deep chest, tucked-up belly, fairly rounded hindquarters, and level back.

LEGS Forelegs are long and straight; well-muscled thighs on the hindlegs.

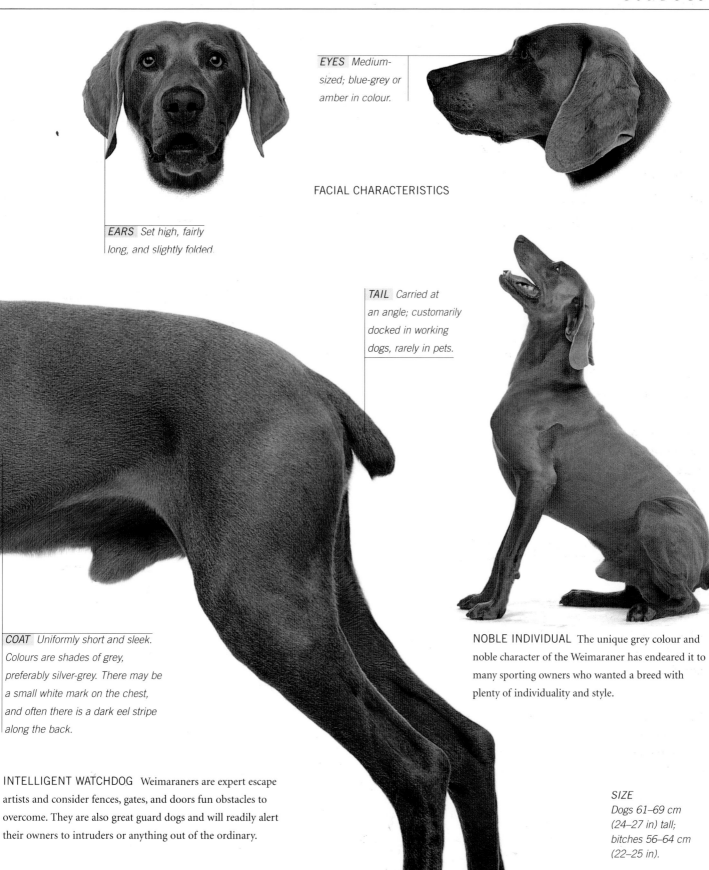

EYES Medium-sized; blue-grey or amber in colour.

FACIAL CHARACTERISTICS

EARS Set high, fairly long, and slightly folded.

TAIL Carried at an angle; customarily docked in working dogs, rarely in pets.

COAT Uniformly short and sleek. Colours are shades of grey, preferably silver-grey. There may be a small white mark on the chest, and often there is a dark eel stripe along the back.

NOBLE INDIVIDUAL The unique grey colour and noble character of the Weimaraner has endeared it to many sporting owners who wanted a breed with plenty of individuality and style.

INTELLIGENT WATCHDOG Weimaraners are expert escape artists and consider fences, gates, and doors fun obstacles to overcome. They are also great guard dogs and will readily alert their owners to intruders or anything out of the ordinary.

SIZE
Dogs 61–69 cm (24–27 in) tall; bitches 56–64 cm (22–25 in).

FEET Compact with arched toes set close together. Nails are grey or amber in colour.

Terriers

If one group of dogs can claim to be "Made in Britain", it is the terriers. These hunting dogs, designed for tackling such burrowing animals as badgers, foxes, rabbits, and rats, were largely developed in the British Isles. When the Romans first invaded, they found these "workers in the earth" already being used, and called them *terrarii* from the Latin for earth, *terra*.

TERRIER TYPES

In some cases the terrier's job was to find and kill the animals underground; in others, they were trained to force the quarry out of its den and up to the surface, where it could be dealt with by the hunter. Terriers are generally small, short-legged, and stocky, with alert and spirited temperaments.

Tough working dogs, terriers come in wide varieties that can be split into two basic coat types: the smooth or shorthaired, such as the Smooth Fox Terrier; and the rough or longhaired, like the Scottish and Skye Terriers.

BRITISH BREEDS

England produced breeds such as the Fox Terrier, Airedale, Bedlington, and Bull Terrier. Scotland gave us the Skye, Cairn, and West Highland, as well as the Scottish. Ireland was the birthplace of the Irish and Kerry Blue, and Wales contributed the Welsh and Sealyham. Almost every British region produced its own variety of terrier; many of these are now extinct, have been absorbed into other breeds, or are narrowly localized. They include the Devon, Poltalloch, Clydesdale, Cheshire, Aberdeen, and Roseneath terriers.

MODEL HEROES

It is possible that more terriers have been declared canine war heroes than any other breed. Billy, a brindled Bull Terrier, served with the Royal Ulster Rifles in the Transvaal during the Boer War, was wounded, and learned how to feign a limp in order to be given a ride on a cavalry horse. Bob was a terrier attached to the Scots Guards during the Crimean War and chased Russian cannonballs when they landed behind the British lines. Drummer Jack, a Fox Terrier, served in World War I with the Coldstream Guards, winning the 1914 Star, Victoria Medal, and General Service Medal. There were many more such valiant terriers.

Terriers have also played a major role in art. Paintings by artists such as Le Nain, Brueghel, and Landseer all feature terriers. Landseer owned a Rough White Terrier, Brutus, who appears in several paintings, including *Rat Catchers* and *Attachment*.

RUGGED INDIVIDUALISTS

No other sort of dog has more gritty tenacity, cockiness, or sparkle than the terriers. These are rugged individuals that you read about being rescued alive after many days down a collapsed mine shaft, or recovering from appalling injuries inflicted by fighting other dogs or badgers in illegal contests organized by barbaric and despicable owners. Most terriers kept in Britain nowadays are not used, fortunately, for any form of hunting, but make delightful, loyal, and lively pets and companions.

WEST HIGHLAND TERRIER (Top right) A terrier through and through, the Westie displays all the characteristics of the type to the highest degree, being spirited, hardy, courageous, and sparkling, as well as possessing considerable self-esteem. It was originally used to keep down foxes, otters, and vermin on Scottish farms.

AIREDALE TERRIER (Below right) A cross between the now extinct Black-and-Tan Terrier and the Otterhound, the Airedale is the biggest terrier. It was developed as a dual-purpose breed to hunt both badger and otter. However, its size stopped it from pursuing game underground.

JACK RUSSELL TERRIER (Left) Another typical small terrier is the Jack Russell – a fun-loving, quick-witted, muscular bundle of energy. Originally developed for rat-catching, the terrier is still used for this purpose today, although it is now most commonly found as a loyal and affectionate companion animal.

Airedale Terrier

This giant among terriers is named after the Yorkshire valley in which it originated. Designed for hunting otters, the Airedale is a strong, energetic dog and a good swimmer. It is never happier than when splashing about in water.

HISTORY

The breed was developed in the 19th century by crossing Otterhounds with the now-extinct Black-and-Tan Terrier, and has been used to hunt bears, wolves, wild boar, and stags, as well as otters. It was one of the first dogs to be recruited by the British Army in World War I, and it was used as a guard and messenger in the trenches of Flanders. An Airedale named Jack even won a posthumous Victoria Cross for gallantry in the field.

TEMPERAMENT

Airedales are friendly and loyal, and they make excellent pets as well as ideal house guards. They can be a bit unruly, and owners must treat them with firmness as well as kindness.

BODY Chest is deep but not broad; back is short, strong, and level.

COAT Stiff, wiry, and lying close to the body. Colours are dark grey, or black, with tan head, ears, underbody, and legs.

WELSH TERRIER This breed looks like a small version of the Airedale. Their common ancestor, the Black-and-Tan Terrier, is probably responsible for this similarity in appearance.

AIREDALE TERRIER One great advantage of these dogs is that they do not shed much hair. They are energetic, however, and will need long daily walks.

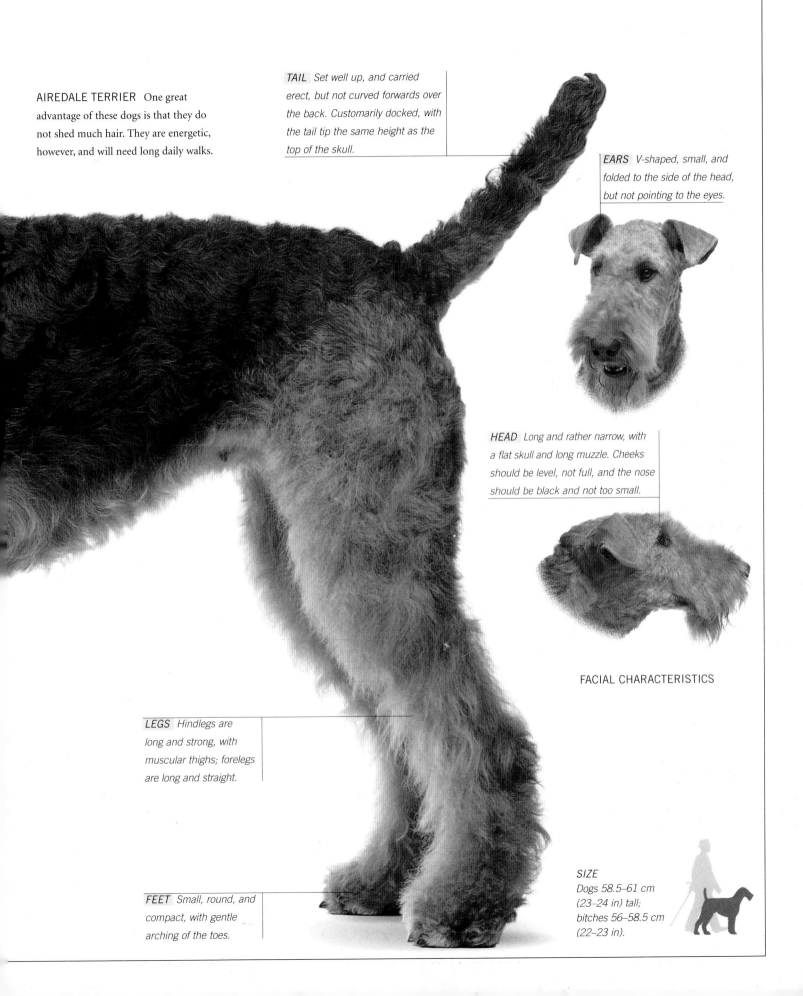

TAIL Set well up, and carried erect, but not curved forwards over the back. Customarily docked, with the tail tip the same height as the top of the skull.

EARS V-shaped, small, and folded to the side of the head, but not pointing to the eyes.

HEAD Long and rather narrow, with a flat skull and long muzzle. Cheeks should be level, not full, and the nose should be black and not too small.

FACIAL CHARACTERISTICS

LEGS Hindlegs are long and strong, with muscular thighs; forelegs are long and straight.

FEET Small, round, and compact, with gentle arching of the toes.

SIZE
Dogs 58.5–61 cm (23–24 in) tall; bitches 56–58.5 cm (22–23 in).

Australian Terrier

One of the few terriers to have been developed outside Great Britain, this breed is tough, energetic, and well suited to the rugged terrain of its homeland. Bred by early settlers to work in the harsh conditions of their new country, it was first used to control rats and kill poisonous snakes but was soon found to make a cheerful and charming pet.

HISTORY

It is likely that the first Australian Terriers were raised in Tasmania by crossbreeding a variety of terrier types. The first hybrids were rough- or broken-coated. In the 19th century, Dandie Dinmont, Skye, Cairn, and Yorkshire Terrier blood (see pp.96–7, 96, 94–5, and 214–15 respectively) was introduced. The first rough-coated terrier, black and tan in colour, was shown in Melbourne in 1868; the first standards for the breed were drawn up a year later; and in 1889 the breed became known as the Australian Rough-coated Terrier. Recognized by the English Kennel Club in 1933 and by the American Kennel Club in 1960, it was the first Australian breed to be recognized by non-Australian dog associations. Although immensely popular in its home country, it has gained favour fairly slowly in Britain, America, and elsewhere.

TEMPERAMENT

Charming, lively, and very bright, the Australian Terrier makes both a good house pet and a plucky guard dog. Easy to keep and adaptable, it is an ideal pet for a city flat.

BODY Long and strong-looking, with a deep chest. This is one of the smallest dogs in the terrier group.

COLOUR VARIANTS The Australian Terrier is clear sandy or red in colour, with a topline lighter in shade; or blue, steel blue, or dark grey-blue with tan markings. The topknot is blue, silver, or a paler shade than the head.

FEET Rather cat-like and bearing rich, tan-coloured hair.

EARS *Small, pointed, and erect.*

EYES *Small, expressive, and dark brown.*

HEAD *Long, with a powerful muzzle and a slight stop. Skull is slightly flattened.*

FACIAL CHARACTERISTICS

TAIL *Docked and set high.*

LEGS *Hindlegs are sturdy with distinctly angled hock (ankle) joints; forelegs are well boned and perfectly straight.*

COAT *Long, harsh outer coat on the body, with shorter hair elsewhere and a soft undercoat. There is a distinct ruff around the neck and a topknot.*

SIZE
Weight: around 6 kg (14 lb).

KILLER OF SNAKES The Australian Terrier is a both a classic terrier and a true Aussie, being lively, sharp-witted, and brave. One of its specialities is killing snakes by leaping up and pouncing on them from behind.

Bedlington Terrier

It may look like a lamb, but this fascinating and rather curious dog is no softie! It is hardy, tough, and quick, and it originated in the coalfields of Northumberland, England, where it was bred for hunting vermin, otters, and even foxes. Despite its unusual shape and curly coat, the Bedlington is a formidable fighter, with very strong jaws.

HISTORY

At first known as the Rothbury Terrier, after its place of origin, the early Bedlington had a heavier body and shorter legs. In the late 18th and early 19th centuries, it was crossed with Whippet *(see pp.52–3)*, Dandie Dinmont *(see pp.96–7)*, and possibly Poodle-type dogs *(see pp.130–31)*, and a taller, finer, speedier breed emerged but still retained its qualities of pluck and endurance. The "new" Bedlington was a poacher's dream and became known as the Gypsy Dog. Gradually the breed was refined into an excellent companion dog, and the arts of clipping and trimming have put the finishing touches to its distinctive appearance.

TEMPERAMENT

Echoing its ancestry, the Bedlington can have a tendency to pick fights with other dogs, but it generally makes a charming and loyal pet.

NON-MOULTING BREED Grooming the Bedlington Terrier can be a fairly intricate process, and first-time clipping should always be done by a specialist. For the house-proud, one great advantage of this breed is that it does not shed its coat.

UK BREED CLUB The Bedlington Terrier Club was founded in the UK in 1875.

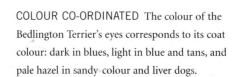

COLOUR CO-ORDINATED The colour of the Bedlington Terrier's eyes corresponds to its coat colour: dark in blues, light in blue and tans, and pale hazel in sandy-colour and liver dogs.

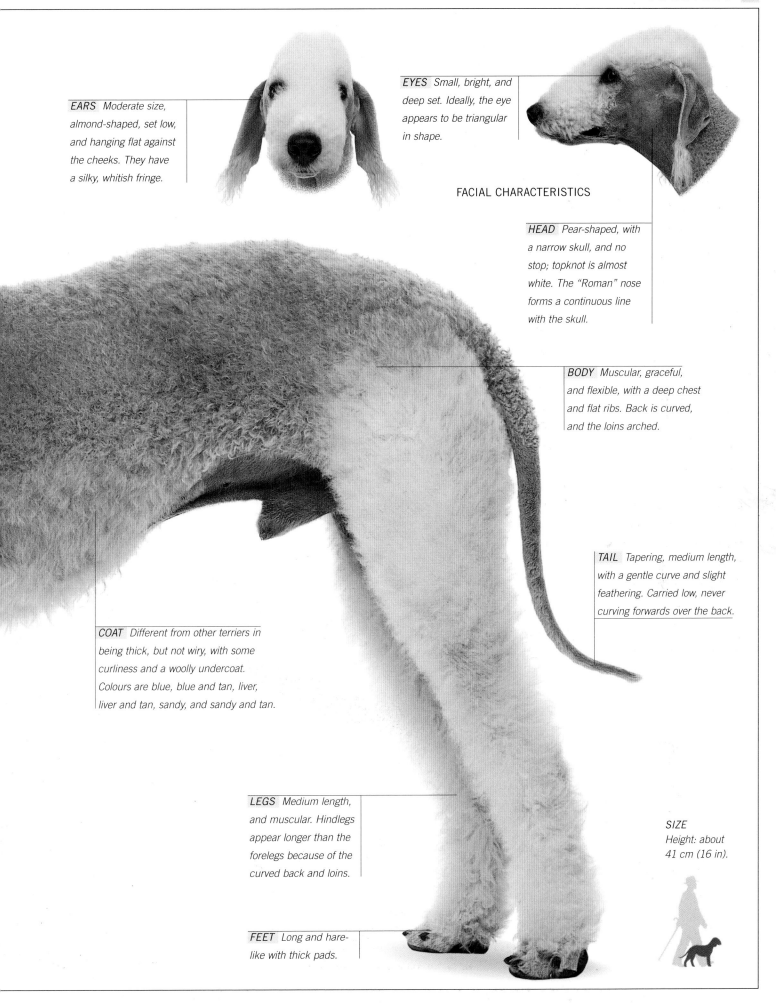

EARS *Moderate size, almond-shaped, set low, and hanging flat against the cheeks. They have a silky, whitish fringe.*

EYES *Small, bright, and deep set. Ideally, the eye appears to be triangular in shape.*

FACIAL CHARACTERISTICS

HEAD *Pear-shaped, with a narrow skull, and no stop; topknot is almost white. The "Roman" nose forms a continuous line with the skull.*

BODY *Muscular, graceful, and flexible, with a deep chest and flat ribs. Back is curved, and the loins arched.*

TAIL *Tapering, medium length, with a gentle curve and slight feathering. Carried low, never curving forwards over the back.*

COAT *Different from other terriers in being thick, but not wiry, with some curliness and a woolly undercoat. Colours are blue, blue and tan, liver, liver and tan, sandy, and sandy and tan.*

LEGS *Medium length, and muscular. Hindlegs appear longer than the forelegs because of the curved back and loins.*

SIZE
Height: about 41 cm (16 in).

FEET *Long and hare-like with thick pads.*

Border Terrier

The rugged and remote frontier country between Scotland and England produced a doughty, no-nonsense breed in the form of the Border Terrier. Its rough, dense coat was ideal for long, wet days following huntsmen in pursuit of the fox, and it was tough and small enough to engage its foe underground at the end of the chase.

HISTORY

The first Border Terrier types came on the scene in the late 17th century, and it shares a common ancestry with other terriers of the region including the Lakeland, Dandie Dinmont (see pp.96–7), Bedlington (see pp.88–9), and the now-extinct, all-white Redesdale. Before 1880, when its modern name was finally established, it was often called the Reedwater or Coquetdale Terrier. The Border Terrier Club was formed in the UK in 1920.

TEMPERAMENT

As a companion dog, the Border is lively, affectionate, and loyal. It is happy in houses and apartments in town, but it needs frequent exercise to burn off its abundant energy.

HEAD Otter-like, with a broad skull and short muzzle. Nose should be black. Neck is fairly long.

COAT A tough and wiry outer coat with a short, dense undercoat. Colours are bluish-grey and tan, blue and tan, red, or fawn, often with a little white on the chest.

BODY Long, narrow, and deep, with strong loins.

TAIL Quite short, thick, and tapering. Set high and carried aloft when active.

FRIENDLY HUNTER Although traditionally tenacious and hostile when in pursuit of the fox, the Border Terrier is generally an amiable creature.

A SPEEDY TERRIER This appealing
breed is renowned for its vitality and is said
to be capable of keeping pace with a horse.

EARS *V-shaped, small,
and falling forward to lie
close to the cheeks.*

EYES *Dark in
colour, with alert
expression.*

FACIAL CHARACTERISTICS

LEGS *Not too heavy.
Forelegs are straight;
hindlegs have
rounded thighs.*

FEET *Small
with thick pads.*

SIZE
Weight: dogs 5.9–7 kg
(13–15½ lb);
bitches 5.2–6.4 kg
(11½–14 lb).

Bull Terrier

Despite its fierce and intimidating appearance, the Bull Terrier is good with people and gentle with children. It does, however, need a firm hand since it is extremely powerful and can be a danger to other dogs.

HISTORY

In the 18th century, Bulldogs *(see pp.120–21)* were crossed with terrier-types to create "Bull and Terrier" fighting dogs. Into these the blood of English Toy Terriers and Whippets *(see pp.52–3)* was introduced, adding speed and agility to ferocity and strength. About 1860, a Birmingham dog dealer named James Hinks refined the breed by incorporating strains of the English White Terrier and possibly Dalmatians *(see pp.124–5)* and Spanish Pointers. This produced a white, well-muscled dog with a smooth head and shorter legs than its forebears. In the 1920s, to avoid the genetic tendency to deafness associated with the all-white breed, some colour was introduced into the dog's coat.

TEMPERAMENT

Although wary of strangers and often fiercely aggressive towards other dogs, this breed will make a devoted pet if given sufficient attention and exercise.

GAMBLER'S DOG
In the second half of the 19th century, white Bull Terriers became particularly fashionable among the gambling classes.

BODY Short and well muscled with a deep, broad chest.

CHAMPION RATTER In March 1865, a brindle Bull Terrier named Pincher set an astonishing ratting record: 500 rats killed in 36 minutes 26.5 seconds!

SIZE
Around 35–45 cm (14–18 in) tall.

STAFFORDSHIRE BULL TERRIER

The Staffordshire Bull Terrier was initially bred for the bloody sports of bull and bear baiting. Although it is now recognized as a faithful, reliable, and affectionate pet, it still enjoys a good fight!

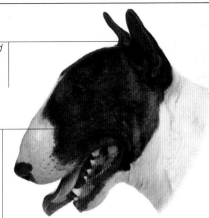

EARS Small, thin, and placed close together; carried erect.

HEAD Long, strong, and egg-shaped, with smoothly curving convex profile. Black nose pad bends downwards at the tip; nostrils are well developed.

EYES Triangular, slanting, and deep set. Black or dark brown in colour.

FACIAL CHARACTERISTICS

TAIL Short, tapering, set low, and carried horizontally.

LEGS Straight and parallel, with heavy bones and powerful thighs.

COAT Short, hard, and flat, with a slight gloss. Colours are pure white, red, fawn, black brindle, or tricolour; blue and liver are undesirable.

FEET Round and compact, with arched toes.

AMERICAN STAFFORDSHIRE TERRIER

The Staffordshire Bull Terrier crossed the Atlantic in the 19th century and gave rise to a heavier, bigger-boned version that is now recognized as a distinct breed known as the American Staffordshire Terrier. In the US, some of these dogs have cropped ears.

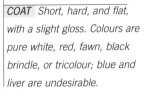

Cairn Terrier

One of the smallest of the working terriers, the Cairn gets its name from the Gaelic word *cairn*, meaning a heap of stones. The landscape of the Scottish Highlands is dotted with cairns, which reputedly mark the graves of ancient Romans. The Cairn Terrier's speciality was to hunt the sort of quarry that would take refuge in such rocky piles – rodents, weasels, foxes, and occasionally the fierce Scottish wildcat.

HISTORY

The history of this engaging and ever-active little terrier goes back at least 500 years. It was developed on the Isle of Skye and has common ancestors with those other Highlanders, the Scottish Terrier *(see p.112)* and the West Highland White *(see pp.112–13)*. When not hunting predators, the Cairn was used to chase rabbits, dig up moles, and take to the water in pursuit of otters. Cairn Terriers were officially recognized by the British Kennel Club in 1912, but some breeders were crossing them with West Highland White Terriers and registering the lighter pups as West Highland Whites and the darker ones as Cairns. In 1924, in an attempt to keep the breeds distinct, the British Kennel Club refused to register the offspring of crosses. The breed was first recognized by the American Kennel Club in 1913.

TEMPERAMENT

As a companion pet, the Cairn is second to none, being intelligent, loyal, friendly, and perky.

BODY Strong and compact, with a deep chest and level back.

PLAYFUL BREED Cairns are easily trained and enjoy learning new games and tricks. Without this sort of mental stimulation they are easily bored and may become destructive or bark incessantly.

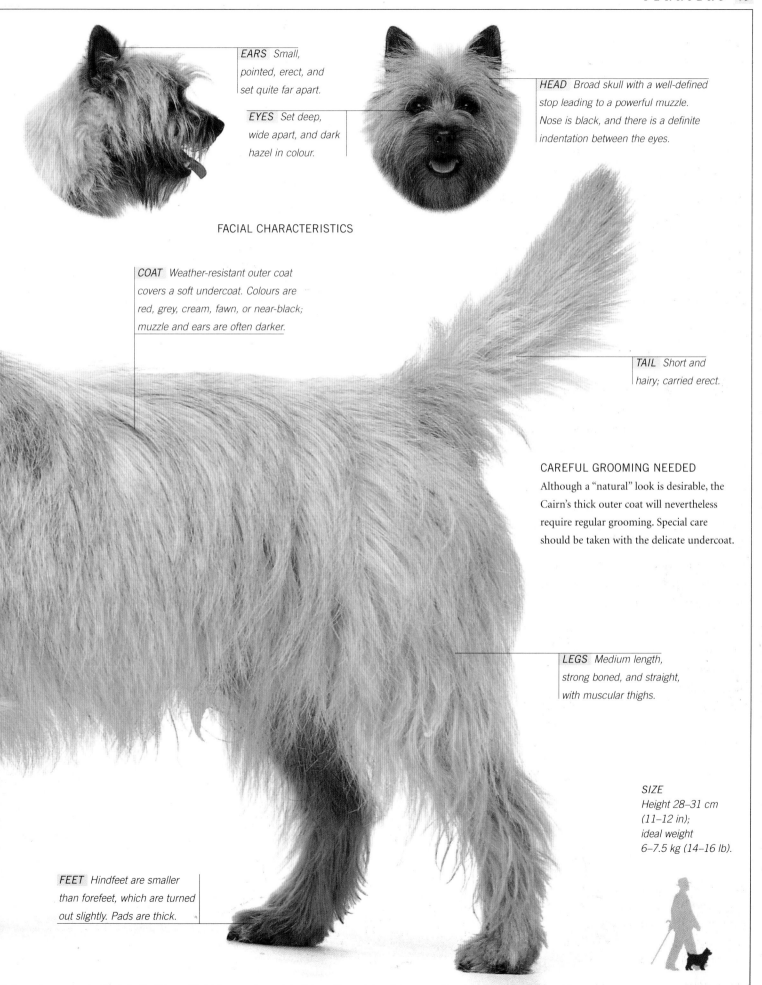

EARS *Small, pointed, erect, and set quite far apart.*

EYES *Set deep, wide apart, and dark hazel in colour.*

HEAD *Broad skull with a well-defined stop leading to a powerful muzzle. Nose is black, and there is a definite indentation between the eyes.*

FACIAL CHARACTERISTICS

COAT *Weather-resistant outer coat covers a soft undercoat. Colours are red, grey, cream, fawn, or near-black; muzzle and ears are often darker.*

TAIL *Short and hairy; carried erect.*

CAREFUL GROOMING NEEDED

Although a "natural" look is desirable, the Cairn's thick outer coat will nevertheless require regular grooming. Special care should be taken with the delicate undercoat.

LEGS *Medium length, strong boned, and straight, with muscular thighs.*

SIZE
Height 28–31 cm (11–12 in); ideal weight 6–7.5 kg (14–16 lb).

FEET *Hindfeet are smaller than forefeet, which are turned out slightly. Pads are thick.*

Dandie Dinmont Terrier

This game little terrier takes its name from a fictional character, a dog-owning farmer in the novel *Guy Mannering* by Sir Walter Scott. Originally an accomplished hunter of vermin, rabbits, otters, and badgers, the Dandie Dinmont is now chiefly valued for its distinctive appearance, and companionable nature.

HISTORY

Originating in the border country between England and Scotland, the Dandie Dinmont can be traced back as a distinct breed to the 17th century. It features in a painting of the Duke of Buccleuch by Thomas Gainsborough and was a favourite pet of Louis Philippe of France. Its long, arched back and scimitar-like tail set it apart from other terriers, and its ancestry may include strains of Otterhound and Basset Hound *(see pp.26–7)*, as well as Skye *(see below)*, Border *(see pp.90–91)*, Cairn *(see pp.94–5)*, Scottish *(see p.112)*, and Bedlington Terriers *(see pp.88–9)*.

TEMPERAMENT

The Dandie Dinmont is friendly, playful, and intensely loyal. It makes an alert house guard, and gives a surprisingly loud bark.

LEGS *Well boned and muscular; forelegs are a little shorter than hindlegs.*

SKYE TERRIER One school of thought has it that the Skye Terrier owes its origins to the shipwreck of a 17th-century Spanish galleon off the coast of Skye in the Scottish Hebrides. On board were Maltese dogs that are said to have mated with the canine inhabitants of the island to produce today's charming, perky little terrier.

EYES *Large and round, set wide and low; dark hazel in colour.*

EARS *Long, hanging close to the cheeks. Set wide apart and well back.*

HEAD *Quite large, with a broad skull, a profuse "pepper" or "mustard" topknot, strongly developed jaws, and a black nose. Its expression is distinctly soulful.*

FACIAL CHARACTERISTICS

DEMANDING DANDIE TOPKNOT Regular, careful grooming is necessary for show dogs, with the fluffy topknot demanding particular attention.

GOOD FOOD AND EXERCISE To keep it in tip-top condition, the Dandie Dinmont needs daily walks and a fairly lean diet.

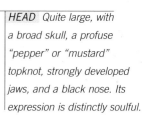

BODY *Deep chest and a long, strong back; slightly arched over the loins.*

COAT *Fairly long with a mixture of hard and soft hairs. Colours are black to pale grey ("pepper"), or reddish-brown to fawn ("mustard").*

TAIL *Thick at the base and tapering to a point. Underside is neatly feathered. Curved, and carried above body level, but perpendicular when excited.*

SIZE *Weight: 8–11 kg (18–24 lb).*

Fox Terriers

These are the classic English terriers – full of energy, irrepressible, and pugnacious. Experts differ as to whether the Wire or the Smooth Fox Terrier is the older type, but both share identical characteristics except for the texture of the coat.

HISTORY

The Wire Fox Terrier was originally developed for fox-hunting in the early 19th century. It carries the blood of several terriers, including the rough-coated Black-and-Tan, while the Smooth variety descends from the smooth-coated Black-and-Tan with a mixture of Beagle *(see pp.28–9)*, Bulldog *(see pp.120–21)*, and Greyhound *(see pp.44–5)*. The breed has an enviable record in the services: one Wire Fox Terrier, Drummer Jack, was attached to the Coldstream Guards during World War I and was awarded the General Service medal. Another, named Igloo, went to the Antarctic between 1928 and 1930 with Admiral Bird (fully equipped with four fur-lined boots and a camel-hair coat). Both Smooth and Wire Fox Terriers have been exported from England all over the world, and their relative popularity has fluctuated over the years. Originally less favoured, the Wire Fox Terrier overtook its rival and reached its zenith of popularity in the 1920s.

TEMPERAMENT

As a companion dog, the Fox Terrier is both affectionate and protective. It does, however, need firm handling to curb its hunting instinct.

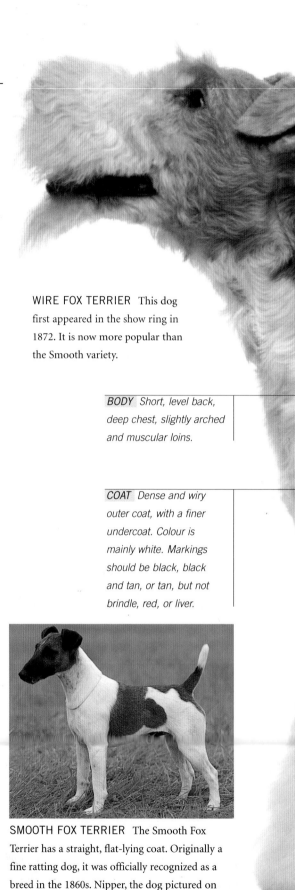

WIRE FOX TERRIER This dog first appeared in the show ring in 1872. It is now more popular than the Smooth variety.

BODY *Short, level back, deep chest, slightly arched and muscular loins.*

COAT *Dense and wiry outer coat, with a finer undercoat. Colour is mainly white. Markings should be black, black and tan, or tan, but not brindle, red, or liver.*

SMOOTH FOX TERRIER The Smooth Fox Terrier has a straight, flat-lying coat. Originally a fine ratting dog, it was officially recognized as a breed in the 1860s. Nipper, the dog pictured on the early His Master's Voice (HMV) record labels, was a Smooth Fox Terrier.

SIZE
Dogs up to 39 cm (15 in) tall; bitches slightly less.

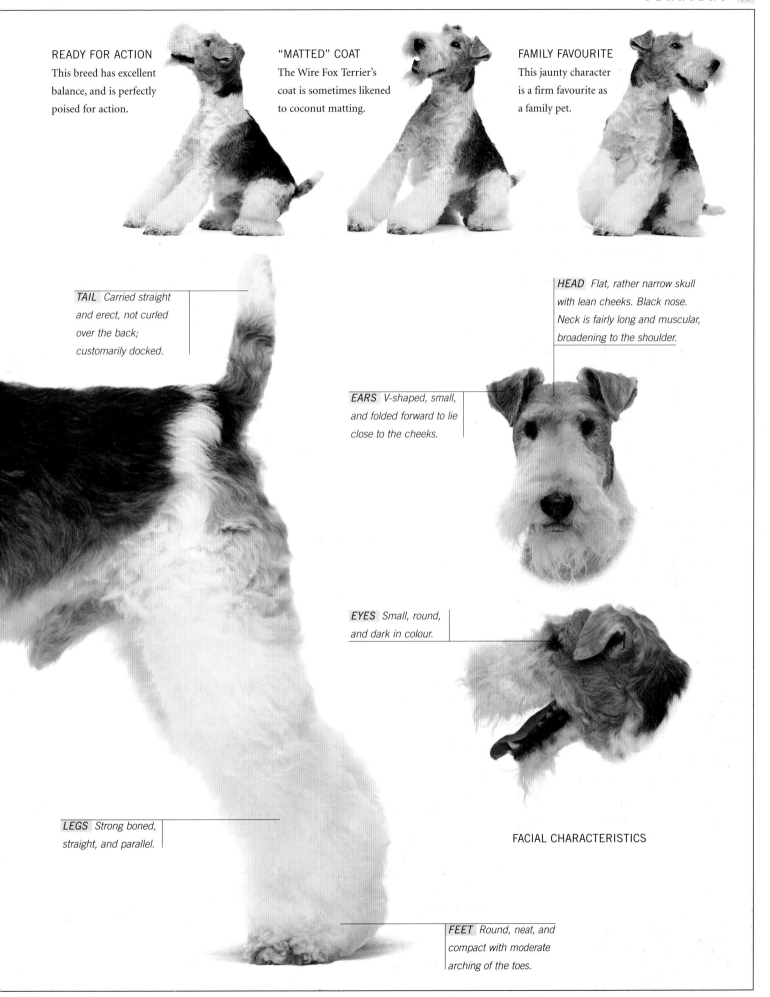

READY FOR ACTION
This breed has excellent balance, and is perfectly poised for action.

"MATTED" COAT
The Wire Fox Terrier's coat is sometimes likened to coconut matting.

FAMILY FAVOURITE
This jaunty character is a firm favourite as a family pet.

TAIL Carried straight and erect, not curled over the back; customarily docked.

HEAD Flat, rather narrow skull with lean cheeks. Black nose. Neck is fairly long and muscular, broadening to the shoulder.

EARS V-shaped, small, and folded forward to lie close to the cheeks.

EYES Small, round, and dark in colour.

LEGS Strong boned, straight, and parallel.

FACIAL CHARACTERISTICS

FEET Round, neat, and compact with moderate arching of the toes.

Jack Russell Terrier

The essential appeal of this exuberant animal is its character – full of intelligence, enthusiasm, and tenacity. Most of the world's major canine clubs refuse to accept the Jack Russell as an official breed, but some aficionados welcome the fact that its excellent practical qualities have not been sacrificed for the show ring. The only dog to have visited both the North and South Poles is Bothy, a Jack Russell Terrier belonging to explorer Sir Ranulph Fiennes.

HISTORY

One of the Church of England's "hunting parsons", the reverend Jack Russell of Devon established the breed in the early 19th century and also gave it his name. The reverend was a keen fox-hunter and he needed a nippy dog with plenty of fighting spirit that could keep up with the hounds and have the courage to face up to its quarry underground. When not pursuing foxes, the Jack Russell was quite happy to perform as a specialist exterminator of vermin. Character has always been the most important ingredient of the breed, so its physical appearance has tended to vary quite widely.

TEMPERAMENT

The Jack Russell Terrier is excitable, cheerful, and loyal, and it makes an excellent guard dog.

COAT There are two main varieties of coat: one is short and smooth, the other is longer and rougher. Colour is predominantly white, with black, tan, or black and tan markings, or all-tan.

BODY Strong, with a straight back, slightly arched loins, and a fairly narrow chest.

TAIL *Short and carried high.*

COURAGEOUS CANINE Despite their diminutive stature, Jack Russells are fearless and tenacious, often willing to take on dogs several times their own size.

EARS V-shaped, small, and falling forwards.

HEAD Flat, rather wide skull, with a gently tapering muzzle and a slight stop. Nose and lips are black.

EYES Dark brown in colour; almond-shaped with lively expression.

FACIAL CHARACTERISTICS

EXERCISE IS A MUST This breed is endowed with abundant energy resources, but it is likely to lose its fine shape if it is not given plenty of vigorous exercise.

LEGS Short with muscular thighs.

SIZE Up to 36 cm (14 in) tall.

FEET Compact with well-arched toes

Kerry Blue Terrier

Sometimes called the Irish Blue, the Kerry Blue Terrier is the national dog of the Republic of Ireland. Its past is steeped in mystery – it could be a descendant of the Spanish dogs that reached the Irish coast from the shipwrecked Armada in 1588, or it is sometimes reputed to be related to the considerably larger Irish Wolfhound (*see pp.46–7*).

HISTORY

Some believe the Kerry Blue to be simply a true native of Ireland, and in the 18th century it was certainly used in the Emerald Isle as a fighting, hunting, herding, and house-guarding dog. Since then, it has probably received some injections of Dandie Dinmont (*see pp.96–7*) and Bedlington Terrier (*see pp.88–9*) blood. Kerry Blues made their show debut in England in 1922, and the American Kennel Club officially recognized them two years later.

TEMPERAMENT

The Kerry Blue is a good-natured, vivacious, and loyal animal, though with a tendency to stubbornness. It makes a good house-dog but requires firm handling.

HEAD Long and well proportioned in relation to the body. Skull is flat with slight stop. Beard is bushy and the moustache profuse.

CHANGING COLOUR Kerry Blues are born black; their coat usually turns to the distinctive blue-grey within 18 months.

NO MOULTING... The Kerry Blue is a very clean character, and does not shed its curly hair.

... BUT GROOMING IS REQUIRED For showing, the Kerry Blue demands elaborate trimming and grooming.

EYES *Small to medium in size, and dark in colour.*

COAT *Very thick, soft, silky, and curly. Colour is blue-grey, sometimes with areas of darker hair.*

TAIL *Medium-length, set high, and carried erect; customarily docked.*

EARS *V-shaped, small, and falling forward to lie close to the cheeks.*

FACIAL CHARACTERISTICS

LEGS *Medium-length and strong. Hindlegs are powerful; forelegs are straight.*

BODY *Short, with a deep, well-sprung chest and a level back.*

SIZE
Ideal height: dogs 46–48 cm (18–19 in); bitches slightly less.

FEET *Moderately small, round, and compact, with black nails.*

Manchester Terrier

Originally bred for the dual purposes of rabbit-coursing and rat-killing, the Manchester Terrier was a quick-tempered, game, and rather snappy dog. Gradually the rougher aspects of its character were bred out, but luckily it retained the lively spirit and alertness so typical of the breed.

HISTORY

This is yet another dog that has the now-extinct Black-and-Tan Terrier as its ancestor. A nimble but powerful ratter, the Black-and-Tan was crossed with a Whippet *(see pp.52–3)* by an 18th-century Manchester breeder, John Hulme, and the first Manchester Terrier was born; West Highland Terrier blood *(see pp.112–13)* may have been introduced later. Until 1959 a separate Toy breed was registered, but now it is considered to be just a smaller variety of Manchester Terrier.

TEMPERAMENT

Although not widely popular, the Manchester Terrier has a devoted following of enthusiasts and is undoubtedly a handsome, active, and affectionate companion.

DOBERMANN CONNECTION This unusually sleek terrier reached the US, Canada, and Germany in the 19th century. Considering the similarities in both coat texture and colour, it is highly likely that the Manchester was involved in the Dobermann's genetic make-up.

TAIL Fairly short and tapering; carried below the level of the back.

CORRECT MARKINGS The Manchester Terrier's jet-black and mahogany-tan markings must be clearly defined in show dogs, but tan outside the hindlegs, known as breeching, should be carefully avoided.

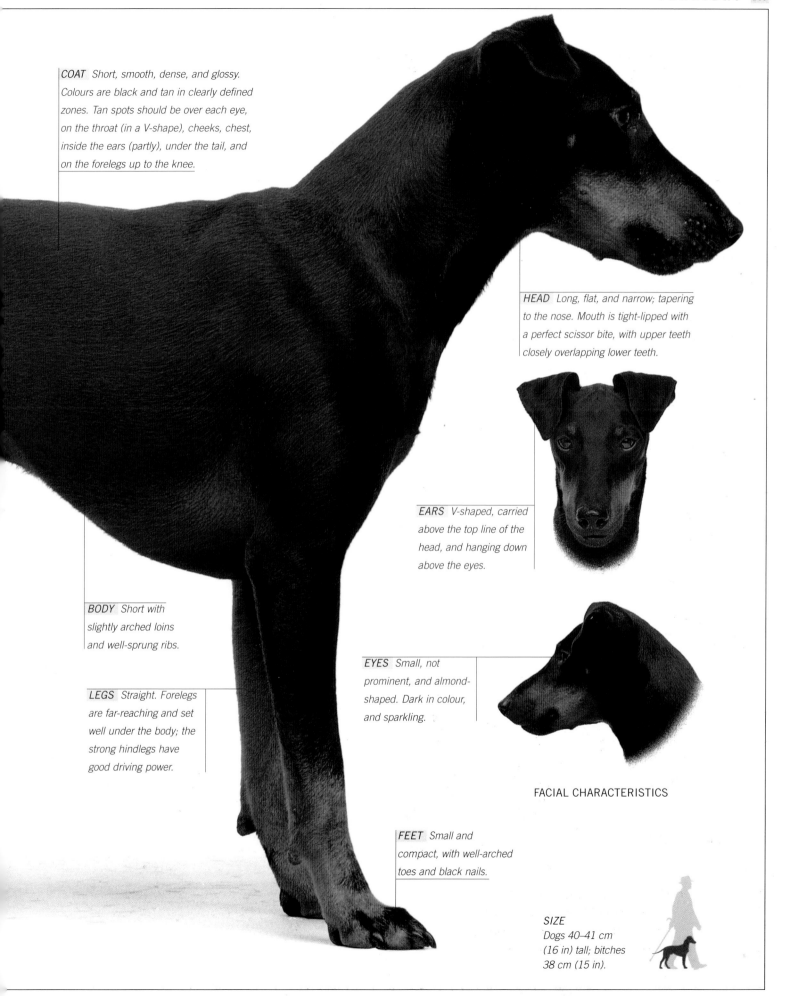

COAT Short, smooth, dense, and glossy. Colours are black and tan in clearly defined zones. Tan spots should be over each eye, on the throat (in a V-shape), cheeks, chest, inside the ears (partly), under the tail, and on the forelegs up to the knee.

HEAD Long, flat, and narrow; tapering to the nose. Mouth is tight-lipped with a perfect scissor bite, with upper teeth closely overlapping lower teeth.

EARS V-shaped, carried above the top line of the head, and hanging down above the eyes.

BODY Short with slightly arched loins and well-sprung ribs.

EYES Small, not prominent, and almond-shaped. Dark in colour, and sparkling.

LEGS Straight. Forelegs are far-reaching and set well under the body; the strong hindlegs have good driving power.

FACIAL CHARACTERISTICS

FEET Small and compact, with well-arched toes and black nails.

SIZE
Dogs 40–41 cm (16 in) tall; bitches 38 cm (15 in).

Norwich Terrier

East Anglia's contributions to the range of British terriers are the Norwich and Norfolk breeds. Very similar apart from the ears, they have only recently been recognized as separate breeds by the American and British Kennel Clubs.

HISTORY

The ancestry of the Norwich Terrier is unclear, but it seems likely that it contains Border *(see pp.90–91)*, Cairn *(see pp.94–5)*, and Irish Terrier blood. Bred for hunting vermin, it became popular with undergraduates at Cambridge University in Victorian times, and consequently was often called the Cantab Terrier. After World War I, the breed crossed the Atlantic, and was known as the Jones Terrier, after Frank Jones, one of the early serious breeders. The Norwich Terrier was first recognized in 1932 in the UK, with both prick-eared and drop-eared varieties being accepted, but in 1965 the drop-eared version was renamed the Norfolk Terrier *(see below)*. In the US, the two separate breeds were recognized in 1979.

TEMPERAMENT

Both East Anglian terriers are tough, lively, loyal, and untroublesome dogs that make ideal pets and watchful house guards.

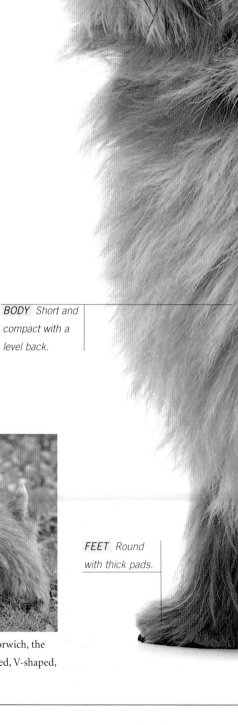

BODY *Short and compact with a level back.*

FEET *Round with thick pads.*

SIZE 25–26 cm (10 in) tall.

NORFOLK TERRIER Unlike the Norwich, the Norfolk Terrier's ears are medium-sized, V-shaped, and slightly rounded at the tip.

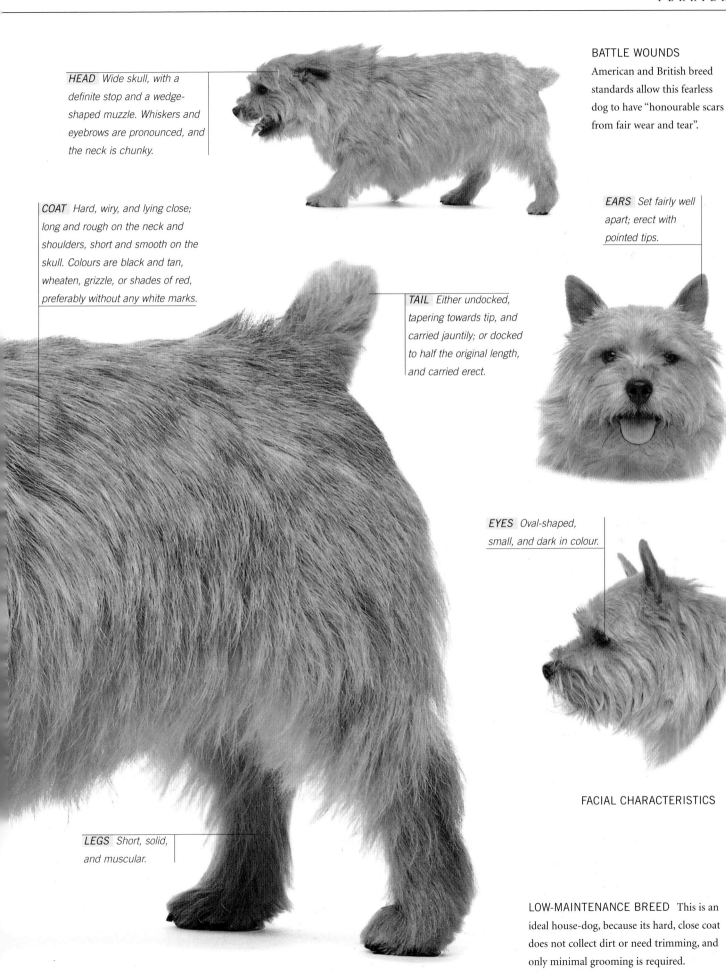

HEAD *Wide skull, with a definite stop and a wedge-shaped muzzle. Whiskers and eyebrows are pronounced, and the neck is chunky.*

BATTLE WOUNDS
American and British breed standards allow this fearless dog to have "honourable scars from fair wear and tear".

COAT *Hard, wiry, and lying close; long and rough on the neck and shoulders, short and smooth on the skull. Colours are black and tan, wheaten, grizzle, or shades of red, preferably without any white marks.*

EARS *Set fairly well apart; erect with pointed tips.*

TAIL *Either undocked, tapering towards tip, and carried jauntily; or docked to half the original length, and carried erect.*

EYES *Oval-shaped, small, and dark in colour.*

FACIAL CHARACTERISTICS

LEGS *Short, solid, and muscular.*

LOW-MAINTENANCE BREED This is an ideal house-dog, because its hard, close coat does not collect dirt or need trimming, and only minimal grooming is required.

Sealyham Terrier

This magnificently bearded animal was bred to accompany hounds in pursuit of the otter, badger, and fox. It therefore had to have stamina, a good turn of speed, gameness to follow its quarry underground, and the bulk, determination, and toughness to battle to the very end.

HISTORY

The Sealyham is a one-man dog in a very special sense; it was created between 1850 and 1891 by the careful selective breeding programme of only one man, Captain John Edwardes of Sealyham, an estate near Haverfordwest in Wales. No one knows exactly how he did it since the Captain kept no records of his work. It is likely, however, that he used the Bull Terrier *(see pp.92–3)*, West Highland White *(see pp.112–13)*, Dandie Dinmont *(see pp.96–7)*, and perhaps the Pembroke Corgi *(see pp.188–9)*. The show debut of the breed took place in 1903, in its home town of Haverfordwest. It was recognized by the American and British Kennel Clubs in 1911, and the American Sealyham Terrier Club was founded in 1913, five years after its British counterpart.

TEMPERAMENT

A typical terrier, with plenty of pluck, the Sealyham makes an affectionate companion.

COAT Long, hard, wiry outer coat covering a weather-resistant, soft, dense undercoat. Colours are white, or white with lemon, with tan or badger markings on the head and ears.

BODY Medium-length and strong, with a level back and a deep, broad chest.

LEGS Short and strong. Forelegs are straight; hindlegs are longer and lighter-boned.

SIZE
Maximum height: 31 cm (12 in).

FURRY FRIEND
This bearded breed is fearless, frank, and friendly.

HIDDEN STRENGTH
Considering the Sealyham's size, its hindlegs are surprisingly powerful.

"LOOK AT ME!"
Bouncy, well balanced, and particularly poised, the Sealyham Terrier has all the attributes of a natural performer.

GROOMING NECESSITIES Careful grooming is a daily requirement for show dogs, in addition to regular attention from a professional groomer.

TAIL Carried erect; customarily docked.

HEAD Long, broad, and powerful, with a black nose. Jaw is square, and the neck is thick and muscular.

EARS Medium-sized with rounded tips. Folded level with the top of the head, with the forward edge lying close to the cheek.

EYES Round and very dark. Set deep and fairly wide apart.

FACIAL CHARACTERISTICS

FEET Large, compact, and round, with well-arched toes pointing forwards.

Soft-Coated Wheaten Terrier

Although the oldest of the terriers native to Ireland, the Soft-coated Wheaten now has its stronghold in the US. It derives its name from its coat, which is the colour of ripening wheat.

HISTORY

Its relations are thought to include the Black-and-Tan, Irish, and Kerry Blue Terriers *(see pp.102–3)*. Originally it was a working terrier on the farm, earning its keep by acting as cattle-drover, guard dog, and foe of badgers, rats, rabbits, and even otters! In the 1930s, its numbers diminished alarmingly, but careful breeding ensured its safety. The Soft-coated Wheaten was recognized by the British Kennel Club in 1943, and although it crossed the Atlantic in 1946, it was not officially recognized by the American Kennel Club until 1973. Soft-coated Wheatens are steadily increasing in popularity, particularly in the US.

TEMPERAMENT

An intelligent, cheerful character, the Soft-coated Wheaten makes an excellent companion dog and loves outdoor exercise.

IRISH THROUGH AND THROUGH Very appropriately for an Irish breed, the Soft-coated Wheaten made its show debut on St Patrick's Day, in Dublin in 1937.

HEAD Medium-length, with flat-topped skull, a definite stop, and a square muzzle. Nose is large and black. Neck is strong, muscular, and slightly arched.

FEET Strong and compact, with black nails. Dewclaws on the hindlegs should be removed.

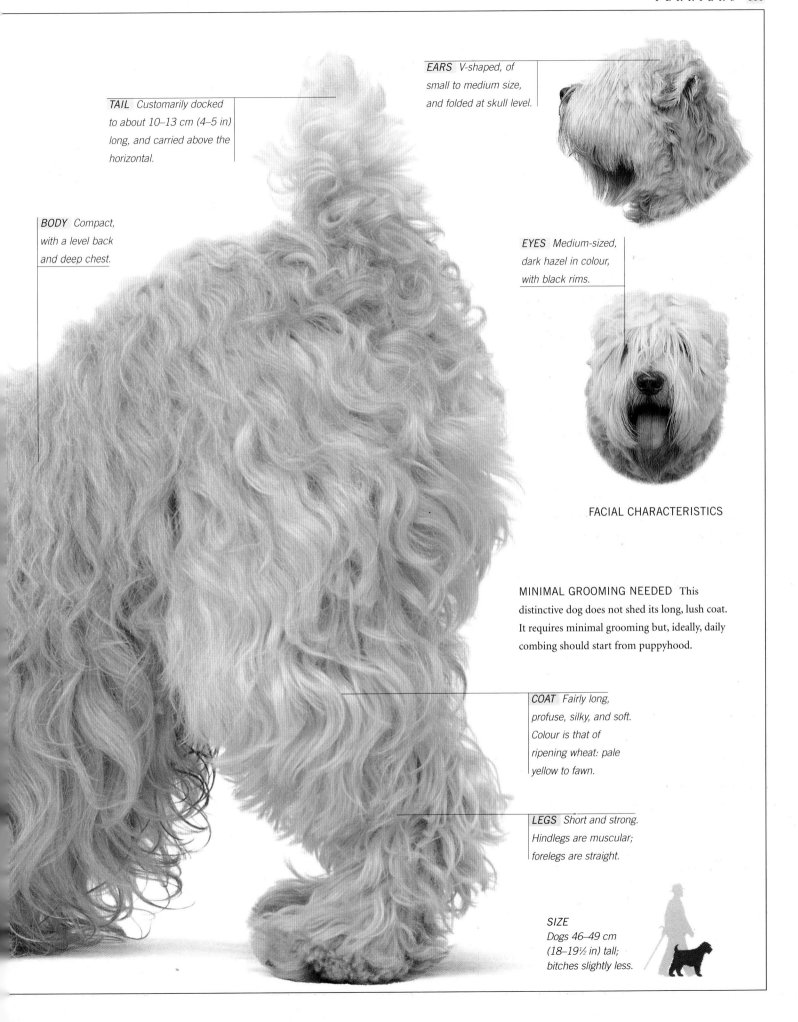

EARS *V-shaped, of small to medium size, and folded at skull level.*

TAIL *Customarily docked to about 10–13 cm (4–5 in) long, and carried above the horizontal.*

BODY *Compact, with a level back and deep chest.*

EYES *Medium-sized, dark hazel in colour, with black rims.*

FACIAL CHARACTERISTICS

MINIMAL GROOMING NEEDED This distinctive dog does not shed its long, lush coat. It requires minimal grooming but, ideally, daily combing should start from puppyhood.

COAT *Fairly long, profuse, silky, and soft. Colour is that of ripening wheat: pale yellow to fawn.*

LEGS *Short and strong. Hindlegs are muscular; forelegs are straight.*

SIZE *Dogs 46–49 cm (18–19½ in) tall; bitches slightly less.*

West Highland White Terrier

Considered by its devotees to be one of the most attractive of the Scottish terriers, the West Highland White is also a hardy and tenacious dog. It requires firm handling and plenty of attention from its owner.

HISTORY

Bred to hunt otters, foxes, and vermin, the West Highland White shares its ancestry with the "Scottie" *(see below)*, Cairn *(see pp.94–5)*, and Dandie Dinmont *(see pp.96–7)*. Selective breeding of all-white dogs around Poltalloch in Argyll in the 19th century established the characteristic features we know today. The "Westie" was once called the Poltalloch Terrier and also the Roseneath Terrier, after the Dumbartonshire estate of the Duke of Argyll, a famous fancier of the breed.

TEMPERAMENT

The Westie is an affectionate, self-confident, and cheeky character. Although small, it is alert and courageous and makes a good guard dog.

"ODOUR-FREE" DOG Westies require regular grooming because the white coat tends to shed hair almost continuously. On the plus side, they have a dry skin with no "doggy" smell, and they need very little trimming for show purposes.

TAIL *About 13–15 cm (5–6 in) long, straight, unfeathered, and carried jauntily, but not curled forward over the back.*

COAT *A harsh, straight outer coat covering a short, soft undercoat. Colour is pure white.*

BODY *Compact and strong with a deep chest and level back.*

SIZE
About 28 cm (11 in) tall.

SCOTTISH TERRIER The Scottie has been known by several names, including the West Highland and the Aberdeen, a reflection of its old and mixed Celtic background. The dog that we know today was developed towards the end of the 19th century.

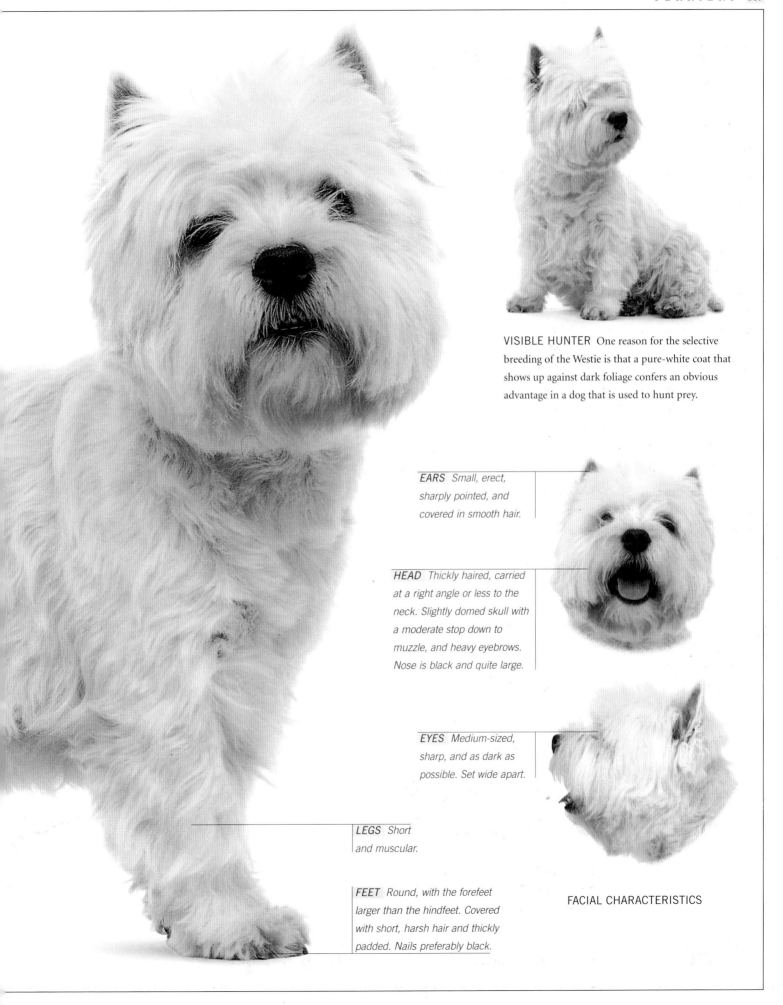

VISIBLE HUNTER One reason for the selective breeding of the Westie is that a pure-white coat that shows up against dark foliage confers an obvious advantage in a dog that is used to hunt prey.

EARS Small, erect, sharply pointed, and covered in smooth hair.

HEAD Thickly haired, carried at a right angle or less to the neck. Slightly domed skull with a moderate stop down to muzzle, and heavy eyebrows. Nose is black and quite large.

EYES Medium-sized, sharp, and as dark as possible. Set wide apart.

LEGS Short and muscular.

FEET Round, with the forefeet larger than the hindfeet. Covered with short, harsh hair and thickly padded. Nails preferably black.

FACIAL CHARACTERISTICS

Utility Dogs

The Utility group of dogs is a miscellaneous collection left over when the other breeds have been neatly pigeon-holed. But they are none the worse for that! Indeed, the group comprises, in many ways, the most interesting, out-of-the-ordinary dogs. All have been selectively bred either for aesthetic effect or to perform a precise function not included in the sporting and working categories, and some of them are among the oldest documented breeds of dog.

UNUSUAL OCCUPATIONS

A good example of practical, but unusual, use of dog is that of the Dalmatian, descended from some form of pointer-cross and employed in days gone by to run alongside carriages to act as a deterrent to highwaymen. The Chow Chow, first bred in Mongolia 3,000 years ago for use in war, was later raised in China and surrounding countries as a source of meat and fur. Sadly, "Red Dogs" of the Chow Chow type are still regarded as table delicacies in Korea and some other parts of the Far East.

DISTINCTIVE BREEDS

The Poodle is a utility dog, now a highly decorative companion, but descended from a German gundog, the Pudel, that retrieved game from water. Most famous, perhaps, and certainly most British of all this group, is the Bulldog. This attractive and surprisingly good-natured fellow has a long record of exploitation by man in the barbaric practice of bull-baiting, which goes back to at least the 14th century. A more recently developed utility dog is the Boston Terrier, one of the few breeds to originate in the US, which had its beginnings in the mid-19th century.

WINNING DOGS

Utility dogs are no reserve team of "also rans" among dog breeds. Four of them – the Shih Tzu, Lhasa Apso, Miniature Schnauzer, and Dalmatian – were among the 20 most popular breeds in the UK in 2001. The Boston Terrier, the Bulldog, the Keeshond, and the Poodle, all Utility breeds, are the proud national dogs of the US, Britain, Holland, and France respectively.

FAMOUS PETS

King William of Orange had his life saved by two Schipperkes in 1572, and Prince Rupert's favourite, a white Poodle called Boy, was thought by some of Cromwell's Roundheads to have supernatural gifts. He was killed at the Battle of Marston Moor in 1644. American President Warren Harding had a white English Bulldog, Oh Boy. An English Bulldog working for the American forces during World War I was decorated with the Bronze star and five other ribbons, and another was promoted to Corporal. Illustrious owners of utility dogs include Sigmund Freud, who owned a Chow, Jo-Fi; John Steinbeck, who had a Standard Poodle called Charley; and Eugene O'Neill, whose Dalmatian was named Blemie.

POODLE (Top right) Poodles were once fairly big dogs (Standard Poodles) used to retrieve game birds that had fallen into water. Nowadays, with Miniature and Toy Poodles more commonly seen, the breed has retired from working and serves as an intelligent, amusing, and good-natured companion animal.

BULLDOG (Below right) Centuries ago, the Bulldog was a brave and tenacious fighting dog pitted against bulls, badgers, and, sometimes, bears and other dogs. Thankfully, with those cruel days long gone, we find the modern English Bulldog to be gentle, sweet-tempered, loyal, and affectionate.

BOSTON TERRIER (Left) Now a non-sporting utility breed, but once used for ratting, the Boston Terrier is a native New Englander and has much to recommend it. It is good-looking, sturdy, entertaining, and nimble, as well as making a fine companion animal.

Japanese Akita

A member of the Spitz family, the Japanese Akita is a strong, athletic breed that derives its name from the Japanese province of Akita, on Honshu Island. In its native land it is primarily used as a police and guard dog, but it has also become a popular family pet around the world.

HISTORY

The Japanese Akita is the largest of Japan's three Spitz-type dogs, and the breed has remained largely unchanged over 300 years. Known in its past as a hunter of wild boar, deer, and even bear, for hundreds of years the Akita was also famous for its dogfighting exploits, a practice that is now illegal in Japan. The breed's devotion is legendary – in Shibuya railway station, Tokyo, there is a statue to Hachiko on the spot where, for nine years, he kept daily vigils awaiting his dead master's return. Japanese Akitas were introduced to the US after World War II by servicemen returning from Japan.

TEMPERAMENT

Renowned for its strength and courage, the Akita is easily trained, affectionate, and loyal.

HEAD Large and broad, with a well-defined stop. Muzzle is blunt, and the nose and lips are black.

COAT Coarse, stiff outer coat, with a soft, dense undercoat. All colours, with clear markings are allowed. Skin is fairly taut.

TOP HUNTERS Japanese Akitas have very good hunting and retrieving skills, particularly in deep snow and water.

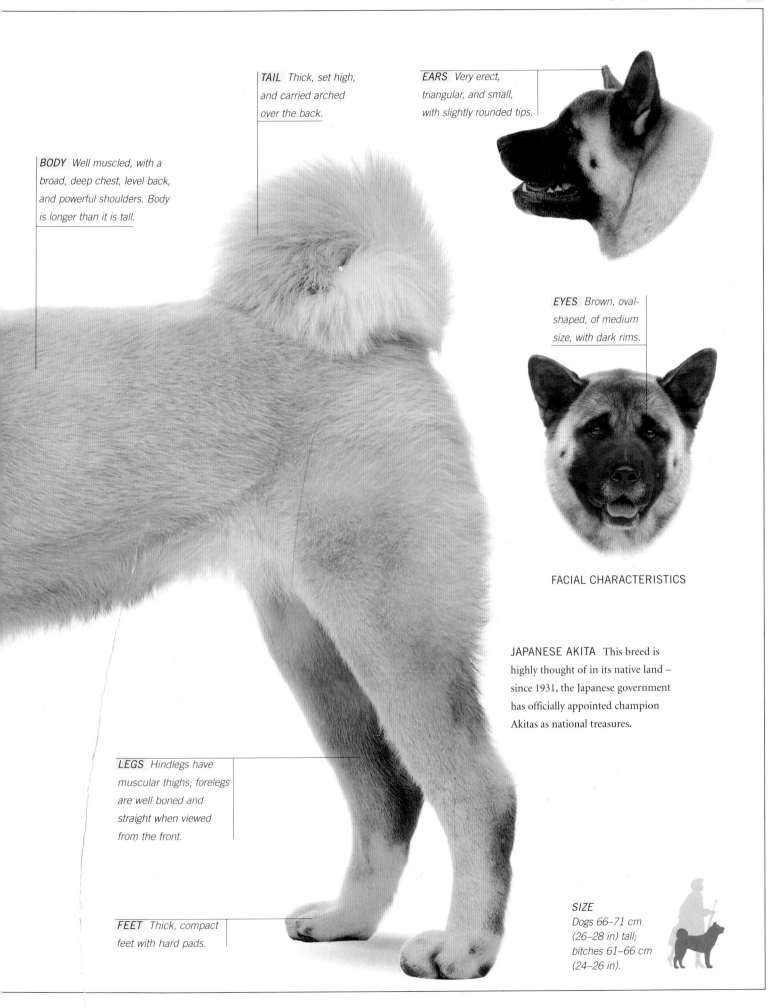

TAIL Thick, set high, and carried arched over the back.

EARS Very erect, triangular, and small, with slightly rounded tips.

BODY Well muscled, with a broad, deep chest, level back, and powerful shoulders. Body is longer than it is tall.

EYES Brown, oval-shaped, of medium size, with dark rims.

FACIAL CHARACTERISTICS

JAPANESE AKITA This breed is highly thought of in its native land – since 1931, the Japanese government has officially appointed champion Akitas as national treasures.

LEGS Hindlegs have muscular thighs; forelegs are well boned and straight when viewed from the front.

FEET Thick, compact feet with hard pads.

SIZE
Dogs 66–71 cm
(26–28 in) tall;
bitches 61–66 cm
(24–26 in).

Boston Terrier

This lively, intelligent, plucky little dog, one of the few breeds to have been developed in the US, has few special requirements and makes an excellent house-dog and companion.

HISTORY

Originally the Boston Terrier was bred for the purpose of dogfighting, a practice that was centred around Boston in the 19th century. The early Boston Terriers were produced by crossing Bulldogs *(see pp.120–21)* with Bull Terriers *(see pp.92–3)*, although later the breed was substantially modified by selective inbreeding and by crossing with French Bulldogs *(see p.121)*. In 1891 the American Bull Terrier Club of Boston applied for breed recognition, which was refused until the offending words "Bull Terrier" were removed. The Boston Terrier Club of America was eventually recognized in 1893. Since then, the breed has become one of the most popular in the US, both as a show dog and a pet. It has also enjoyed popularity in Britain, Canada, and Australia, but to a lesser extent. In the 1960s, a Boston Terrier named Missie was credited with powers of divination and made predictions by moving the hands of a toy clock. Apparently, she predicted the time of her own death precisely.

TEMPERAMENT

The Boston Terrier is an intelligent, boisterous, and affectionate dog with none of the aggressive tendencies of its ancestors.

BOSTON TERRIER Because of the structure of the puppy's head, most Boston Terriers have to be delivered by Caesarean section. This surgery is expensive, and breeding tends to be limited to those of very fit stock.

COAT Short, fine hair, giving a smooth, shiny coat. Colour is preferably brindle with white markings.

WEIGHING IN There are three recognized weight classes of Boston Terrier: lightweight is under 6.8 kg (15 lb), middleweight is 6.8–9.1 kg (15–20 lb), and heavyweight is 9.1–11.4 kg (20–25 lb).

EYES Large, dark in colour, wide apart, and round. Alert, intelligent expression.

HEAD Should be in proportion to the size of the dog, square, flat-topped, and with a short muzzle. Flews completely cover the teeth when the mouth is closed.

EARS Erect, thin, and set to the corner of the skull.

FACIAL CHARACTERISTICS

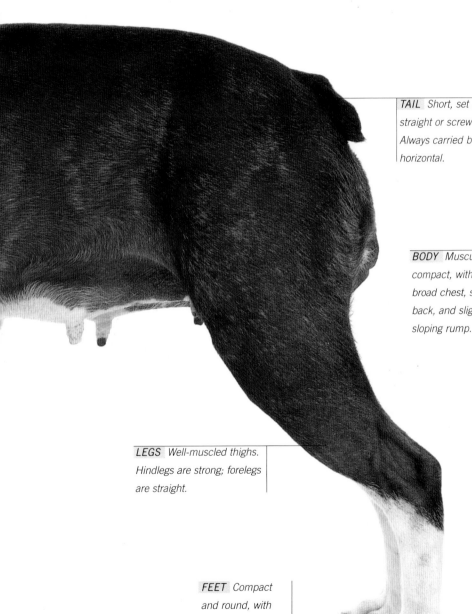

TAIL Short, set low, straight or screwed. Always carried below horizontal.

BODY Muscular and compact, with a deep, broad chest, short back, and slightly sloping rump.

LEGS Well-muscled thighs. Hindlegs are strong; forelegs are straight.

A TRUE BOSTONIAN The ancestor of this perky breed was called Hooper's Judge. Owned by Mr Hooper of Boston, this early Boston Terrier was a cross between a Bulldog and an English Terrier.

FEET Compact and round, with clearly arched toes.

SIZE
Weight should not exceed 11.4 kg (25 lb).

Bulldog

Despite its formidable appearance, the Bulldog is a gentle, affectionate, and loyal creature. These qualities, plus its reputation for courage and dogged endurance, prompted the British to adopt it as their national dog and to preserve the breed after the abolition of bull-baiting.

HISTORY

The practice of setting dogs to attack bulls for the purposes of public entertainment had been established in Britain for over 600 years before it was finally made illegal in 1835. By the 17th century the dogs used for this "sport" had become known as Bulldogs, but they probably had longer legs and were certainly more aggressive than the breed we know today. This may reflect the Bulldogs' ancestry, since they were probably derived from a Mastiff-type dog (*see pp.158–9*) introduced into Britain by the Phoenicians in the 6th century BC.

TEMPERAMENT

Today's Bulldog has a very different temperament from that of its forebears. It is an affectionate and dependable animal, gentle with children, but known for its courage and its excellent guarding abilities.

EYES Very dark, round, set wide apart and low down in the skull.

BODY Heavily built, but narrower at the loins. Shoulders are broad; back is short and slightly arched; chest is wide and round.

GROUP DIFFERENCES

The Bulldog is classified as a Utility Dog in the UK and as a Non-Sporting Dog in the US and Australia.

COAT Fine, short, and smooth. Colours include brindle, white, red, and fawn, some with a black mask or muzzle. Also pied, with white areas in any of the colours.

TAIL Medium-length, round, smooth, and tapering. Juts out straight, then turns downwards.

HEAD Large, broad, and square. Cheeks are well rounded and heavily wrinkled. Upper lips hang over lower jaws at the sides but join lower lip at the front and completely cover teeth.

EARS Small, thin, set high and wide apart. The "rose ear" exposes the pink inside.

FACIAL CHARACTERISTICS

FRENCH BULLDOG Probably derived in part from smaller examples of the English Bulldog, the French Bulldog is a muscular, energetic, little dog with an affectionate and dependable nature.

DIRECT ATTACK This prizefighter of a dog won a place in Englishmen's hearts for its tremendous courage: scorning a less direct approach, it would always attack from the front.

LEGS Straight and muscular; hindlegs are longer than forelegs.

FEET Compact and round, with forefeet turning slightly outwards. Toes are well spaced.

SIZE Weight: dogs 25 kg (55 lb); bitches 22.7 kg (50 lb).

Chow Chow

This exotic animal has two unique anatomical features – its mouth and tongue are blue-black in colour, and it walks with a stilted gait, due to its virtually straight hindlegs.

HISTORY

Also known as the Tartar Dog, Dog of Barbarians, and the Chinese Spitz, the Chow Chow probably originated in Mongolia. In ancient times, the breed was the adversary of evil spirits, guarding temples against their malign influence. Following its introduction into China, it performed the roles of guard dog (against intruders rather than spirits) and hunting dog of emperors and aristocrats. Later, the breed unfortunately became a source of both food – its flesh is still considered a delicacy in many parts of Asia – and fur. The Chow's coat can be rough or smooth: the rough is more common and has the distinctive ruff on the neck and culottes on the legs, but the smooth coat is still quite thick and dense, and it stands up from the body.

TEMPERAMENT

The Chow's rather independent and quiet nature contrasts sharply with the loyalty and affection it characteristically shows towards its owner.

BEAR DOG In China, the Chow Chow's appearance has given it the name *hsiung kon*, meaning "bear dog".

COAT Dense and abundant, standing out from the body. Colours are black, blue, cream, white, red, or fawn. Usually lighter shading on the backs of the thighs and underneath the tail.

TAIL Set high, and arching forwards over the back.

FEET Fairly small, round, and cat-like.

LEGS Hindlegs are muscular and almost straight; forelegs are long and well boned.

SIZE
Dogs 48–56 cm (19–22 in) tall; bitches 46–51 cm (18–20 in).

DECEPTIVE APPEARANCE With its leonine ruff, massive bear-like face, and scowling expression, the Chow Chow can look a daunting creature, but it is unlikely to fight unless provoked.

BODY Muscular and well balanced, with a broad, deep chest, and a short, straight back.

EARS Small and thick; set erect and wide apart.

EYES Almond-shaped, small, and usually dark in colour.

FACIAL CHARACTERISTICS

HEAD Broad, with a flat-topped skull, and a small stop. Muzzle is broad and square. Mouth and tongue are blue-black.

FAITHFUL FRIEND Aloof and self-contained, this breed is remarkably faithful to its owners, but remains wary of strangers.

Dalmatian

With its white coat and distinctive dark spots, the Dalmatian is one of the most elegant and eye-catching of breeds. In 19th-century Europe, and particularly in Britain, it trotted alongside horse-drawn carriages – reputedly to protect passengers from the unwanted attentions of highwaymen, but probably also for its marvellous decorative effect.

HISTORY

Although the Dalmatian is often considered a British dog because of its association with the aristocracy's stately processions, its history remains the subject of some debate. Some say its origins can be traced to northern India, and that it reached Europe by travelling with gypsy caravans in the Middle Ages via Dalmatia, Yugoslavia, from where its name derives. Others, however, claim that it may have had its roots in Egypt or Greece. Also called the Firehouse Dog in America, the Dalmatian was used by fire departments in the 1800s to run with the horses pulling the fire trucks to keep them in order. Apart from its spots, the Dalmatian resembles the Pointer *(see pp.56–7)*, and the dogs are probably related.

TEMPERAMENT

A lively, extrovert, and intelligent dog, the Dalmatian is naturally friendly, and a favourite with children. It likes regular exercise, and has great stamina.

HEAD Wrinkle-free, with a long, flat-topped skull, and a moderate stop. Muzzle is long and powerful.

COAT Glossy, with short, fine hairs. Colour is white with either brown or black spots.

POPULAR FILM DOG The 1961 animated Disney film *One Hundred and One Dalmatians* – along with its live-action remake – has helped ensure the breed's continuing popularity.

PHYSICAL PERFECTION An important requirement of the breed is a well-balanced physique.

CHANGING WITH AGE Unlike leopards, Dalmatians do change their spots! They are born white, then, as puppies, develop faint smudges that change to bold, distinctive marks as they get older.

EYES Round in shape. Dark-coloured if spots are black, amber if brown. Dark rims should match the spots.

EARS Set high and carried close.

FACIAL CHARACTERISTICS

BODY Deep-chested, but not too wide. Loins are well muscled.

TAIL Slightly curved and long. Ideally it should be spotted.

LEGS Well-developed thighs. Hindquarters are rounded; forelegs are straight.

FEET Round and compact, with arched toes. Nails are white, or match the colour of the spots.

SIZE
Ideal height: dogs
58.4–61 cm
(23–24 in); bitches
55.9–58.4 cm
(22–23 in).

Keeshond

This typical Spitz-type breed could have derived its name from Jan Kees, a very common Dutch name, or from the two patriots Kees de Witt and Kees de Gyselaer. Used extensively as a guard dog on canal boats, it became known as the Dutch Barge Dog, although in Victorian England it was perhaps rather unkindly named the Overweight Pomeranian!

HISTORY

In 18th-century Holland, the Keeshond was known as "a dog of the people". It symbolized resistance against the rule of William of Orange, and one of the Dutch patriot leaders, Kees de Gyselaer, actually owned one of these dogs. The Keeshond's ancestors remain rather obscure, but it was probably derived from earlier types of Spitz dogs, such as the Wolf Spitz. Keeshonds were first introduced into the UK by Mrs Wingfield-Digby, and by the late 1920s the breed had arrived in the US.

TEMPERAMENT

A bright, friendly character, quick to learn, and very alert. It makes a good guard dog.

HEAD *Fox-like and wedge-shaped from above, with a large ruff, dark, medium-length muzzle, and black nose.*

BODY *Short, compact, and powerful, with a deep, well-rounded chest.*

COAT *Pale grey, dense, soft undercoat with a long, hard, grey outer coat, standing out from body. Thorough daily grooming is required.*

A DOG FOR LIFE Keeshonds tend to be one-person dogs, and usually enjoy a very long life.

DUTCH BARGE DOG Although it is quite a large dog, the Keeshond does not take up much room in the home and, like its ancestors on the barges in Holland, can comfortably curl up to keep out of the way.

GRAND SPITZ The doyen of the Spitz group of Northern dogs, this breed differs from the Keeshond and Wolf Spitz in being somewhat smaller and carrying a black, brown, or white coat.

TAIL Moderate length, set high, with a black tip. It is carried tightly curved over the back. A double curl is highly desirable.

EYES Almond-shaped, dark eyes, with distinctive "spectacle" markings.

EARS Small, set high, velvety, and erect.

FACIAL CHARACTERISTICS

LEGS Hindlegs are muscular; forelegs are straight, with good bones.

FEET Cream-coloured and compact, with black nails. Short, smooth hair on feet and lower legs.

SIZE
43–46 cm
(17–18 in) tall.

Lhasa Apso

Prior to the 20th century, this Tibetan breed was rarely seen outside its native land. The exact origins of its name remain obscure – Lhasa is probably taken from Tibet's capital city, but Apso could have been derived from the Tibetan *abso seng kye*, meaning "barking sentinel dog", or from a version of *rapso*, Tibetan for goat, perhaps referring to the breed's long, wiry coat.

HISTORY

For at least 2,000 years, the Lhasa Apso was bred only in Tibet by holy men and nobles. It was used as a watchdog in temples and monasteries and was considered sacred, for when its master died, his soul was thought to enter the Lhasa Apso's body. Although they were thought to bring good luck to their owners, Lhasa Apsos were virtually impossible to buy. Happily, these very precious dogs spread to other parts of the world, mainly because the Dalai Lama, Tibet's ruler, would present them to visiting foreign diplomats. The breed was first seen in Britain in the 1920s, and it was introduced to the United States in the 1930s.

TEMPERAMENT

This is a hardy dog with a friendly, assertive manner. Intelligent and lively, it makes a good pet, but it is naturally suspicious of strangers.

SIZE
*Ideal height:
dogs 25.4 cm (10 in);
bitches slightly less.*

COAT *Long, coarse, and straight outer coat, with thick undercoat. There is a definite parting along the spine. Colours should be sandy, honey, golden, slate, dark grizzle, smoke, black, white, brown, or particolour.*

MANE MAINTENANCE Because of the golden-honey colours in its coat, the Lhasa Apso is sometimes referred to as the Lion Dog of Tibet. This long, beautiful coat can easily become matted, so it requires regular and thorough grooming from an energetic owner.

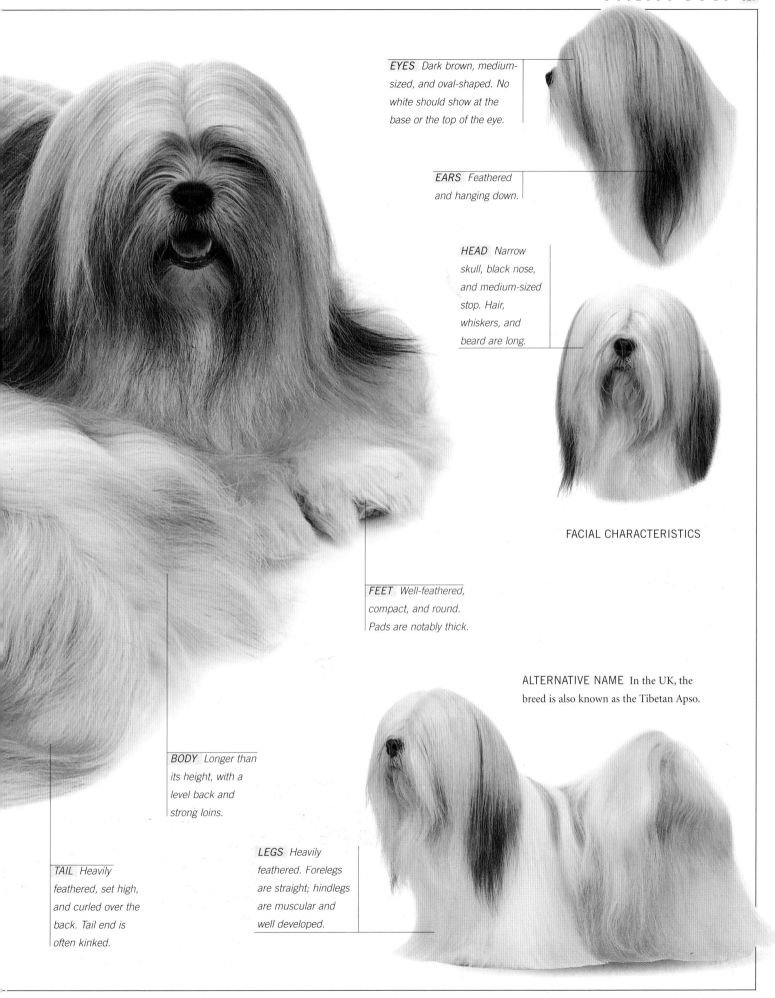

EYES Dark brown, medium-sized, and oval-shaped. No white should show at the base or the top of the eye.

EARS Feathered and hanging down.

HEAD Narrow skull, black nose, and medium-sized stop. Hair, whiskers, and beard are long.

FACIAL CHARACTERISTICS

FEET Well-feathered, compact, and round. Pads are notably thick.

ALTERNATIVE NAME In the UK, the breed is also known as the Tibetan Apso.

BODY Longer than its height, with a level back and strong loins.

LEGS Heavily feathered. Forelegs are straight; hindlegs are muscular and well developed.

TAIL Heavily feathered, set high, and curled over the back. Tail end is often kinked.

Poodles

It is perhaps unfortunate that this animal has received more attention for the unique way it is clipped for showing, than for its exceptional intelligence and sporting past. Nevertheless, it has become one of the world's best-loved breeds.

STANDARD POODLE It is generally accepted that the Standard is the healthiest of the three varieties of Poodle.

HISTORY

Although the Poodle has been known throughout western Europe for at least 400 years, its exact origins are uncertain. Very versatile, it can happily perform in various environments. On the battlefield, Boy, the constant companion of Prince Rupert of the Rhine, was killed at the Battle of Marston Moor in 1644; in the field, French Poodles were used to retrieve game birds from water (Caniche, the French name for the Poodle, derives from the word *canard*, meaning duck); and at the circus, the combination of distinctive looks and a "show-off" nature meant that Poodles always pulled in the crowds. There are three varieties of Poodle: Standard, Miniature, and Toy; they differ only in size.

TEMPERAMENT

Lively and good-natured, Poodles are intelligent and friendly, and they can be extremely loyal.

MINIATURE POODLE The Miniature is smaller than the Standard but larger than the Toy. It was particularly popular in the 1950s.

LEGS Forelegs and hindlegs are straight and muscular.

FEET Small and compact, with well-arched toes, ample pads, and dark nails.

SIZE
Toy up to 28 cm (11 in) tall;
Miniature 28–38 cm (11–15 in) tall;
Standard over 38 cm (15 in) tall.

EYES Almond-shaped, dark, and set fairly wide apart.

EARS Wide and long, set low, and hanging down close to the face.

HEAD Lean, well chiselled, and carried high, with flat cheeks and tight-fitting lips. Nose, lips, eyes, and eye rims are usually black, but may vary according to the coat colour.

FACIAL CHARACTERISTICS

TOY POODLE All Poodles have the advantage that they do not shed their frizzy hair, but it does grow continuously and will need regular clipping.

CLIPPING STYLES

Lion clip	
Dutch clip	
Lamb clip	
Puppy clip	

BODY Deep chest, short back, and muscular loins.

COAT Profuse, with firm texture, and characteristically frizzy. All solid colours.

TAIL Set high and carried at a slight angle from the body; customarily docked.

Schipperke

This rather fierce-looking creature probably derives its name from its work on the waters of lowland Belgium, being used as a guard dog and rat catcher on the canal boats. *Schipperke* means "little captain" or "boatman" in Flemish, but its name could also refer to its spruce, dark coat and proud military bearing.

HISTORY

The Schipperke has its roots in Flanders, where it has existed as a distinct breed for centuries. Some believe that it is descended from a now-extinct Belgian sheepdog breed, or from the Northern Spitz family, or that it may be a terrier and Pomeranian *(see pp.208–9)* cross. Whatever its origins, this lively, intelligent animal was, and is, much loved and has become one of Belgium's national breeds. It reached the UK and the US in the late 19th century, and the Schipperke Club of America was established in 1929.

TEMPERAMENT

The "Schip" is a loyal, energetic, inquisitive little dog. These characteristics, together with a robust constitution, make it ideally suited to life as a house-dog.

BODY Compact and muscular, with a broad chest and powerful loins. Back is straight and strong.

LEGS Straight forelegs and strong, muscular hindlegs. Thighs are powerful with longish hair on the backs.

RISING HAIR When the Schipperke becomes excited, its mane of thick rough hair appears to rise.

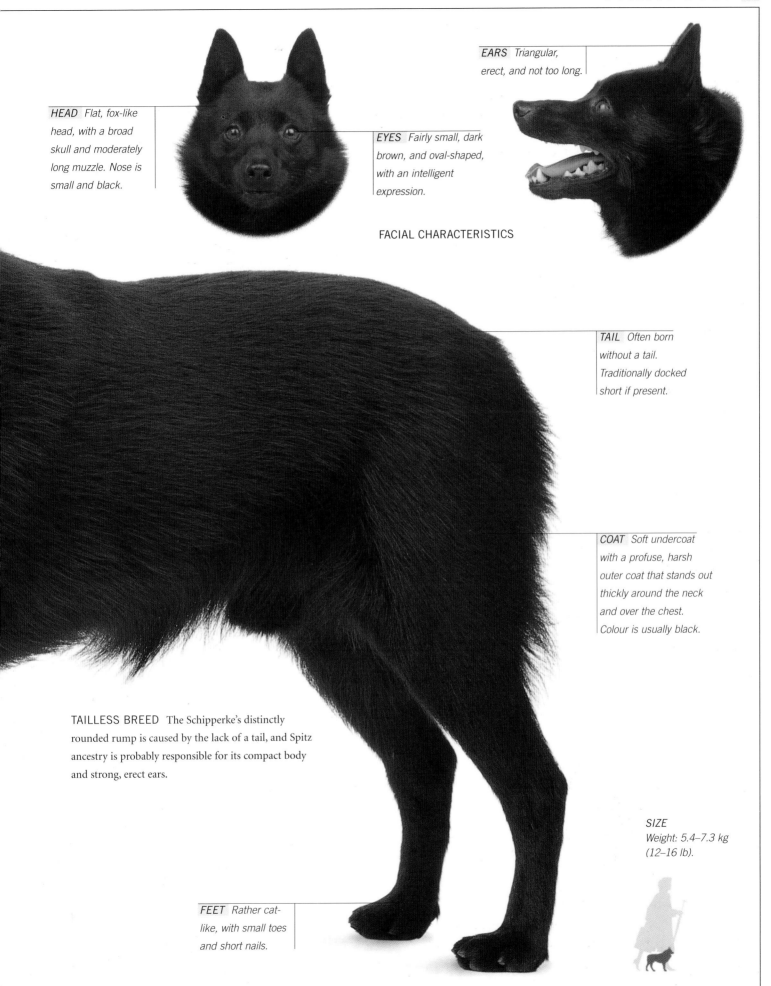

HEAD *Flat, fox-like head, with a broad skull and moderately long muzzle. Nose is small and black.*

EARS *Triangular, erect, and not too long.*

EYES *Fairly small, dark brown, and oval-shaped, with an intelligent expression.*

FACIAL CHARACTERISTICS

TAIL *Often born without a tail. Traditionally docked short if present.*

COAT *Soft undercoat with a profuse, harsh outer coat that stands out thickly around the neck and over the chest. Colour is usually black.*

TAILLESS BREED The Schipperke's distinctly rounded rump is caused by the lack of a tail, and Spitz ancestry is probably responsible for its compact body and strong, erect ears.

SIZE
Weight: 5.4–7.3 kg (12–16 lb).

FEET *Rather cat-like, with small toes and short nails.*

Schnauzers

Currently, there are three types of Schnauzer – Giant, Standard, and Miniature. Their name is derived from the German word *Schnauze*, meaning muzzle. The Schnauzer's muzzle is remarkable in that it is adorned with a distinctive, prominent moustache.

HISTORY

The Schnauzers originally came from the cattle- and sheep-farming areas of Württemberg and Bavaria in southern Germany, where a standard-sized, Schnauzer-like dog was recorded in the 16th century. Its forebears probably included Poodle-type dogs, as well as the Wire-haired German Pinscher. The early Schnauzers were general-purpose dogs, being very good ratters and guards, and they were also popular as coach dogs because of their great stamina. Today, the Standard and Giant Schnauzers are classified as Working Dogs in the US, and as Utility Dogs in the UK and Australia.

TEMPERAMENT

Generally, all three Schnauzer types are alert and energetic. They make good companions and family pets.

BODY Deep chest of moderate width and straight, sloping back.

GIANT SCHNAUZER The strongest of the Schnauzers stands 60–70 cm (23½–27½ in) tall at the shoulder. It was originally used as a cattle dog in Bavaria.

SMALL FAVOURITE
The Miniature Schnauzer is a brisk, bright little dog and is the most popular of the Schnauzers.

LEGS Forelegs are fine and straight; thighs on the hindlegs are well muscled.

TAIL Set high and carried above the horizontal; customarily docked.

DIFFERING GROUPS The Miniature Schnauzer is classified as a Terrier in the US, and as a Utility Dog in the UK and Australia. The dog illustrated here has cropped ears, which would be illegal in the UK, but is optional in the US and other countries.

HEAD Broad and gradually tapering to a blunt muzzle. Moderate stop down from skull to muzzle accentuates prominent eyebrows. Nose should be black with wide nostrils. Prominent moustache.

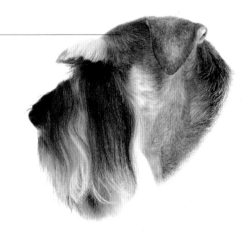

EYES Medium-sized, oval, and dark.

EARS V-shaped, set high, and falling forwards.

FACIAL CHARACTERISTICS

COAT Coarse, wiry outer coat and dense undercoat; long on legs and head, short elsewhere. Colours are "pepper and salt" (a mixture of dark- and light-grey hairs), pure black, or black and silver.

MINIATURE SCHNAUZER As its size suggests, this dog is not only smaller and more manageable than both the Giant and Standard Schnauzers, but it also tends to be less aggressive in temperament.

FEET Round and short. Toes are arched with dark nails.

SIZE
Ideal height:
dogs 35.6 cm (14 in);
bitches 33 cm (13 in).

Shar Pei

One of the world's rarest dogs, this baggily wrinkled creature is likely to cause a stir wherever it goes! It derives its name from its bristly coat – *shar pei* means sharkskin or sandpaper in Chinese. It is a pleasant, amiable breed and at first may seem undeserving of its other name – the Chinese Fighting Dog. In the past, however, it has achieved considerable success in canine combat, for its seemingly oversized skin makes it a difficult dog to get to grips with!

HISTORY

The Shar Pei's Oriental ancestors can possibly be traced back to between 206 BC and AD 220, for works of art from the Chinese Han Dynasty feature a dog resembling it. Some believe the breed to be descended from a much larger dog, now extinct, found in Tibet and China's Northern Province around 2,000 years ago, while others consider it to be related to the Service Dogs of China's Southern Province. Its future has sometimes looked very bleak indeed – in 1947, the dog tax in China rose so steeply that many Shar Pei owners could no longer afford to keep them and their numbers diminished alarmingly. In the 1970s, the Shar Pei's plight was taken up by breeders in the US, and in 1981 the first Shar Pei arrived in Britain.

TEMPERAMENT

The Shar Pei is a joy to be with – it is independent and well behaved, and it loves people.

HEAD *Large, with a flat skull, broad stop, and fairly long muzzle. Nose is preferably black, or should conform to the coat colour, and has a bulge at its base. Wrinkles on the forehead and the cheeks. A solid blue-black tongue is preferred.*

LEGS *Muscular and strong. Forelegs are straight; hindlegs are fairly angulated.*

EYE PROBLEMS Shar Peis are generally healthy dogs, but they are prone to entropion (inward rolling of the eyelids), an eye disease that can result in blindness unless treated promptly.

SIZE
46–51 cm
(18–20 in) tall.

COAT Stiff, short, and bristly, standing off the body, and lying flatter on the limbs. It should not be longer than 2.5 cm (1 in). Colours are black, red, fawn, and cream, often with lighter shading on backs of the thighs and tail.

TAIL Rounded, with a high-set base, narrowing to a fine point. Carried in a curl, curved over, or high and curved.

CHINESE FIGHTING DOG In its Chinese Fighting Dog days, it is likely that Shar Peis were drugged by their owners to stimulate sufficient aggression to ensure a long and profitable fight.

EYES Dark, medium in size, with a frowning expression.

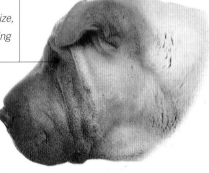

BODY Broad, deep chest and short, strong back. Mature dogs should not have excessive skin.

EARS Small, thick, and rectangular, pointing towards the eyes.

HOUSE-PROUD DOG This extremely uncommon breed makes a fine house-dog. It has a splendid reputation for cleanliness, and Shar Pei puppies are sometimes credited with the ability to house-train themselves.

FEET Compact and not too large. Toes are well knuckled.

FACIAL CHARACTERISTICS

Shih Tzu

The flowing mane-like locks of the Shih Tzu are probably responsible for its name, meaning "Lion Dog" in Chinese. Today it will happily adorn and protect the home, but its ancestors were used to rather grander surroundings, such as the palaces of the Manchu emperors in Imperial China.

HISTORY

Secrecy shrouds the exact origin of the Shih Tzu, but Lamaism, the religion of Tibet and a form of Buddhism, offers some clues. Maujusri, the Lamaist god of learning, was often accompanied by a small dog that could transform itself into a lion. Because of its leonine looks, the Tibetan Lhasa Apso (*see pp.128–9*) became strongly associated with this "Lion Dog". The Chinese emperors were presented with Lhasa Apsos by Tibet's ruler, the Dalai Lama, and it is likely that, having reached China, these exotic-looking dogs were crossed with the Pekingese (*see pp.206–7*) to create the breed we see today. The Shih Tzu is classed as a Non-Sporting Dog in Australia, as a Toy in the US, and as a Utility Dog in the UK.

TEMPERAMENT

Playful and energetic, the Shih Tzu makes an appealing pet and a very alert watchdog.

SIZE
Weight 4.5–8.1 kg (10–18 lb); height not more than 26.7 cm (10½ in).

LEGS Short and muscular, with abundant hair.

FEET Round and seemingly large because of the hair between pads and over feet.

AVOIDING TANGLES Long daily grooming sessions are necessary, otherwise combing out the tangles can be a painful process for both dog and owner!

PONYTAIL PUP To avoid eye infections, the Shih Tzu's long crown-hair should be tied up in a topknot.

TAIL Set high, well-plumed, and carried curved over the back. Ideal height is approximately level with the skull.

FAST-GROWING POPULARITY Due to the reluctance of the Chinese to sell or export Shih Tzus, they only reached the UK and the US in the 1930s, but they have rapidly enjoyed popularity in the show ring.

HEAD Broad, with a short, square muzzle. Nose is tip-tilted or level, with open nostrils. Abundant hair on the muzzle and the crown.

EYES Large and well spaced. Usually dark in colour, but lighter shades are permitted in liver-marked or liver dogs.

BODY Length greatly exceeds height of the dog. Level back, broad chest, and firm shoulders.

EARS Large and drooping, with abundant hair. They appear to blend into the neck.

FACIAL CHARACTERISTICS

COAT Long, soft, and dense, with a good undercoat. Wavy or straight, and all colours. White forehead blaze and tail-tip are desirable.

Working Dogs

Man first domesticated the dog as far back as 10,000 years ago, and perhaps even 35,000 years ago. It is likely that, to begin with, he used dogs for food and fur, killing the adults and fattening up the pups. Before long, he realized that this, his earliest animal companion, could be useful to him in other ways, as a watchdog and as a helper in the pursuit of game.

As time passed, various breeds of dog emerged, and the first were hunting dogs of the hound kind. From then on, the potential of the dog – which as a wild species was, and still is, a versatile, multipurpose creature – was gradually cultivated. Breeds specializing in a wide range of tasks, not just hunting, evolved, and the dog became far more than merely "man's best friend".

The variety of skills that the different dog breeds could master derived from the biological make-up of the dog family, *Canis*, one of the most successful types of mammal on earth. Intelligence, strength, stamina, speed, excellent sight and a remarkable sense of smell, the sociability of the pack animal, and the natural hunting skills of a predatory carnivore were all there; man had simply to select, concentrate, and exaggerate some of these features by controlled breeding.

DEVELOPING SKILLS

Over the centuries dogs became guards, sentries, and weapons of war. They pulled and carried loads, herded cattle, sheep, and other beasts, tracked criminals, and located people in trouble. In modern times, their role has been expanded, with some dogs acting as police auxiliaries, seeing-eyes, and sniffers-out of truffles, drugs, gas leaks, and explosives. Now there are even "hearing-ear" dogs that aid deaf people.

DRAUGHT BREEDS

Up to the late 19th century, dogs were used in teams to draw the Sussex Mail between the towns of Steyning and Storrington in Britain and to take fish from Southampton to London. Dog teams were also used in the early 1800s to pull the carts of butchers, bakers, hawkers, and knife grinders, as well as the travelling sideshows that visited country fairs.

Other draught breeds include the snow dogs, such as the Alaskan Malamute, Siberian Husky, and the Samoyed, which still perform great feats of strength and endurance, not only for sport, but also for more serious purposes in the Far North.

SPECIALIZATION

The Working Dogs group also contains some rather less well-known "specialist" dogs, like the Portuguese Water Dog, which would dive to retrieve nets and other fishing gear and also bring back fish that had escaped the trawl, and the Bernese Mountain Dog, which worked for Swiss farmers pulling loads of milk and cheese to market.

And finally, if there is one rare breed with the strangest occupation, it has to be the Norwegian Lundehund, otherwise known as the Puffin Hound, which is trained to work in caves and cliffs as a raider of puffin nests.

NEWFOUNDLAND (Top right) This breed is renowned for rescuing people in danger of drowning. Its large size, strong hindquarters, webbed paws, and excellent lung capacity make it easy for the Newfoundland to carry out its task and safely bring a person to shore.

BOXER (Below right) Thanks to their intelligence and acute sense of smell, dogs such as the Boxer, Rottweiler, German Shepherd, Great Dane, and Giant Schnauzer can work as part of the "police group" – they have all been trained as sentry aids and guard dogs.

ALASKAN MALAMUTE (Left) Snow dogs, such as this handsome example of Alaskan Malamute, have been known to run 160 km (100 miles) in just under 18 hours, and a four-dog team can pull a load of 180 kg (400 lb) for over 48 km (30 miles) a day.

Alaskan Malamute

This powerful Spitz-type breed is one of the oldest sled dogs. Stronger than the Siberian Husky *(see pp.166–7)*, it could not only pull heavier loads, but was also used to carry back-packs over very long distances.

HISTORY

The Alaskan Malamute probably derives its name from the Mahlemuts, an Inuit people, and early records of the first North American settlers mention the breed. These handsome creatures possess remarkable powers of fortitude and endurance; before the snowmobile, when sturdy dogs were still necessary for travel in the Far North, the Mahlemuts were much envied for their dogs by the other Inuit peoples. The Malamute was nearly lost through crossbreeding with imported dogs after Alaska was opened up to exploitation, but in 1926 steps were taken in the US to preserve the pure strain.

TEMPERAMENT

This loyal animal is a good worker, a fine guard dog, and an affectionate family pet.

COAT *Dense woolly undercoat with a thick, hard outer coat standing out from body. Colours are white, light grey to black, or gold to liver, with white on the underbody, feet, parts of legs, and face.*

POLAR DOG Alaskan Malamutes are renowned for their strength and endurance, and they have often been used in Arctic and Antarctic expeditions.

*SIZE
Dogs 64–71 cm
(25–28 in) tall; bitches
58–66 cm (23–26 in).*

TAIL *Well furred and set high. Hangs down when the dog is resting; carried over its back when working.*

OUTDOOR DWELLER This rugged breed thrives on plenty of exercise and actually prefers to live outside.

HUNTER AND GUARD The Inuit peoples thought highly of the breed and used it to hunt polar bears and wolves and to guard their herds of caribou.

EARS *Small, triangular, set wide apart, and erect or folded back.*

EYES *Brown, medium-sized, almond-shaped, and set obliquely.*

BODY *Powerfully built, with a deep chest; straight back slopes down to the hindquarters.*

HEAD *Wolf-like in appearance. Broad skull, with a large muzzle, powerful jaws, and "smiling" lips.*

LEGS *Broad, powerful hindlegs; heavy, muscular forelegs.*

FEET *Fairly large but compact. Toes are well arched and close-set, with hair in between. Pads are thick and tough.*

FACIAL CHARACTERISTICS

Bernese Mountain Dog

Of the four breeds of Swiss Mountain Dog in existence, the Bernese Mountain Dog is by far the most popular. In Switzerland's Berne district, it was developed as a draught animal, pulling carts for cheesemakers and weavers.

HISTORY

It is likely that the Bernese Mountain Dog's ancestors came to Switzerland as guard dogs with the Roman legions and were left behind to crossbreed with the local sheepdogs when the invaders departed. The result was four Swiss mountain breeds: the Bernese Mountain Dog, also known as the Bernese Sennenhund; the Great Swiss Mountain Dog; and the Appenzeller and Entlebuch Sennenhunds. In the 19th century, the Bernese Mountain Dog was in danger of extinction, but it was revived to the extent that a breed club was established in Switzerland in 1907. The breed reached the United States 30 years later.

TEMPERAMENT

Bernese Mountain Dogs are self-confident and cheerful, and they make excellent pets for all the family.

EYES *Almond-shaped, and dark brown in colour.*

STILL WORKING The Bernese Mountain Dog still shows traces of its working past, often being used to pull children's carts at shows and fairs.

FEET *Rounded and short, with close-set toes and white nails.*

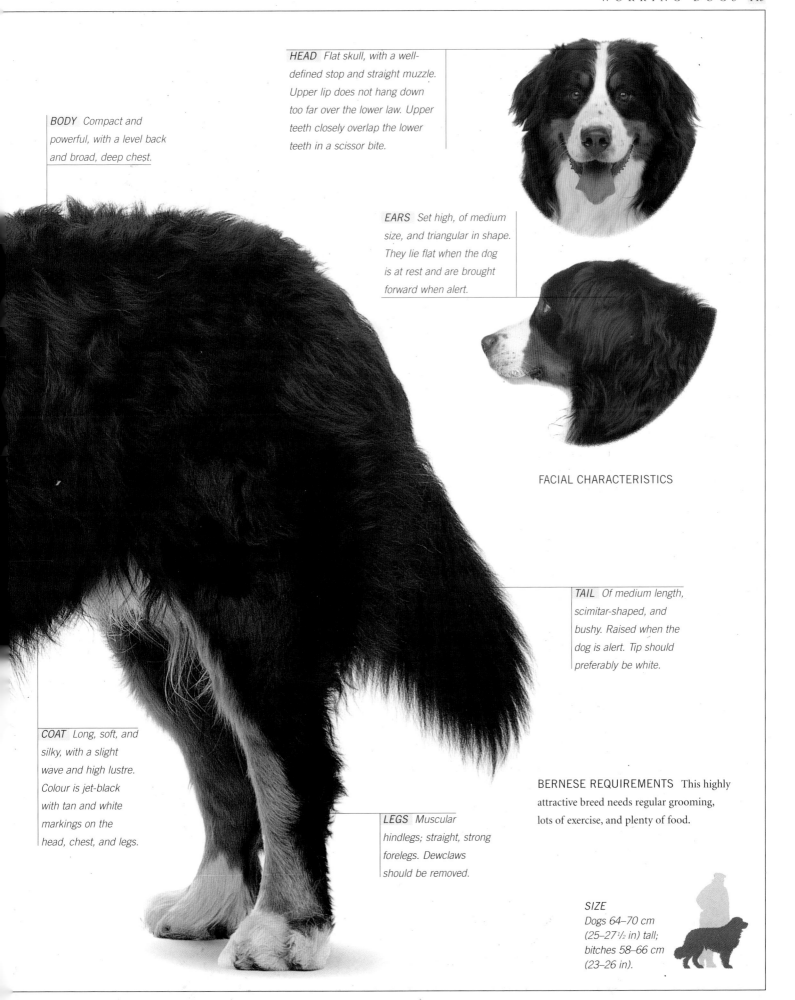

HEAD *Flat skull, with a well-defined stop and straight muzzle. Upper lip does not hang down too far over the lower law. Upper teeth closely overlap the lower teeth in a scissor bite.*

BODY *Compact and powerful, with a level back and broad, deep chest.*

EARS *Set high, of medium size, and triangular in shape. They lie flat when the dog is at rest and are brought forward when alert.*

FACIAL CHARACTERISTICS

TAIL *Of medium length, scimitar-shaped, and bushy. Raised when the dog is alert. Tip should preferably be white.*

COAT *Long, soft, and silky, with a slight wave and high lustre. Colour is jet-black with tan and white markings on the head, chest, and legs.*

BERNESE REQUIREMENTS This highly attractive breed needs regular grooming, lots of exercise, and plenty of food.

LEGS *Muscular hindlegs; straight, strong forelegs. Dewclaws should be removed.*

SIZE
Dogs 64–70 cm (25–27½ in) tall; bitches 58–66 cm (23–26 in).

Bouvier des Flandres

Formerly one of the most skilful cattle dogs in western Europe, the shaggy Bouvier is now employed as a guide dog, guard dog, and tracker. It originated around the Franco-Belgian border, and a literal translation of its name is "Ox-drover of Flanders".

HISTORY

The exact origins of the Bouvier are unclear, but around 100 years ago Flanders boasted several types of cattle dog. Bouviers were first shown in 1910 at the Brussels International Dog Show, but a breed standard was not established until 1912. World War I brought the breed widespread recognition for its strength and courage in army work, carrying messages, and finding wounded soldiers. Unfortunately, Belgium and north-eastern France bore the brunt of the fighting, and the Bouvier nearly died out through wartime casualties and the obliteration of its homeland. Dedicated Flemish breeders revived the Bouvier in the 1920s.

TEMPERAMENT

The Bouvier is intelligent and lively, but also calm and sensible. It is capable of extreme loyalty and courage.

BRIARD Not dissimilar in looks to the Bouvier, the Briard is a descendant of several ancient breeds, including perhaps the Alaunt and the Persian Sheepdog. It was once a hunting and guard dog of the French aristocracy, but after the 1789 Revolution its role became that of a general-purpose farm dog. It first took part in dog shows in France at the end of the 19th century, and it served its country well during World War II.

SIZE
Height 59–68 cm (23–27 in); weight 27–40 kg (60–80 lb).

FLEMISH GIANT This is an imposing dog, its body giving an impression of great power without clumsiness, while its beard adds a forbidding expression.

TAIL Customarily docked short to the second or third joint. Should be carried jauntily when on the move.

HEAD Rectangular, flat skull, powerful muzzle. Cheeks should be flat. Nose is black and well developed, with wide nostrils.

EARS Set high, triangular, and supple.

EYES Dark, oval, medium-sized, well-spaced, and alert in expression.

FACIAL CHARACTERISTICS

BODY Deep chest and broad, powerfully built, compact trunk.

LEGS Long, muscular, and heavy-boned. No dewclaws.

FEET Round and short. Toes are well-arched and held close together. Robust pads; strong black nails.

CROP-EARED BOUVIER DES FLANDRES
The Bouvier's working role was the original reason for cropping the breed's ears, which might otherwise have got in its way. These days, although the practice is still allowed in some countries – notably the US and Canada – an increasing number of dogs are left with their ears intact. Almost certainly, the numbers of crop-eared Bouviers will continue to fall.

Boxer

Gifted with seemingly boundless reserves of energy, the Boxer is one of the canine world's great characters. The breed only became well known in Britain and the US after World War II, but since then it has gained enormous popularity both as a family pet and guard dog.

HISTORY

The Boxer's main ancestors were two German dogs of the Mastiff type *(see pp.158–9)* – the Bullenbeiszer and the Barenbeiszer – that were used in the Middle Ages for bull-baiting and hunting boar and deer. In the 19th century they were crossed with other breeds, particularly the Bulldog *(see pp.120–21)*, to create the Boxer. Despite its German origins, Boxer is an English name that aptly describes the dog's punchy fighting style.

TEMPERAMENT

The Boxer is always keen to work and play, but it can be rather boisterous and even in old age it is still extremely athletic. Noted for courage as well as discipline, it makes an excellent guard dog. Also well suited to family life, the Boxer is very affectionate, loyal, and fond of children.

VISIBLE EXCITEMENT Because its tail is docked short, when the Boxer is pleased, happy, or excited, it tends to wag its whole body instead.

COAT Short, smooth, shiny, and lying flat to the body. Colours are fawn or brindle. Any white markings should not take up more than one third of the coat colour.

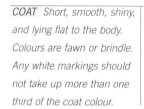

HEAD Square, with a deep, broad muzzle and upturned nose. Nose is broad and black, with a line between its wide nostrils. Lower jaw projects beyond the upper and curves slightly upwards. Neither teeth nor tongue should be visible when the mouth is closed.

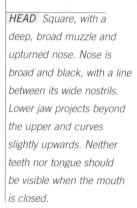

SIZE Dogs 57–63 cm (22½–25 in) tall; bitches 53–59 cm (21–23 in).

FEET Small, with ample pads and well-arched toes. Hindfeet are longer than the forefeet.

EYES Medium-sized, dark brown, with dark eye-rims.

EARS Thin, set high, and wide apart. Lying flat and close to the head when the dog is in repose; falling forward when alert.

FACIAL CHARACTERISTICS

TAIL Set high, carried erect, and usually docked short to 5 cm (2 in).

POINTED EARS In the US and other countries (but not the UK), it is traditional for most Boxers to have ears that are cropped to a point.

BODY Deep chest, with well-arched ribs. Back is broad, short, and well muscled; the abdomen tucked in; and the loins short.

DISTINCTIVE GUARD DOG One of the more distinctive dogs in appearance, the Boxer needs plenty of exercise to keep it looking and feeling its best. It is generally trustworthy but has a strong guarding instinct.

LEGS Hindlegs are well muscled, with broad, curved thighs; forelegs are long, straight, and parallel.

Bullmastiff

A true "designer dog", the Bullmastiff was bred in England in the 19th century by crossing the Bulldog (*see pp.120–21*) with the Mastiff (*see pp.158–9*) to combine their qualities. Now used as a guard dog by police forces and the military, it can also be a lovable pet.

HISTORY

Poaching was often a necessary way of life in 19th-century England, and the heavy penalties imposed upon offenders meant that poachers were often prepared to shoot gamekeepers to escape justice. The Bullmastiff was the ideal protector and companion for a gamekeeper, for it combined the courage and ferocity of the Bulldog, with the power, speed, and nose of the Mastiff. The breed became known as the "Gamekeeper's Night Dog" and would attack on command, knocking down and pinning a poacher to the ground without mauling him. The Bullmastiff is classified as a Working Dog in the US and the UK, but as a Utility Dog in Australia.

TEMPERAMENT

Once renowned for its aggression, the Bullmastiff is now an energetic and bright breed, with a calm, loyal, and affectionate nature.

HEAD Large, square skull, with a pronounced stop and a short, broad, black-masked muzzle. Upper lips do not hang below the lower jaw.

SIZE
Dogs 63.5–68.5 cm (25–27 in) tall; bitches 61–66 cm (24–26 in).

ACCEPTABLE COLOURS This fine specimen is a brindle Bullmastiff. Other colours include shades of red or fawn. Any white markings should be on the chest only.

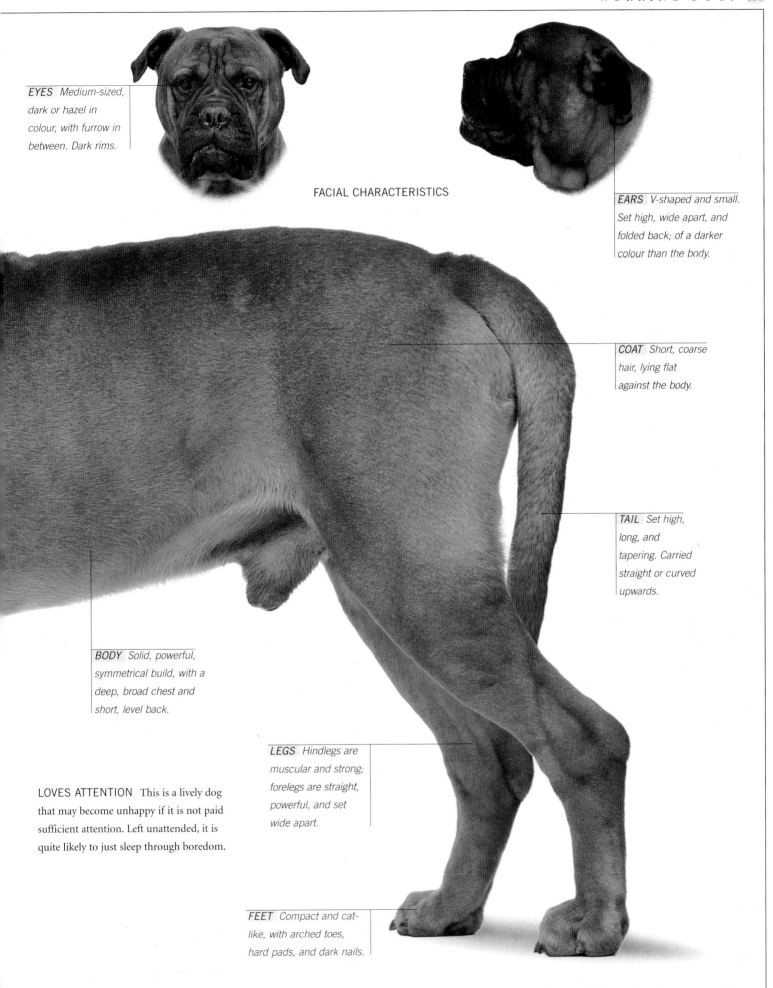

EYES Medium-sized, dark or hazel in colour, with furrow in between. Dark rims.

FACIAL CHARACTERISTICS

EARS V-shaped and small. Set high, wide apart, and folded back; of a darker colour than the body.

COAT Short, coarse hair, lying flat against the body.

TAIL Set high, long, and tapering. Carried straight or curved upwards.

BODY Solid, powerful, symmetrical build, with a deep, broad chest and short, level back.

LEGS Hindlegs are muscular and strong; forelegs are straight, powerful, and set wide apart.

LOVES ATTENTION This is a lively dog that may become unhappy if it is not paid sufficient attention. Left unattended, it is quite likely to just sleep through boredom.

FEET Compact and cat-like, with arched toes, hard pads, and dark nails.

Dobermann

Despite its current popularity, the Dobermann has only existed as a breed for a little over 100 years. An exceptionally powerful animal, its principal role is that of a guard dog, but it can also be trained for tracking, retrieving, and even sheep herding.

HISTORY

Between 1865 and 1870, a German tax inspector named Louis Dobermann endeavoured to create the perfect guard dog by crossing a variety of breeds. His exact formula remains a secret, but probably involved local cattle dogs, the Rottweiler *(see pp.162–3)*, Pinscher, the Manchester Terrier *(see pp.104–5)*, and maybe even the Greyhound *(see pp.44–5)*. Dobermanns were officially recognized by the German Kennel Club in 1900, and the breed then quickly reached the US and Britain. In World War I Dobermanns served the German Army in the front lines as guard and patrol dogs, and they have since been used by police forces all over the world.

TEMPERAMENT

The Dobermann is a natural guard dog – intelligent, strong, and aggressive when necessary. Consequently, it needs firm control, but it can still become a loyal and even affectionate companion.

EAR CROPPING In the US and some other countries, it is traditional for the breed to have cropped ears.

HEAD Long, with a blunt, wedge-shaped profile. Top of skull is flat, and parallel to top of muzzle. Lips are set tightly over jaws. Nose colour depends on coat colour.

TAIL Continues the line of the spine. Usually docked at either the first or second joint.

DECEPTIVE APPEARANCE The moderate size of the Dobermann belies its surprising weight and muscular power.

EYES Almond-shaped, with a keen, alert expression. Colour is dark brown in black dogs, or tones with coat colours.

FACIAL CHARACTERISTICS

EARS Small, set high, and folded or erect.

BODY Squarely built, with a well-developed, muscular chest and tucked-up belly. Back is short and straight.

DIFFERENT CLASSIFICATION The breed is classified as a Working Dog in the US and the UK, but as a Utility Dog in Australia.

COAT Short, smooth, and hard, lying close to the body. Colours are black, blue, brown, or fawn, with rusty markings above the eyes, on the muzzle, throat, chest, and legs, and below the tail.

LEGS Hindlegs are powerful, set fairly wide apart, and parallel. Forelegs are straight.

TRAINING IS ESSENTIAL This sleek, streamlined breed requires careful training to curb its latent aggression. Plenty of exercise will ensure its excellent shape.

FEET Cat-like and compact, with well-arched toes. Dewclaws should be removed.

SIZE Ideal height: dogs 69 cm (27 in) tall; bitches 65 cm (25½ in).

Great Dane

One of the gentle giants of the canine world, the Great Dane possesses enormous strength as well as a kindly nature. Although its name suggests Danish origins, the breed was actually developed in Germany, where it is known as the *Deutsche Dogge* or German Mastiff.

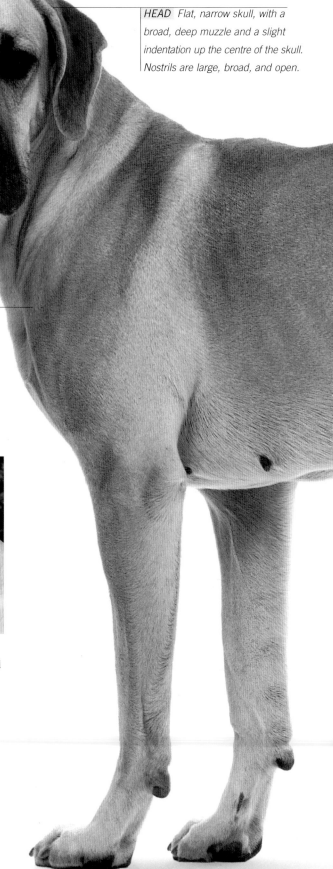

HEAD *Flat, narrow skull, with a broad, deep muzzle and a slight indentation up the centre of the skull. Nostrils are large, broad, and open.*

HISTORY

Large Mastiff-like dogs *(see pp.158–9)* are portrayed in the artefacts of many ancient civilizations. It may have been Phoenician traders who brought these animals to Mediterranean countries, or Roman legions who brought them directly to Germany. Either way, the forebears of today's Great Dane were to be found in the households of royalty and nobles throughout Europe in the Middle Ages. Not only mediaeval status symbols, Great Danes showed their considerable mettle by hunting wild boar, stags, and wolves.

COAT *Short and thick, with great lustre. Colours are brindle, fawn, blue, black, and harlequin (white with black markings).*

TEMPERAMENT

The Great Dane is a very affectionate, kindly dog, capable of great loyalty. Because of its large size, however, early training is essential if an effective but controllable guard dog is required.

CROP-EARED GREAT DANE
It is usual practice in the US and Canada for Great Danes to have their ears cropped between two and three months of age.

DRAWN TO THE HEAT This truly "great" breed likes to be physically cosseted – it needs, and relishes, somewhere warm to sleep.

CANINE APOLLO A dog closely resembling the Great Dane appears on Greek coins dating from the 1st century BC. This "Greek connection" is probably responsible for the breed's nickname – the "Apollo of dogs".

EYES Medium-sized, set deep in the face, and preferably dark in colour.

EARS Medium-sized, triangular, set high, and folded forwards.

FACIAL CHARACTERISTICS

BODY Very deep chest, strong back, and arched loins.

LEGS Hindlegs are long and powerful; forelegs are straight and flat-boned.

TAIL Long and tapering, with a slight curve towards the end. Carried in line with the back when the dog is moving.

FEET Toes are well arched and set close together; nails are preferably dark.

SIZE
Minimum height: dogs 76 cm (30 in); bitches 71 cm (28 in).

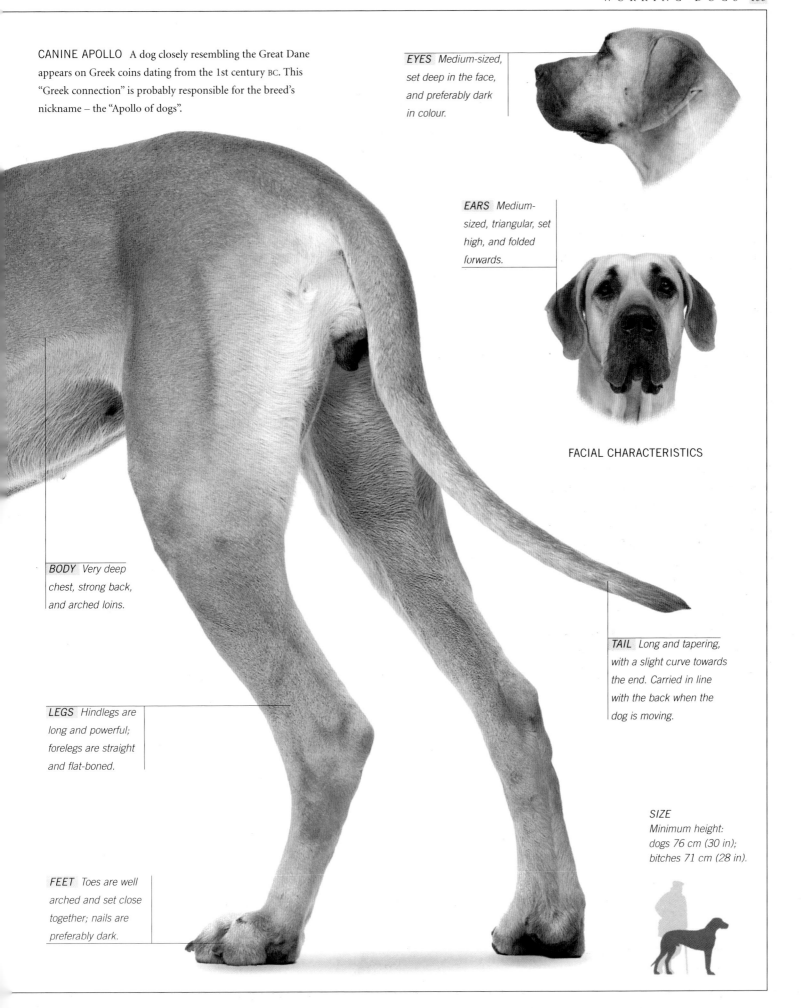

Leonberger

This gentle giant of a dog has a name meaning "lion of the mountains", and indeed it possesses the thick, yellow-brown coat, mane, and dark gold eyes of the lion. However, it is genial and affectionate, rather than ferocious. Like all very big dogs, its average life-expectancy is about 11 years.

HISTORY

Although some believe the Leonberger originated in Switzerland, it is more probable that it arose in the early 19th century in the town of Leonberg, Germany, from the crossing of St Bernards, Newfoundlands, and, perhaps, Pyrenean Mountain Dogs (see pp.164–5, 160–61, and 182–3 respectively). It almost became extinct during World War II, but it is now increasing both in numbers and popularity in Britain and the United States, as well as in its native land.

TEMPERAMENT

With its loving and lovable character, the Leonberger is excellent with children and devoted to the family. It is an intelligent and brave breed and makes a superb guard dog. It needs, of course, plenty of space and opportunity for exercise.

BODY *Powerfully built, with a fairly short, wide, straight, muscular back and deep chest.*

COAT *Thick, with a woolly undercoat and carrying a thick mane and "trousers". It is golden to reddish-brown in colour.*

LEGS *Muscular, with long thighs. Forelegs are set wide.*

WATER-LOVING BREED This good-looking dog is tough and hardy and adores messing about in water – even in winter.

EYES Medium in size
and brown in colour, with
a frank expression.

EARS As wide
as they are long,
and drooping.

FACIAL CHARACTERISTICS

HEAD A slightly rounded
skull. Nose is jet black.

HIP PROBLEMS As with some other large breeds
of dog, hip dysplasia – a congenital disease of the hip
joints – can cause trouble in some lines of Leonberger.

AN OUTDOOR DOG The Leonberger
is a keen, strong swimmer. Because of its
love – and need for – the great outdoors,
it is not a dog suited to town life.

TAIL Long, bushy,
and set low.

FEET Big and rounded, with
webbing (good for swimming)
and black pads.

SIZE
Weight: 34–50 kg
(75–110 lb); height:
65–80 cm (25½–31½ in)

Mastiff

The Mastiff is one of the oldest dog breeds, and despite its warrior past it is nowadays another of our gentle canine giants. Although still used for guard-dog duties, the Mastiff is more often simply an affectionate member of the family!

HISTORY

Mastiff-like dogs are depicted in Egyptian artefacts dating back to 3000 BC, and the breed may have been introduced into Britain by Phoenician traders or by invading Angles and Saxons. The native Celts certainly had Mastiffs fighting with them when Julius Caesar invaded Britain in 55 BC, and they were used as dogs of war up until the 17th century. Their other uses were as hunters of bears and wolves, and as participants in the practice of dogfighting and bear-baiting. After these were banned, in the 19th century, the Mastiff's popularity waned in Britain, but the breed has been maintained in two strains, those of Lyme Hall Kennels in Cheshire, and the dogs bred by the Duke of Devonshire at Chatsworth.

TEMPERAMENT

Although Mastiffs are generally even-tempered, gentle, and loyal, they retain the ability to guard and must be handled firmly.

HEAD Squarish, with a heavy, broad skull, a short, broad muzzle, and a depression in the centre of the forehead between the eyes. Ears, nose, and muzzle should be black.

BODY Powerful build, with a broad, deep chest and wide back and loins.

FEET Large and round, with arched toes and black nails.

LEGS Forelegs are strong and set wide apart; hindlegs are muscular and squarely set.

EYES *Small, set wide apart, and dark, hazel brown in colour.*

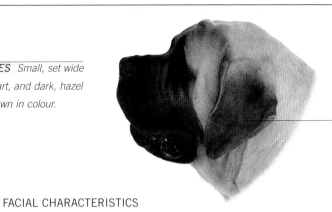

EARS *Small, thin, and set wide apart. Lying close to cheeks when at rest.*

FACIAL CHARACTERISTICS

BRITAIN'S PRIDE A very English dog – featured in the poetry of Chaucer and present at the Battle of Agincourt in 1415 – the Mastiff is now seldom seen in Britain. However, it has flourished in the US in recent years.

NEAPOLITAN MASTIFF Less popular at present than the Mastiff, this dog can trace its ancestry back for over 2,500 years to the Molossus, a fighting dog of ancient Greece and Rome. A heavy, muscular breed, often employed as a formidable guard dog, it can nonetheless make a loyal and affectionate pet if properly trained.

SIZE *Minimum height: dogs 75 cm (30 in); bitches 70 cm (27½ in).*

COAT *Short, coarse, and lying flat. Colours are apricot-fawn, silver-fawn, or dark fawn-brindle.*

TAIL *Long, set high, and tapering. Curved when excited, but not over the back.*

Newfoundland

Developed on the island of Newfoundland, this bear-like dog possesses remarkable skills as a life-saver from water. One of the strongest working dogs ever developed, it is also intensely loyal, and fits superbly into family life.

HISTORY

The ancestors of this breed remain largely unknown. Some claim that the Vikings brought its forebears to Newfoundland in the 10th century, while others claim that it is a descendant of the Pyrenean Mountain Dogs (*see pp.182–3*) that accompanied emigrating French fishermen. Whatever the truth, the breed evolved on Newfoundland into an outstanding sea-rescue dog and draught animal. In the 18th century Newfoundlands were imported into Britain and France and rapidly became popular with English sailors as ship dogs. The Scottish author JM Barrie based the dog Nana in *Peter Pan* on his own Newfoundland.

TEMPERAMENT

The Newfoundland is a particularly pleasant and docile dog. Despite its considerable bulk, it is very gentle with children.

NATURAL SWIMMER The Newfoundland is a powerful swimmer, with a natural passion for water. It should have access to the sea, a pond, or a river.

BODY *Deep, broad chest, level back, and powerful loins.*

FEET *Large and broad, with webbing between the toes for swimming.*

SIZE
Approximate height: dogs 71 cm (28 in); bitches 66 cm (26 in).

HEAD Broad, massive skull, with a short, square muzzle covered in short, fine hair. Mouth is very soft.

EARS Small, set back, and lying flat.

EYES Small, deep-set eyes, dark brown in colour.

HOT COAT This densely coated dog is understandably unhappy in high temperatures.

FACIAL CHARACTERISTICS

TAIL Thick, well covered with hair, and slightly curved. Hangs downwards when the dog is at rest; raised on the move.

COAT Outer coat is coarse, straight, and flat, with an oily, water-resistant quality; undercoat is dense. Colours are chocolate-brown, black, bronze, or white with black markings (known as a "Landseer"). Black and brown dogs can have splashes of white on the chest, toes, and tail-tip.

LEGS Hindlegs are partially feathered; forelegs are straight and well feathered.

Rottweiler

One of the strongest and most powerful dogs in the world for its size, the Rottweiler, a former cattle dog, is intelligent, robust, and companionable. It is now a highly valued guard and police dog but can also make a rewarding pet.

HISTORY

After the Roman legions retreated, their large, Mastiff-type dogs *(see pp.158–9)* were left in southern Europe and became known as hunters of wild boar. By the Middle Ages, in Rottweil, Germany, the Roman dogs had been crossed with local sheepdogs to create the *Rottweiler Metzgerhund* ("Rottweil butchers' dog"). Butchers were using their dogs as drovers and security guards, because livestock was only able to be moved around on foot. In the 19th century, with cattle-driving becoming illegal in Germany, and livestock being transported by railway, the Rottweiler suffered a decline in popularity. Enthusiasts came to the rescue around 1900, and the breed reached the US and Britain in the 1930s.

TEMPERAMENT

The Rottweiler is a natural guard dog and can be aggressive towards intruders. Obedience training and firm handling may be required, but Rottweilers can, and do, make affectionate, calm-tempered pets.

LOW MAINTENANCE
Grooming the Rottweiler is an easy task, for daily brushing is adequate to keep the coat in good condition.

HEAD Of medium length, with a broad skull and deep muzzle. Forehead is fairly arched and cheeks are well boned. Nose is well developed and always black, and the skin on the head can form a wrinkle.

COAT Medium-length, coarse top coat, and fine undercoat. Colour is black, with tan to mahogany markings, not exceeding one tenth of the body colour. Undercoat colours are black, grey, and fawn and should not show through.

BODY Squarely built, compact, and powerful. Deep, broad chest, straight back, and sloping rump.

EYES *Almond-shaped, dark brown in colour, and medium-sized.*

EARS *Small, set high, and lying flat.*

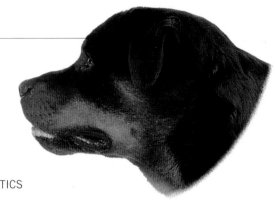

FACIAL CHARACTERISTICS

TAIL *Set high, and carried horizontally. It is traditionally docked to the first joint.*

BEAUCERON A superb, instinctive herding dog, the Beauceron is the sheepdog star of France. Powerfully built, intelligent, and with a reputation for aggressiveness akin to that of the Rottweiler, it needs equally careful raising and training. If correctly brought up, its loyalty and protective nature can make it a loving companion. The Beauceron is not, however, a dog for the town.

ROBBERY-PROOF DOG The talents of this breed as a guard dog have long been recognized. In the Middle Ages, rich merchants would cleverly avoid robbery by fastening their money bags around Rottweilers' necks.

LEGS *Hindlegs are well angled; forelegs are straight and muscular.*

FEET *Compact, with round front feet, and longer hindfeet. Hard pads, short black nails, and well-arched toes, preferably with black pencil markings. The rear dewclaws should be removed.*

SIZE
Dogs 63–69 cm (25–27 in) tall; bitches 58–63.5 cm (23–25 in).

St Bernard

During three centuries of arduous mountain-rescue work, St Bernards have saved an estimated 2,500 human lives. Modern roads and transport have now made the breed's life-saving skills redundant – today it is highly prized as an intelligent and soft-hearted family dog.

HISTORY

The breed takes its name from the Hospice of the Great Saint Bernard Pass. It was founded in AD 980 by St Bernard de Menthon as a refuge for travellers through the perilous Alpine pass between Switzerland and Italy. Early records have unfortunately been lost, but by the 18th century the monks of the hospice were breeding St Bernards to guide, find, and recover people in the treacherous mountain conditions. The original St Bernard dogs had short coats, but the introduction of Newfoundland blood (see pp.160–61), to reverse the effects of inbreeding, has produced a rough-coated variety.

TEMPERAMENT

Despite their tremendous bulk, St Bernards are extremely gentle and friendly. Very tolerant of children, they make ideal family pets as long as they have plenty of space, food, and exercise.

HEAD Large, broad, and rounded skull, with a definite stop, down to a short, deep muzzle. Flat cheeks and long upper lip. Large, black nose has well-developed nostrils.

BODY Deep, broad chest, powerful back, and sloping hindquarters.

A TRUE LIFE-SAVER The most successful mountain-rescue dog ever was a St Bernard named Barry, who died in 1814 with a total of 40 lives to his credit.

EYES *Dark brown in colour, and medium in size.*

EARS *Medium-sized, and lying against the cheeks.*

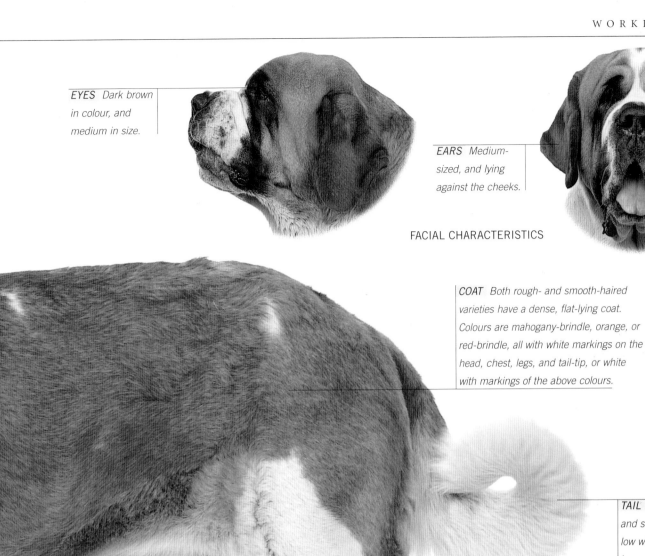

FACIAL CHARACTERISTICS

COAT *Both rough- and smooth-haired varieties have a dense, flat-lying coat. Colours are mahogany-brindle, orange, or red-brindle, all with white markings on the head, chest, legs, and tail-tip, or white with markings of the above colours.*

TAIL *Long, heavy, and set high. Carried low when the dog is in repose; raised during activity.*

THE IMPORTANCE OF TEAMWORK In mountain-rescue work, the dogs worked in teams of four. On locating a victim of avalanche or exposure, two St Bernards would lie down next to him to keep him warm, one would lick his face to revive him, and one would return to the hospice to get human help. If the victim began to recover, he could revive himself further by drinking brandy from a barrel, firmly attached to each dog's collar.

LEGS *Hindlegs are heavy-boned and powerful; forelegs are straight and long.*

SIZE
Great height and proportionate bulk.

FEET *Very large, with well-arched toes. Dewclaws should be removed.*

Siberian Husky

Strictly speaking, this is the only breed that should be called a husky, although the term is loosely applied to many sled dogs. It has a handsome, rather wolf-like appearance, an excellent temperament, and enormous stamina.

HISTORY

Siberian Huskies were developed by the nomadic Chukchi, an Inuit people of eastern Siberia, for pulling sleds, herding reindeer, and for use as watchdogs. They were the perfect working dogs for the harsh Siberian conditions – hardy, able to integrate into small packs, and quite happy to work for hours on end. Huskies remained isolated in Siberia for hundreds of years, until the beginning of the 20th century, when fur traders took them to North America. They soon became the undisputed champions of competitive sled-racing and are now popular as companion dogs.

TEMPERAMENT

This breed has an extremely amiable character – docile but alert – and is always willing to work.

HEAD Domed skull, with a definite stop down to a tapering muzzle. Skull and muzzle are of equal length. Lips are black and close-fitting. Nose is black, liver, or pink in colour, toning with the coat.

COAT Dense undercoat and straight, soft outer coat of medium length. Colours are various, often with unusual head markings.

BODY Deep chest and muscular, level back. Loins are slightly arched.

FEET Compact, well furred, and oval, with strong pads and a slight web between the toes. Dewclaws should be removed.

SIZE
Dogs 53–60 cm (21–23½ in) tall; bitches 51–56 cm (20–22 in).

GENTLE GIANT Despite its great strength, the Siberian Husky makes an ineffective guard dog since its disposition is too gentle.

HOWLING DOG A characteristic of the Siberian Husky is that it usually howls rather than barks.

TAIL Well furred, like a fox's brush; carried hanging when the dog is at rest or working, curved over the back when attentive.

MINIMAL GROOMING This hardy breed has a beautiful, odour-free coat that needs no trimming, except around the feet.

EYES Almond-shaped and obliquely set. Colours are any shade of blue or brown, and sometimes one of each colour.

EARS Medium-sized, triangular, set close together and high. Well furred on both the insides and the outsides.

LEGS Hindlegs are parallel and muscular; forelegs are strong and straight.

FACIAL CHARACTERISTICS

Pastoral Dogs

For many centuries, clever, thinking dogs have been working alongside shepherds, herdsmen, and farmers in the gathering and controlled moving of cloven-footed animals, such as sheep and cattle. Some of the dogs in the Pastoral group also have additional talents, such as the ability to guard against predators.

These dogs are accustomed to hard work, often in rugged terrain and certainly in all weathers, and usually they possess a waterproof double coat.

VARYING SPECIALITIES

Some of the breeds in the Pastoral group, such as the Australian Kelpie, Appenzell Mountain Dog, and Portuguese Cattle Dog, were, and in some cases still are, used to work with a variety of stock; the Kelpie even enjoys herding poultry! Dogs such as the Komondor, which once guarded Hungarian sheep and cattle against wolves, are now employed in North American farms to deter marauding coyotes. The beautiful Samoyed was originally, in its native Russia, a super-efficient herder and protector of reindeer. Smaller pastoral breeds, such as the Lancashire Heeler, are now rarely used as working animals. The Heeler, so named because of its way of running behind and, if necessary, nipping the heels of recalcitrant cattle, is more often a cheerful companion pet, though it can still make a wonderful rat hunter.

AMERICAN FAVOURITE

The dog most commonly used on American farms for herding work is an unofficial breed called the American Shepherd, English Shepherd, or Border Collie. It is a Collie-type dog, but it has a shorter muzzle and smaller body, and is usually black-and-white in colour. The Border Collie is also the most popular working sheepdog in Great Britain and Ireland, each summer entertaining many thousands of spectators at sheepdog trials, agricultural shows, and on television. This is a dog that needs to work. Without the stimulus and interest of doing the job for which it was bred, it can become difficult to handle. Border Collies are generally not very happy when kept solely as house pets.

INTERNATIONAL HERDERS

Almost every nation has a breed of dog used for herding. Thus we have the Collie from Scotland, the Puli from Hungary, the Corgi from Wales, and the Maremma from Italy. The Puli is a sheep herder and driver. These black individuals spend long hours out on the mountains and may show red tints to their coats due to the bleaching effect of the sun. Corgis were first used as cattle dogs by the ancient Celts. They worked like Heelers, controlling movement of the stock by nipping their heels. Nowadays, they make loyal companion animals to doting owners, among them Queen Elizabeth II. Maremmas, usually white in colour, are handsome dogs that live quite spartan lives on the high pastures of central Italy.

SAMOYED (Top right) Sometimes called the "Reindeer Dog" or the "Smiling Dog", the Samoyed for centuries herded reindeer, pulled sledges, and was a household companion for the ancient semi-nomadic tribespeople of Siberia and the Russian Arctic. In more recent times, Samoyeds have served as sled dogs for innumerable Arctic explorers.

BORDER COLLIE (Below right) One of the most popular breeds of dog, loved and admired for its intelligence, skill, loyalty, and excellent temperament, the Border Collie is an expert herder of sheep, found working in all weathers to the whistle and voice of the shepherd, particularly in Great Britain and Australia.

GERMAN SHEPHERD (Left) Originally a herder of sheep, the German Shepherd is nowadays working with energy, skill, and intelligence in other fields. Trained as a guard of military installations, as an assistant to police, as a detector of drugs, guns, and explosives, and to track human beings, the breed has never been more valued.

Australian Cattle Dog

Formerly known as the Queensland Heeler, the Australian Cattle Dog is notable for its powerful bite, an essential attribute for a dog required to drive cattle over long distances in the outback. Bred to survive in a harsh environment, it is essentially an energetic, out-of-doors dog that needs plenty of exercise.

HISTORY

In the 1830s, Australian stockmen developed a tough working breed, because, in the words of an Australian breed historian, the existing cattle dogs "bit like an alligator and barked like a consumptive". Various dogs were involved in the creation of the Australian Cattle Dog; they include Dingoes for their hardiness and silence, an obscure, rugged breed known as the Smithfield, blue merle Collies, Dalmatians *(see pp.124–5)*, Australian Kelpies *(see p.177)*, and Old English Sheepdogs *(see pp.180–81)*.

TEMPERAMENT

An intelligent and alert animal, the Australian Cattle Dog is courageous, reliable, and very hard-working.

BODY *Strong, level back and deep, fairly broad chest.*

SNAPPING DOG This breed has also been known as the Australian Heeler, or Blue Heeler. Heeler refers to its herding skill of snapping and biting cattle's heels.

SIZE
Dogs 46–51 cm (18–20 in) tall; bitches 43–48 cm (17–19 in).

HEAD *Broad and strong, with top of skull parallel to top of muzzle. Powerful lower jaw. Cheeks are muscular but not prominent. Nose is always black.*

EARS *Thick, triangular, set wide apart, and pricked when alert. Hair inside.*

EYES *Medium-sized, dark brown, and oval-shaped.*

FACIAL CHARACTERISTICS

COAT *Dense undercoat with a coarse, straight, weather-resistant outer coat. Colours are red-speckled or blue, blue-mottled, or blue-speckled, with or without additional markings.*

TAIL *Well furred and set low. Carried hanging with a slight curve when the dog is at rest, or raised when working.*

LOYAL COMPANION This is a highly protective and loyal dog, wary of strangers yet responsive to firm command, and very well suited to guard-dog duties.

LEGS *Hindlegs have broad, muscular thighs; forelegs are straight.*

FEET *Rounded, with short, well-arched, close-set toes. Pads are hard; nails are strong.*

Belgian Shepherd Dogs

As their name indicates, up to the 20th century Belgian Shepherd Dogs were widely used to guard flocks in and around Belgium. Nowadays their main work is as guard dogs – for the police, for the army, and even for publicans – but they also make endearing family pets.

HISTORY

Many closely related breeds of sheepdog existed in Belgium up to the late 19th century, but as shepherding became increasingly unnecessary, breeders refined these dogs to produce one basic type with four colour and coat varieties. In most countries they are accepted as different forms of the same breed, but in the US three are recognized as separate breeds (Groenendael, also known as the Belgian Sheepdog, or Belgian Shepherd Dog; Belgian Tervuren; and Malinois). The Laekenois has yet to achieve recognition in the United States.

TEMPERAMENT

Belgian Shepherd Dogs are alert, intelligent, and very watchful. Although primarily outdoor dogs, they can adapt well to home life, providing they can stretch their legs at regular intervals.

COAT Long, straight outer coat, with a dense undercoat. Hair is short on the head and lower legs. Colours are red, grey, or fawn, with black shading on the tip of each hair.

LAEKENOIS This is the only rough-coated variety of Belgian Shepherd Dog. Its hair is wiry, dry but never curled, and its coat colour is a ruddy fawn, with black shading.

BODY Athletic and muscular. Deep chest, level back, and broad, sloping rump. Neck is slightly elongated.

LEGS Long, lean, and muscular.

TAIL Well furred, and of medium length. Hangs with the tip curved up when the dog is resting; lifted when active.

GROENENDAEL The most popular of the four types of Belgian Shepherd Dog, the Groenendael has a long, black outer coat and sometimes has white markings.

TERVUEREN Known as the Belgian Tervuren in the US (note the subtle difference in spelling), this finely proportioned breed is full of vitality and is constantly on the move when not relaxing.

EARS Set high, triangular, and erect.

EYES Medium-sized, almond-shaped, and preferably dark brown in colour.

HEAD Long and finely chiselled, with flat cheeks. Skull and muzzle are of equal length. Black mask on the face.

FACIAL CHARACTERISTICS
Tervueren

FEET Forefeet are rounded; hindfeet are oval. Arched toes, thick pads, and dark nails.

SIZE
Ideal height: dogs 61–66 cm (24–26 in) tall; bitches 56–61 cm (22–24 in).

Bearded Collie

Previously known as the Highland Collie, the Bearded Collie is an active dog that retains its enthusiasm for the outdoors, yet makes a perfect household companion. Similar in looks to the Old English Sheepdog (*see pp.180–81*), this breed is smaller, leaner, and has an undocked tail.

HISTORY

The exact origins of the collie family are unclear, but their ancestors may have been ancient breeds native to Scotland. Some authorities suggest, however, that Magyar dogs brought by Polish traders to the north of Britain in the Middle Ages may have been one of the main ancestors of the Bearded Collie. The breed almost disappeared in the early part of the 20th century but was rescued through mating a pair in 1944.

TEMPERAMENT

Noted for its friendliness, the Bearded Collie is a lively, intelligent, and even-tempered dog. It thrives on regular exercise.

LEGS *Covered with shaggy hair all round. Straight, well-boned forelegs and well-muscled hindlegs.*

FEET *Oval and well haired, with ample pads. Well-arched, close toes.*

BORDER COLLIE Originally from the Scottish border country, this breed is an outstanding sheepdog valued by farmers all over the world.

CONFIDENT HERDER This is an intelligent working dog, and should have a bright, inquiring look in its eyes. There should be no sign of nervousness or aggression.

EYES Large and set wide apart. Colour tones with coat.

EARS Medium-sized, drooped when resting.

HEAD Broad, flat-topped, square skull with a strong muzzle. Large, arched eyebrows do not obscure the eyes. Nose, lips, and eye-rims are usually black, but can follow coat colour in blue and brown dogs.

FACIAL CHARACTERISTICS

COAT Soft undercoat with a long, harsh outer coat, straight or wavy. Colours are black, blue, all shades of grey, brown, reddish fawn, and sandy, all with or without white markings on the head, chest, legs, and tip of the tail.

BERGAMASCO This dog takes its name from the Italian province of Bergamo, where it was first bred. It is thought that the Bearded Collie contributed to its development.

TAIL Set and carried low, with an upward curl at the tip. Well haired.

SIZE
Dogs 53–56 cm (21–22 in) tall; bitches 51–53 cm (20–21 in).

BODY Long, with a deep chest and level back. Chest profile straight in front.

Rough Collie

For centuries the Rough Collie was hardly known outside Scotland, but it is now one of the world's most popular breeds. Descended from generations of hard-working herding dogs, it is a conscientious creature of immense intelligence.

HEAD Long and tapered, with a flat skull and black nose. End of the muzzle is blunt, not square.

HISTORY

Rough Collies originated in the Lowlands of Scotland, and they probably take their name from a local type of black sheep known as the Colley. Like many dogs, they owe much of their popularity to Queen Victoria. She became enchanted by these attractive animals while visiting her Scottish estate at Balmoral in the 1860s and took some Collies back home with her to Windsor Castle. It quickly became a highly sought-after show dog in England, and, by the late 1880s, in the US too. In the 1940s the breed shot to even greater fame when a Rough Collie was chosen to star as Lassie in the much-loved series of films based on Eric Knight's classic novel *Lassie Come Home*.

TEMPERAMENT

This is a good-natured, friendly dog, energetic out of doors, wary of strangers, and very affectionate to its owner and family.

COAT Abundant, with a thick undercoat, and long, straight, harsh outer coat. Colours are sable (light gold to rich mahogany) and white, tricolour (black, tan and white), or blue merle (silvery blue, marbled with black, with white markings, and optional tan markings).

CALM, ASSURED DOG This gregarious creature usually shows no trace of nervousness or aggression.

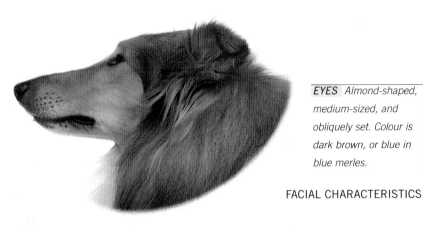

EYES Almond-shaped, medium-sized, and obliquely set. Colour is dark brown, or blue in blue merles.

EARS Small and neither too close together nor too far apart.

FACIAL CHARACTERISTICS

BODY Greater in length than height. Chest is deep. Back is slightly arched over the loins.

AUSTRALIAN KELPIE This excellent working dog is notorious for its rather odd skill of running along sheep's backs to reach the head of the flock. It is a tough, durable breed that can go without water for long periods.

ACUTE HEARING The Rough Collie is endowed with expressive ears – thrown back when the dog is in repose, and carried forwards and semi-erect when it is alert. They are also highly functional appendages that can reputedly detect a shepherd's whistle or a voice from a distance of up to 1.5 km (1 mile).

TAIL Long and set low, with the tip turned upwards. Carried proudly when the dog is excited.

LEGS Hindlegs are powerful and sinewy; forelegs are straight and muscular.

FEET Oval-shaped, with well-padded soles, and arched toes.

SIZE Dogs 63.5–68.5 cm (25–27 in) tall; bitches 61–66 cm (24–26 in).

German Shepherd Dog

Also known as the Alsatian, the German Shepherd is one of the most versatile working dogs ever developed. Throughout the world it is used by police forces and armies as a guard and sniffer dog, by the blind as a guide dog, and by farmers as a sheepdog. It is also a popular pet, providing personal protection and companionship.

HISTORY

The breed was established in Germany in the 1880s, although there is still some debate about its ancestry. Initially it was a farm dog but, having shown its versatility in the German army during World War I, it was soon introduced into the US and the British Commonwealth by returning Allied soldiers. Since then, it has rapidly achieved widespread popularity, undoubtedly with the help of scene-stealing "character" roles such as Rin Tin Tin in the 1920s, and Bullet, Roy Rogers' companion, in the 1950s.

TEMPERAMENT

The German Shepherd is extremely intelligent and generally dependable. Given correct and early training, it can make an obedient and loyal companion for all the family.

HEAD Broad skull and wedge-shaped muzzle are of equal length. Nose is always black. Lips are firm and close tightly over teeth.

EARS Medium-sized, broad-based, and set high and erect.

EYES Medium-sized, almond-shaped, and usually dark brown in colour.

LEGS Straight forelegs; hindlegs have broad and powerful thighs.

FACIAL CHARACTERISTICS

SIZE Approximate height: dogs 62.5 cm (25 in); bitches 57.5 cm (23 in).

SHOW-RING DARLING Once known as the Alsatian Wolf Dog, this breed is a star performer in the show ring. It made its show debut in Hanover in 1922.

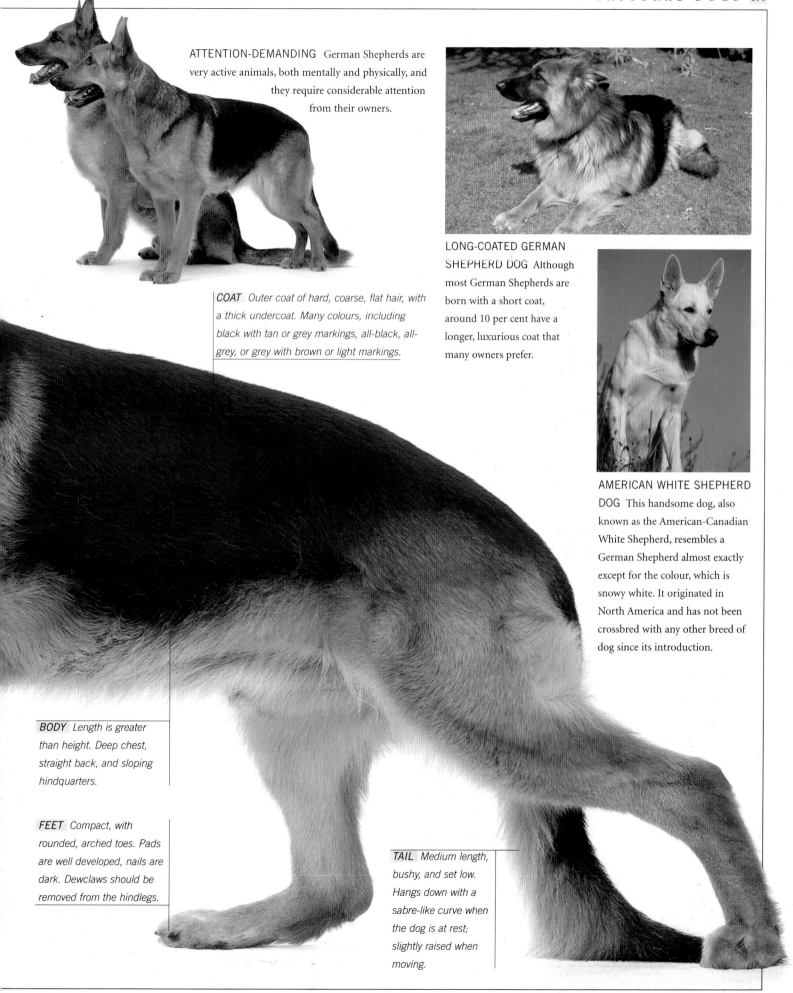

ATTENTION-DEMANDING German Shepherds are very active animals, both mentally and physically, and they require considerable attention from their owners.

LONG-COATED GERMAN SHEPHERD DOG Although most German Shepherds are born with a short coat, around 10 per cent have a longer, luxurious coat that many owners prefer.

COAT Outer coat of hard, coarse, flat hair, with a thick undercoat. Many colours, including black with tan or grey markings, all-black, all-grey, or grey with brown or light markings.

AMERICAN WHITE SHEPHERD DOG This handsome dog, also known as the American-Canadian White Shepherd, resembles a German Shepherd almost exactly except for the colour, which is snowy white. It originated in North America and has not been crossbred with any other breed of dog since its introduction.

BODY Length is greater than height. Deep chest, straight back, and sloping hindquarters.

FEET Compact, with rounded, arched toes. Pads are well developed, nails are dark. Dewclaws should be removed from the hindlegs.

TAIL Medium length, bushy, and set low. Hangs down with a sabre-like curve when the dog is at rest; slightly raised when moving.

Old English Sheepdog

One of England's most ancient sheepdog breeds, the Old English Sheepdog has now become a much-loved and highly distinctive family pet. With its rolling gait and abundantly shaggy coat, it can easily be mistaken for a bear.

HISTORY

The breed was developed in England's West Country by farmers who needed an agile cattle drover and sheep herder to take their animals to market. Its ancestors probably include the Bearded Collie *(see pp.174–5)* and a variety of imported European herding dogs. By the 19th century, the Old English Sheepdog was widely used in agricultural areas. It made its British show debut in 1873.

TEMPERAMENT

Several generations ago, the breed was described as fierce and untrustworthy, but these characteristics have long since disappeared. Although still capable of guarding, the Old English Sheepdog is friendly, faithful, and even-tempered, with an intelligent and boisterous manner. The breed is exceptionally good – and popular – with children.

HEAD Squarish, broad skull, arched over the eyes. Muzzle is strong and of equal length to the skull. Large, black nose, with wide nostrils.

BODY Short and compact, with a deep chest and fairly arched loins. Long, strong, gently arched neck.

BOBTAIL BREED The completely cropped tail gave the breed its nickname of "Bobtail" or "Bob".

FEET Compact, round, and small, with well-arched toes and thick, robust pads. Dewclaws should be removed.

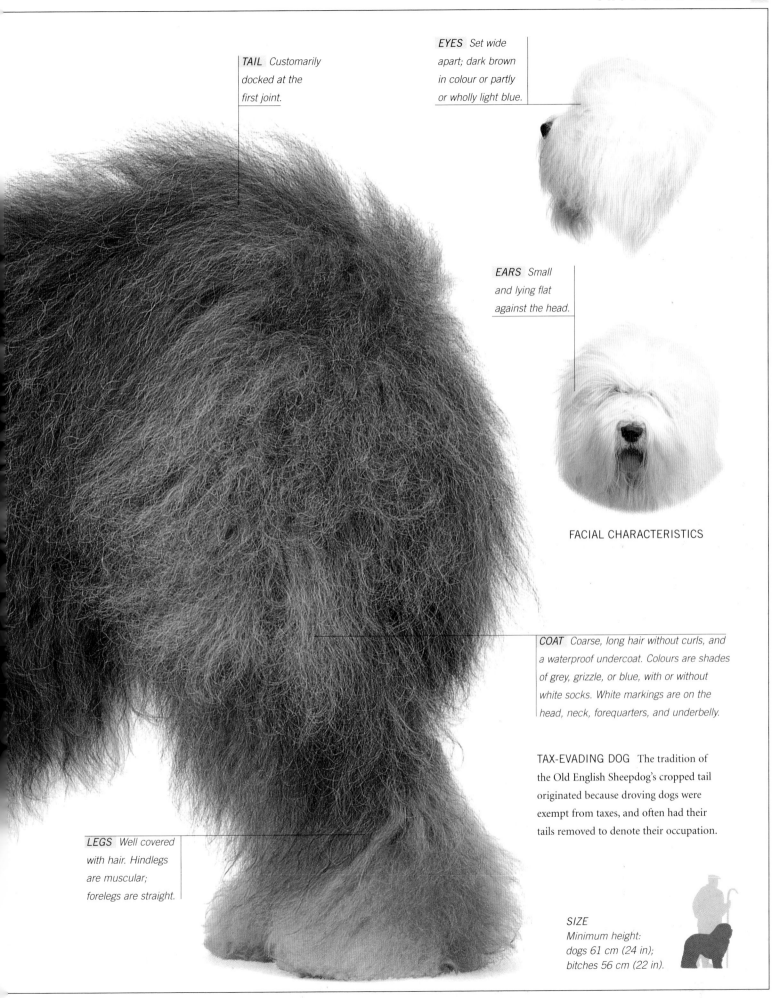

TAIL *Customarily docked at the first joint.*

EYES *Set wide apart; dark brown in colour or partly or wholly light blue.*

EARS *Small and lying flat against the head.*

FACIAL CHARACTERISTICS

COAT *Coarse, long hair without curls, and a waterproof undercoat. Colours are shades of grey, grizzle, or blue, with or without white socks. White markings are on the head, neck, forequarters, and underbelly.*

TAX-EVADING DOG The tradition of the Old English Sheepdog's cropped tail originated because droving dogs were exempt from taxes, and often had their tails removed to denote their occupation.

LEGS *Well covered with hair. Hindlegs are muscular; forelegs are straight.*

SIZE *Minimum height: dogs 61 cm (24 in); bitches 56 cm (22 in).*

Pyrenean Mountain Dog

Probably the most powerful breed in existence, the Pyrenean Mountain Dog fortunately carries a kindly nature within its immense frame. Though suited to family life, it is not a dog to be kept indoors.

HIGH-MAINTENANCE DOG These dogs need an enormous amount of food, lots of exercise, and frequent grooming to keep them happy, healthy, and looking their best.

HISTORY

For centuries these dogs were used in the Pyrenees to protect sheep flocks from marauding bears and wolf packs. Their ancestor was probably the Tibetan Mastiff, brought from Asia over 1,000 years ago, but there may have been a certain amount of crossbreeding with indigenous marsh dogs present in the area since prehistoric times. In the 15th century, Pyrenean Mountain Dogs were used as guards and became particularly fashionable during the reign of Louis XIV, after he installed one at the Louvre as a watchdog. It was not long before they were to be found guarding chateaux all over the country. However, their popularity in France declined markedly following the Revolution of 1789.

COAT *Abundant undercoat of fine hairs; long, thick, and coarse outer coat, straight or wavy. Colours are white or white with patches of badger, wolf-grey, or pale yellow.*

TEMPERAMENT

A kind-natured, gentle dog, obedient, loyal, and affectionate, but also capable of guarding.

LEGS *Straight, well-muscled forelegs. Hindlegs are well feathered, with double dewclaws.*

SIZE
Minimum height: dogs 70 cm (28 in); bitches 65 cm (26 in).

HEAD Big, domed skull, with a deep, strong muzzle. Skull and muzzle are joined by a gentle slope, with only a slight furrow between. Nose and lips are black, and the roof of the mouth is marked with black.

EYES Dark amber-brown, almond-shaped. Dark rims.

FACIAL CHARACTERISTICS

EARS Small, triangular, and lying flat. May be raised slightly when alert.

MAREMMA SHEEPDOG
The Maremma is to the shepherds of Italy what the Beauceron and the Collie are to their counterparts in France and Britain. Usually white, but sometimes fawn or lemon in colour, this handsome dog may be related to the Kuvasz and the Pyrenean Mountain Dog.

BODY Solidly built, with a broad, deep chest, and wide, muscular, straight back.

FEET Short, compact feet, with slightly arched toes. Thick, strong nails.

DOG OF WAR The Pyrenean Mountain Dog has not always been known for its gentleness. At one time it was used in battle as a dog of war, often with iron spikes fitted to its collar.

TAIL Long, tapering, and well feathered, with tip slightly curled. Tail rises from low position to high above the back as the dog becomes excited.

Samoyed

The lavish, snow-white coat and famous "Samoyed smile" ensure that this glamorous creature will turn heads and make friends wherever it goes! Elegant and agile, it is now one of the most fashionable show and companion breeds, yet it has a history of hard work in severe conditions.

HISTORY

The breed's ancestors were the tough European Spitz dogs. A nomadic Siberian people, the Samoyed gave the dogs their name and used them to pull sledges and herd reindeer. The breed became renowned for its endurance and hardiness, and European explorers used Samoyeds in their polar expeditions. Originally "Sammy" (as the breed is affectionately known) was a multicoloured dog, usually black, black and white, or black and tan, but eventually the white in the coat became dominant. In the late 19th century, fur traders recognized the potential profit of Sammy's glistening white coat and started to import the breed into the US and Europe. The first Samoyeds reached Britain in 1889, and Queen Alexandra was among their many admirers.

TEMPERAMENT

The Samoyed is a lively creature, with an intelligent and independent nature. It will gladly be friendly to all, including intruders!

TELL-TALE SIGNS The erect ears, tail carried over the back, and coat standing off the body all point towards the Samoyed's Spitz ancestry.

LEGS Hindlegs are very muscular; forelegs are straight and well boned.

HEAD Powerful and wedge-shaped. Flat, broad skull, and fairly long muzzle. Nose is preferably black. Lips are black, with a smiling expression.

FEET Long, flat, and feathered. Pads are hairy; toes are well spaced.

BODY Muscular back, strong loins, and deep, moderately broad chest.

SMILING HAPPY DOG Appearances are not deceptive in this case; the characteristic "Samoyed smile" – caused by the lips being slightly curved at the corner of the mouth – does seem to reveal the breed's true character. It is an even-tempered, good-natured, and generally very happy dog, with a natural affinity for human company.

COAT Thick, soft undercoat, with a long, harsh outer coat growing through. Straight outer coat should stand away from the body and have silver tips. Colours are white, white and biscuit, and cream.

EARS Set wide, erect, and well haired.

EYES Fairly wide apart, almond-shaped, and set slanted; medium to dark brown in colour.

TAIL Long, thick, and carried over the back. When alert, it is carried to the side; when resting, carried dropped.

FACIAL CHARACTERISTICS

SIZE
Dogs 51–56 cm (20–22 in) tall; bitches 46–51 cm (18–20 in).

Shetland Sheepdog

A particularly well-proportioned, handsome animal, the Shetland Sheepdog, or "Sheltie", is easily mistaken for a small Rough Collie *(see pp.176–7)*. Despite being bred as a sheepdog, it makes an excellent family pet and competent guard dog.

MULTIPURPOSE DOG These animals are easily trained, which makes them ideal as working dogs, show dogs, or pets. Shelties thrive on regular exercise, and their long coats reward frequent grooming.

HISTORY

For centuries these little dogs were used to herd and guard the sheep flocks of the Shetlands – those rugged islands off the Scottish coast, where many of the animals are rather small in stature. Their ancestors are thought to have been either the Scottish Rough Collie or the Icelandic Yakki, brought to the islands by whalers. Refinement of the breed took place mainly in the 20th century, after the export of Shelties to mainland Scotland and beyond.

TEMPERAMENT

A dog of remarkable intelligence and trainability, the Sheltie has retained many of the characteristics of its working forebears. It makes a fine guard dog in the home, since it is loyal and affectionate to its owners but wary of strangers.

LEGS Forelegs are straight and well feathered; hindlegs have powerful, muscular thighs.

SIZE
Ideal height:
dogs 37 cm (14½ in);
bitches 35.5 cm (14 in).

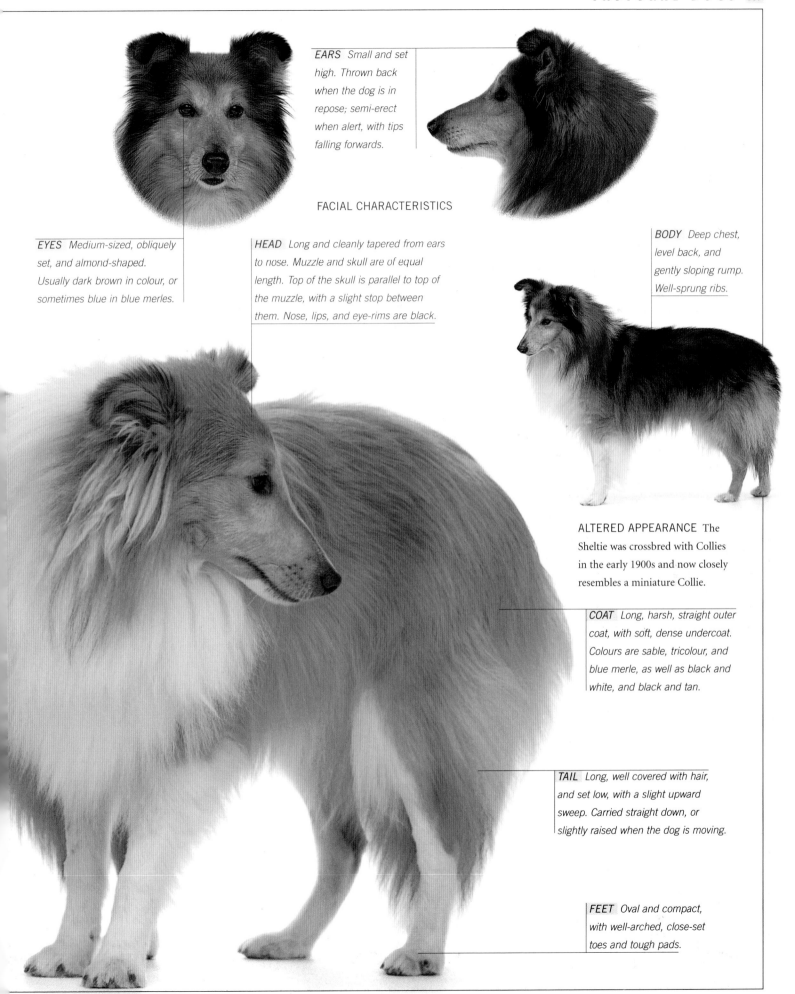

EARS *Small and set high. Thrown back when the dog is in repose; semi-erect when alert, with tips falling forwards.*

FACIAL CHARACTERISTICS

EYES *Medium-sized, obliquely set, and almond-shaped. Usually dark brown in colour, or sometimes blue in blue merles.*

HEAD *Long and cleanly tapered from ears to nose. Muzzle and skull are of equal length. Top of the skull is parallel to top of the muzzle, with a slight stop between them. Nose, lips, and eye-rims are black.*

BODY *Deep chest, level back, and gently sloping rump. Well-sprung ribs.*

ALTERED APPEARANCE The Sheltie was crossbred with Collies in the early 1900s and now closely resembles a miniature Collie.

COAT *Long, harsh, straight outer coat, with soft, dense undercoat. Colours are sable, tricolour, and blue merle, as well as black and white, and black and tan.*

TAIL *Long, well covered with hair, and set low, with a slight upward sweep. Carried straight down, or slightly raised when the dog is moving.*

FEET *Oval and compact, with well-arched, close-set toes and tough pads.*

Welsh Corgis

Welsh Corgis probably derive their name from the Welsh word *corrci*, meaning dwarf dog. There are two closely related varieties – the Pembroke and the Cardigan. The Pembroke enjoys much more popularity than the Cardigan, perhaps because it has always had friends in high places, despite its small size! Through the ages it has been a big favourite of royalty, from Richard I to Queen Elizabeth II.

HISTORY

The Pembroke Welsh Corgi is thought by most to have arrived in Wales in 1107 with the Flemish weavers. Some claim that its Flemish history and fox-like head point towards Spitz ancestry, while others suspect that trading between Wales and Sweden introduced the Swedish Vallhund into the local canine stock. Like the Cardigan, the Pembroke enjoyed most success in herding cattle. Being quick and agile, Welsh Corgis could nip their herd's heels, then nimbly elude the angry hoof! The Pembroke and the Cardigan were recognized as separate breeds in Britain in 1934.

TEMPERAMENT

Welsh Corgis are loyal, affectionate, friendly, and very good with children. They tend to be wary of strangers and, therefore, make good guard dogs.

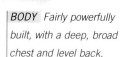

WATERPROOF COAT The Pembroke Welsh Corgi's water-resistant coat needs daily brushing to keep it looking trim.

TAIL Naturally short tail is preferred, otherwise docked close.

BODY Fairly powerfully built, with a deep, broad chest and level back.

SIZE 25.4–30.5 cm (10–12 in) tall.

LEGS Short, well boned, and strong.

FEET Oval, with short nails, strong pads, and well-arched toes. The two centre toes are longer than the outer toes.

EARS Medium-sized, pricked, and slightly rounded.

HEAD Flat, wide skull, moderate stop, and black nose. Tapering muzzle gives a fox-like facial appearance.

EYES Of medium size, round, and brown, blending with coat colour.

FACIAL CHARACTERISTICS
Pembroke Welsh Corgi

COAT Medium length and quite dense. Colours are red, sable, fawn, or black and tan, with or without white markings. The Corgi "bib" is like no other.

PEMBROKE WELSH CORGI
Since its cattle-herding days, the Pembroke Welsh Corgi has always enjoyed a quick nip, but this tendency is unendearing and should be discouraged in a family pet.

CARDIGAN WELSH CORGI The Cardigan can be distinguished from the Pembroke by its longer body and brush-like tail. Because it is a blue merle, this Cardigan's right eye is brown and its left is pale blue. Blue merles' eyes can be pale blue, blue, or have blue flecks.

Toy Dogs

Toy dogs are specialists in their own right – as companion animals, and as small, conveniently sized, and aesthetically pleasing pets. They play a vital role in the lives of many people who live alone, and their beneficial effects on the wellbeing of the old, the ill, and the housebound, are increasingly acknowledged.

THE SMALLEST OF DOGS

Applied to dogs, as it has been since 1863, the word "toy" means simply "diminutive". Toy dogs are, of course, a varied and decorative group, but they usually develop a strong protective instinct towards their human friends and their home. This quality often makes them effective sentries who warn of the presence of strangers with loud barks and yelps. Some are so protective of their property, that, despite their small size, they have no compunction in attacking intruders.

A FAIR SELECTION

Mostly, toy dogs have been selectively bred for a pleasing appearance. Some, such as the Italian Greyhound and Toy Spaniels, are mini-versions of full-sized breeds in the Hound and Gundog groups; and the Pomeranian is the tiny representative of the Spitz group of dogs, which includes the Finnish Spitz, Samoyed, Akita, and Keeshond. But there are also toys that were developed for special purposes. The Turnspit, for example, paddled a wheel that turned the spit on which game or sucking-pig were roasted over the fire.

A LONG HISTORY

Four thousand years ago the Chinese kept "lion dogs" that were almost identical to the Pekingese of today, and "lapdogs" were popular with the Romans. Toy dogs were also particular favourites of noble ladies, and they have been associated with such royal names as Mary Queen of Scots, Queen Victoria, and Queen Marie Antoinette of France. And long ago, when the Empress of China entered her court, a hundred Japanese Chins would stand up on their hindlegs and remain so until she was seated. Men have been just as devoted to toy dogs, from Charles II and the little spaniels named after him, through Louis XV of France, who adored tiny "truffle" dogs, to the Dalai Lamas of Tibet, who exchanged Lhasa Apsos for Shih Tzus with visiting officials from China.

A CHARMING TALE

In mediaeval times people would often take dogs with them when they went to church for use as "footwarmers". A story tells of how once, when the Bishop of Gloucester was holding a service in Bath Abbey with a goodly sprinkling of dogs, including some Turnspits, in the congregation, the first lesson happened to be from the Book of Ezekiel. The reading included the verses in the tenth chapter that refer to "wheels" and the "animals that control them". The Turnspits were only too familiar with the word "wheel" and what it implied, and a witness reported that "they all clapt their Tails between their Legs and ran out of the Church"!

PUG (Top right) The Pug, with its small, squat body, black, wrinkled face, and tightly curled tail, was for a long time a popular, amusing companion, particularly in some of the royal houses of Europe, where it almost took the place of the court jester. Pugs appear in a number of paintings by the Old Masters.

YORKSHIRE TERRIERS (Bottom right) Looking at the exquisitely coiffed and beribboned Yorkies of today, it is hard to believe that this was once a working breed. It was developed in the early 19th century by Yorkshire miners who wanted a terrier that could be carried in a pocket and used for ratting in the mines and woollen mills.

PEKINGESE (Left) A truly ancient breed, the Pekingese was already fully established when first mentioned in records of the 8th-century Tang dynasty. Small enough to be carried in the wide sleeves of robed Imperial courtiers, they were referred to as "sleeve dogs".

Bichon Frise

Companion of sailors, a favourite at the 16th-century French court, successful circus performer, a rising star at today's shows – the Bichon Frise has had a career as glamorous as its extraordinary looks suggest.

HISTORY

Although it is thought of as a French breed, the Bichon Frise may have originated on the Canary Islands, from where it was brought to the European mainland by Italian travellers during the 14th century. At that time, there were four varieties – the Maltais, Bolognais, Havanais, and Tenerife – but the French Revolution was to see the decline not only of the aristocracy but also of the little dog that it had favoured. The Bichon Frise traded the golden life of palaces and chateaux for the gilt and spangles of the circus ring, where, like the Poodle *(see pp.130–31)*, it was employed as an easily trained, cheerful trooper. Its numbers fell, however, especially during World War I, and it was not until the 1930s that the dog enjoyed a resurgence in France. A standard was drawn up in 1933, when the dog became known by its present name, which translated means "curly lapdog". Although classified as a Non-Sporting Dog in the US, the breed is a Toy Dog in the UK and also in Australia, where it is known as the Bichon Frisé.

TEMPERAMENT

A dog that loves human company, the Bichon Frise nevertheless has a strong, independent spirit.

SIZE
Up to 30 cm
(12 in) tall,
ideally smaller.

TAIL *Set low; usually carried curved, but not curled, over the back.*

EASILY RECOGNIZED A charming puffball of a dog, with a coat that makes it literally stand out from the crowd, the Bichon Frise has a robustness and tenacity that belies its "child's-toy" appearance.

LEGS *Thighs are broad and well rounded. Forelegs are straight and perpendicular when seen from the front and should not be too finely boned.*

KEEPING UP APPEARANCES Maintaining the "powder-puff" appearance of the Bichon Frise takes extensive trimming, brushing, and bathing. For pets that are not destined for showing, normal grooming keeps the coat in a pleasant, curly condition.

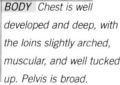

BODY Chest is well developed and deep, with the loins slightly arched, muscular, and well tucked up. Pelvis is broad.

COAT Fine and silky, with corkscrew curls when not brushed out. Colour should be white. Under the coat, a dark pigment is desirable.

FEET Tight, rounded, and well knuckled up. Pads are black, with black nails a desirable feature.

EYES Fairly large and round; dark in colour. White of the eye should not be visible when the dog looks forwards.

HEAD Lines drawn between the outer corners of the eyes and the tip of the nose should create an equilateral triangle. Nose is large, round, and black.

EARS Narrow, delicate, hanging close to the head, and covered with long, fine hair.

FACIAL CHARACTERISTICS

Chihuahuas

The tiniest of a tiny group, the Chihuahua's enormous popularity is out of all proportion to its size. It manages to combine the delightful appeal of a toy breed with the hunting and protective instincts of a much larger dog.

HISTORY

Up until 1898, when it was imported into the US from Mexico, the history of the Chihuahua is open to conjecture. Is it a truly indigenous South American breed, descended from the dogs held sacred first by the Incas and then by the Aztecs? Was it introduced into the New World by the conquistadors? Or did it arrive from China as recently as the 19th century? Evidence for the Chihuahua's antecedents include carvings in the monastery of Huejotzingo that can be dated back to the Toltecs; remains of small dogs found on archaeological digs in Mexico; and records of a small dog, such as the Chinese Crested, being brought across from Asia. In all probability, the breed is not the product of just one type of dog, but of several that are both ancient and relatively modern.

TEMPERAMENT

Unintimidated by other dogs, whatever their size, the Chihuahua is nevertheless fussy about the company it keeps and tends to prefer its own kind.

HEAD Graceful in appearance, slightly rounded, with an elongated skull. Cheeks should be cleanly chiselled, lean, and flat. Nose is narrow and can be any colour.

COAT Fur is long and soft in texture, either flat or slightly wavy. A large neck ruff is a desirable feature. Any colour or combination of colours is acceptable.

BODY Back should be level, shoulders lean, and chest deep. Ribs are rounded without being "barrel-shaped".

SIZE As diminutive as possible; weight up to 2.7 kg (6 lb).

SHIVERING DOG Despite its ample covering, the Long-coat Chihuahua is as prone to "the shivers" as its Smooth-coat cousin – although it is no more likely to catch a chill than any other type of breed.

FEET Small, dainty, and cushioned, with toes that are well divided but not spread apart.

EYES *Large, round, and set well apart. Colours are dark or ruby, or light in light-coloured dogs.*

EARS *Large, flared, and set at an angle of approximately 45 degrees.*

FACIAL CHARACTERISTICS

TAIL *Medium in length, set high, and carried up and over the back. It should be long and plume-like.*

LONG-COAT CHIHUAHUA

The Aztecs had no wool or cotton and so depended on dog hair to make cloth. It is more than possible that their raw material came from dogs very similar to the Chihuahua. The modern longhaired version of the breed may have arisen through crossing the Smooth-coat Chihuahua with other miniature breeds such as the Papillon, Pomeranian, and Yorkshire Terrier.

LEGS *The hindquarters should be muscular and the forelegs straight.*

SMOOTH-COAT CHIHUAHUA Fur that is glossy, close-lying, smooth, and soft is the only difference between this variety of the breed and the Long-coat. The two varieties are now equally popular.

King Charles Spaniel

HEAD *Well-domed, with a black, snub, turned-up nose, and a well-defined stop. Skull is large in comparison to the dog.*

Perhaps the most royal of breeds, the King Charles Spaniel was a favourite of both Mary Queen of Scots and Charles II of England. At Mary's beheading, "one of the executioners espied her little dog which was crept under her clothes which could not be gotten forth but by force"; and Charles was so enamoured with the breed that Samuel Pepys noted that all he observed at court "was the silliness of the King playing with his dog all the while and not minding his business."

HISTORY

The King Charles Spaniel probably originates from China or Japan. In the 16th century it crossed the English Channel from France, where it had long been established as a sporting breed. In the early 19th century it was still used as a "cocker" on woodcock shoots, but selective breeding produced a shorter-nosed dog, with both good looks and nature.

TEMPERAMENT

It is affectionate, level-headed, good with children, and it mixes well with other dogs.

SIZE
Height 26–32 cm (10–12½ in); weight 3.6–6.3 kg (8–14 lb).

CAVALIER KING CHARLES SPANIEL
Crossbreeding during the 19th century led to the creation of a separate type of dog that is somewhat larger than the King Charles, with a flat skull and longer muzzle.

LEGS *Short, straight, strong, and stout. Heavily feathered.*

EYES Large, dark in colour, and set wide apart. Eyelids should align horizontally.

EARS Very long, set low, and hanging beside the cheeks. Heavily feathered.

FACIAL CHARACTERISTICS

COAT Silky in texture, long, and glossy. A slight wave is permitted.

BODY Cobby and compact in appearance, with a short, broad back and a deep chest.

PRINCE CHARLES AND BLENHEIM KING CHARLES SPANIELS A tricoloured dog, the Prince Charles has a pearly white coat with black-and-tan markings. The Blenheim has the same white coat, but with chestnut-red patches. The two other varieties of the breed are the original Black and Tan, and the Ruby, which is a solid-coloured red.

TAIL A square "flag" shape, well feathered, and carried below the level of the back.

FEET Should be compact and round, well padded, and heavily feathered.

ROYAL CANINE It was Charles II's inordinate fondness for the dog that gave this breed its name. Such was his affection that he allowed his numerous pets access to all parts of the palace of Whitehall. On occasion, it was rumoured at the time, he neglected affairs of state in order to play with them.

Japanese Chin

Despite its name, the Japanese Chin
is of Chinese extraction. It shares
the same family tree – rooted in
the ancient Tibetan Spaniel – as
the Pug *(see pp.210–11)* and
Pekingese *(see pp.206–7)*.

HISTORY

The long and venerable history of the
Japanese Chin extends back over 2,700
years, when the breed was introduced to
Japan from China. At the Imperial Japanese
court, Chins were often kept in gilded
hanging cages, much like rare exotic birds.
In 1853, when Commodore Perry brought
out several examples of the breed, the West
was at last able to enjoy the company of these
graceful and elegant little dogs. Although the
breed was almost decimated by the distemper
virus shortly after its entry into the US,
numbers on both sides of the Atlantic are
now healthy and increasing steadily.

TEMPERAMENT

The Chin is a zestful, affectionate, and
entertaining pet with excellent manners and
a great sense of humour. It
likes to be the centre of
attention, and makes a
good show dog.

HEAD Broad skull, well rounded
at the front and between the
ears. Nose is black in the Black-
and-White variety, or flesh-
coloured in the Red-and-White.

BODY Short, square,
and compact. About
as long as it is tall,
with a broad, deep
chest.

SIZE
Weight
1.8–3.2 kg
(4–7 lb).

A DOG TO BE WORSHIPPED The status
of the Chin became particularly elevated at
one stage, when a devoted Japanese emperor
decreed that it should be worshipped.

CHOICE OF COLOURS The Black-and-White is the original and most popular variety of the breed, but various shades of red – including sable, lemon, and orange – with white are also permitted.

COAT Should be long, lush, silky, and straight, without any waves or curls. There is a ruff at the neck and profuse feathering.

CROSS-EYED DOG The wide distance between its eyes gives the Japanese Chin a bemused, slightly cross-eyed expression when it looks straight ahead.

TAIL Lushly feathered, with long hair to form a plume that falls to one side as the tail is carried curled over the back.

EARS V-shaped, small, set wide apart, and high on the head. Should be feathered and carried slightly forwards.

LEGS Small and fine, with good feathering.

EYES Large, rather prominent, and dark. Set wide apart.

FEET Small but longish, with a slight tendency to stand on tiptoe.

FACIAL CHARACTERISTICS

Maltese

Issa, the Maltese owned by Publius, the Roman Governor of Malta, in the 1st century AD, received this most moving of poetic tributes: "Issa is more frolicsome than Catulla's sparrow. Issa is purer than a dove's kiss. Issa is gentler than a maiden. Issa is more precious than Indian gems. Lest the last days that she sees light should snatch her from him for ever, Publius has had her painted."

HISTORY

The Maltese may well have originated either in Malta or in the Sicilian town of Melita. It is one of the oldest breeds: statues of similar dogs have been found in Egyptian tombs of the 13th century BC, and the dog may have arrived in Great Britain with the Roman legions as early as 55 BC. In any event, by the Middle Ages it was a regular consort of European nobility, and from that point on its popularity has never waned.

TEMPERAMENT

Loving and loyal, as well as tough, the Maltese makes a first-class pet as well as an efficient watchdog.

HEAD Medium in size, with a slightly rounded top to the skull and a well-defined stop. Muzzle is broad. Nose should be black.

BAD-WEATHER ALERT Not surprisingly, the long, silky coat of the Maltese needs a great deal of care and attention to keep it in top condition. These dogs should not be exposed to extreme cold or heavy downpours of rain.

FEET Small and round, covered with hair. Pads should be black in colour.

EARS Long, set low, hanging close to the head, and heavily feathered.

EYES Fairly large, oval in shape, and dark brown with black rims.

FACIAL CHARACTERISTICS

COAT Very long, straight, silky, without curls, and of a pure-white colour.

TAIL Abundant, long hair forming a plume that is carried curled over the back.

EARLY SHOW DOG A truly ancient breed, the Maltese was one of the first dogs to be shown – in Britain in 1862, and in the US in 1877.

BODY Low-slung and compact, with a short, level back, and a fairly deep, well-sprung chest.

LEGS Strong hindlegs with muscular thighs; short, straight, fine forelegs.

SIZE 20–25.5 cm (8–10 in) tall.

Miniature Pinscher

This lively, robust little dog, with its characteristic high-stepping gait, has gained widespread popularity in the US in recent years, but was almost unknown outside Germany before 1900. Although it looks like a miniature version of the Dobermann (*see pp.152–3*), there are no genetic ties.

HISTORY

The small Pinscher (the word means "terrier" in German) existed in Germany and Scandinavia for centuries before the Miniature Pinscher emerged as a distinct breed. In 1895 the German Pinscher Klub (later the Pinscher Schnauzer Klub) was formed in Germany, and the Miniature Pinscher was officially recognized. The dog's popularity increased in the 1920s, after having been exported to the US, and in 1929 the Miniature Pinscher Club of America was founded. Only six years later, an American-bred Miniature Pinscher was awarded the accolade of Best in Toy Group at the Chicago Show.

TEMPERAMENT

Alert, intelligent, and loyal, the breed is very courageous for its diminutive size. It makes a good watchdog and family pet, and is an excellent rat-catcher.

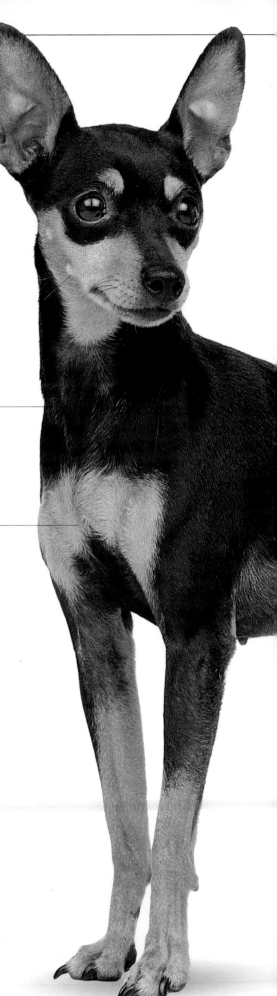

COAT Short, smooth, and shiny. Colours are black, blue, or chocolate, all with tan markings, or solid red of various shades.

BODY Squarely built, with a deep chest, straight back, and tucked-up belly.

COURAGEOUS CANINE This is a distinctive little animal, with a precise hackney gait, an animated manner, and the fearless spirit of a dog twice its size.

SIZE
25.5–30 cm
(10–12 in) tall.

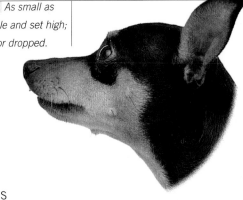

EARS *As small as possible and set high; erect or dropped.*

HEAD *Narrow, tapering skull with a flat top. Muzzle is strong and in proportion to the head. Colour of the nose matches the coat. Upper teeth closely overlap the lower teeth.*

EYES *Medium-sized, slightly oval, and black in colour.*

FACIAL CHARACTERISTICS

TAIL *Set and carried fairly high. Customarily docked short.*

ERECT EARS The ears can be cropped to a point in the US and some other countries. Since ear cropping is illegal in the UK, British breeders are producing "Min Pins" with naturally erect ears.

PURE SHOW DOG The Miniature Pinscher is a born show dog – elegant and vivacious, with a close coat that is easy to groom.

LEGS *Muscular hindlegs, set wide apart; straight forelegs.*

CORRECT COLORATION On a typical black-and-tan Miniature Pinscher, there are tan markings on the cheeks, lips, lower jaw, throat, over the eyes, on the chest, forelegs, hindlegs, feet, and on the area beneath the tail. There are preferably no white markings on the chest.

FEET *Short, round, well-arched feet with dark nails.*

Papillon

The French word for butterfly gives this delightful dog its name, at least for the prick-eared variety; the original drop-eared form of the breed is called a Phalène, meaning moth. These canine moths and butterflies have been flitting through history since at least the 16th century, and there are some experts who claim that they are the oldest European breed.

HISTORY

Although little is certain about the Papillon's origins, its history after 1545, when there is a record of one being sold, is well documented. The Dwarf Spaniel is thought to be the ancestor of the breed, which may have been brought to Spain from China. By the 16th century it was firmly established as the favourite lapdog of the Spanish and French nobility. Indeed, like Mary Queen of Scots and her King Charles Spaniel (see pp.196–7), Marie Antoinette had her much-loved Papillon with her when she went to the scaffold. By the late 19th century, French and Belgian breeders had developed the erect-eared type, which was first shown in Britain in 1923 and received recognition in the US in 1935.

TEMPERAMENT

The Papillon is a friendly, intelligent dog that is tougher than it looks, and loves outdoor exercise. It may be very possessive of its owner and resent outsiders.

TAIL Long and set high, curled over the back, with a heavy plume.

COAT Long, silky, and flat, with slight wavy areas. Colour is white with patches in black or any other shade apart from liver.

*SIZE
20–28 cm
(8–11 in) tall.*

SQUIRREL DOG The Papillon was once known as a Squirrel Spaniel because of the way it carries its tail over its back.

BODY Rather longer than it is tall, not stocky, with a straight back and medium-deep chest.

HEAD Small, medium-wide and with a slightly domed skull. Nose is round and black. Stop is well defined, and the muzzle is finely pointed.

BUTTERFLY EARS Heavily fringed ears that look like open butterfly wings earned this breed its name. American and British breeders have developed a slightly smaller dog than elsewhere.

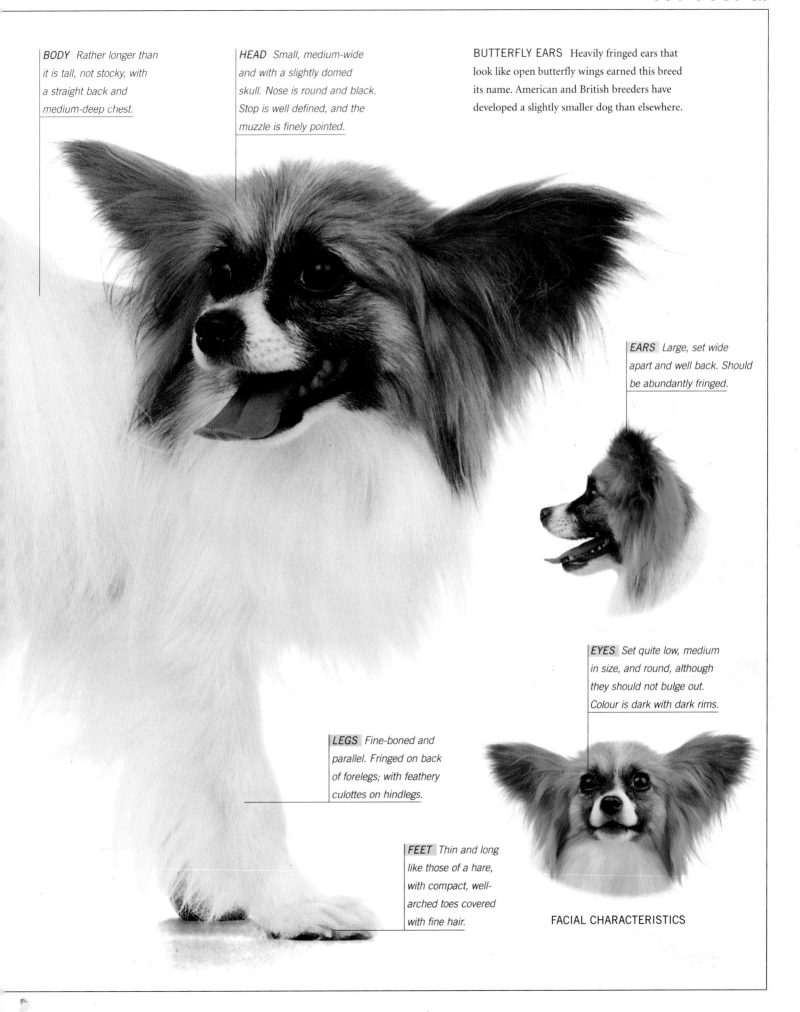

EARS Large, set wide apart and well back. Should be abundantly fringed.

EYES Set quite low, medium in size, and round, although they should not bulge out. Colour is dark with dark rims.

LEGS Fine-boned and parallel. Fringed on back of forelegs; with feathery culottes on hindlegs.

FEET Thin and long like those of a hare, with compact, well-arched toes covered with fine hair.

FACIAL CHARACTERISTICS

Pekingese

Toy dogs are renowned for their royal and aristocratic connections, but the Pekingese is undoubtedly the leader of the pack, having been at one time the sacred animal of the Chinese Imperial House. A Pekingese was one of only two dogs to survive the sinking of the *Titanic*; the other was a Pomeranian *(see pp.208–9).*

HISTORY

Regarded as manifestations of the legendary Foo Dog that drove away evil spirits, Pekingese were venerated as semi-divine by the Chinese. Commoners had to bow to them; to steal one was punishable by death; and when an Emperor died, his Pekingese were sacrificed so that they could go with him to give him protection in the afterlife. The breed reached the West after 1860, when British troops overran the Summer Palace during the Second Opium War. The Imperial Guards were ordered to kill the little dogs to prevent them falling into the hands of the "foreign devils", but five survived. These were taken to England, where one was presented to Queen Victoria, who named it, appropriately, Looty. It is from these canine spoils of war that the modern Pekingese is descended. The breed was first shown in Britain in 1893, arriving in the US a few years later.

TEMPERAMENT

Pekingese are brave, combative, and loyal. They may be prone to breathing difficulties, so owners should keep an especially close watch on their health.

COAT Very long, straight, coarse top coat over a thick undercoat. Ears, backs of legs, tail, and toes should be profusely feathered. All colours.

HEAD Large, broad, and flat between the ears. Nose is very snub, broad, and black. Profile is very flat, with a pronounced stop. Wide, wrinkled muzzle.

LEGS Short. Upper forelegs are bowed; hindlegs are lighter-boned.

FEET Flat and large, with front toes turned out.

EYES *Prominent, dark, and round. Set wide apart.*

EARS *Heart-shaped and drooping, but not long. Profusely feathered.*

FACIAL CHARACTERISTICS

SNUG FIT Quintessentially Oriental, these remarkable little dogs were carried in the wide sleeves of Chinese courtiers, making them true "sleeve dogs". Other names for them were Lion Dog – they do have a leonine look – and Sun Dog, so golden-red were their coats.

TAIL *Set high and curled over the back to either side.*

BODY *Short, but well built in front, with broad, well-sprung chest, and straight back. Lion-like shape.*

SIZE
Weight should not exceed 5 kg (11 lb) in dogs and 5.5 kg (12 lb) in bitches.

Pomeranian

Although the Pomeranian is one of the first breeds to spring to mind when the term "toy dogs" is mentioned, it was once a larger, very hard-working dog that earned its keep by the sweat of its brow. These days, however, it is one of the most expensive breeds to buy and one that demands extensive care to keep in top show condition.

HISTORY

A Spitz-type dog, the Pomeranian is almost certainly descended from the sledge-pulling dogs of the Arctic, and is probably related to the Keeshond, Norwegian Elkhound, and Samoyed *(see pp.126–7, pp.38–9, and pp.184–5 respectively).* The first reliable records of dogs similar to the breed came, not surprisingly, from Pomerania, a region bordering the Baltic in what is now partly Poland and partly Germany, where it was used to herd sheep. By the mid-18th century, Pomeranians had spread to several European countries, including Italy; it was in Florence that Queen Victoria was presented with the "Pom" that was to lead to her lifelong attachment to the breed. Early Pomeranians were relatively big, mostly white dogs, but selective breeding from the early 19th century has produced a diminutive animal prized for its full, flowing, colourful coat.

TEMPERAMENT

At one stage, the Pomeranian had a reputation for being a snappy, volatile dog, but that has now given way to a personality that is agreed to be loyal and friendly while still lively. It makes an excellent watchdog as well as being very much at home in the show ring.

BODY Short and compact, with a relatively deep, well-rounded chest.

LEGS Should be fine-boned, of medium length, and well feathered.

SIZE Weight is 1.8–2 kg (4.5–5.5 lb) for a dog; 2–2.5 kg (4–4.5 lb) for a bitch.

HIGH MAINTENANCE The "Pom" is not a breed for those who cannot make time for a regular grooming regime. Its spectacular double coat requires meticulous daily brushing as well as frequent trimming.

HEAD *Fox-like, with a wide, flattish skull and a fine, wedge-shaped muzzle. Nose colour depends on colour of the coat. Fairly short neck is set well into the shoulders.*

TAIL *Turned over the back and carried flat in typical Spitz fashion. It should be covered with profuse, long hair.*

FAMOUS PATRONS Not only was the Pomeranian a favourite of Queen Victoria, who founded a kennel and exhibited the breed, but also of Napoleon's wife Josephine and of Mozart.

EARS *Small, not too far apart, and pricked like those of a fox.*

EYES *Medium-sized, a slight oval in shape, and dark brown in colour. They should not be set too wide apart. Rims are black.*

COAT *A long, hard, straight, and gleaming outer coat should overlie a soft and fluffy undercoat to give the impression of a ball of fluff from which the limbs protrude. All coat colours are allowed, including orange, brown, cream, black, blue, and particolours.*

FEET *Very small and compact.*

FACIAL CHARACTERISTICS

Pug

The old word for a goblin, snub nose, or small monkey became appended to this charming, most fastidious of dogs in the late 18th century.

HISTORY

The family tree of the Pug is a matter of debate. Some experts think it came from the Lowlands, brought back from the Far East by Dutch traders. It is possibly of Oriental stock, descended from a shorthaired relative of the Pekingese *(see pp.206–7)*, but another school of thought claims it to be the result of crossing small Bulldogs *(see pp.120–21)*. Yet another theory is that it is a miniature form of a rare French mastiff called the Dogue de Bordeaux. The breed was a favourite of the artist Hogarth, who included Trump, his pet Pug, in several of his works. From the 16th century, it became a fashionable adornment of the European courts, reaching its peak of popularity in Victorian times.

TEMPERAMENT

The Pug is a very loving and attentive dog that does not need much grooming or exercise but does demand company.

HEAD Large and round, with much wrinkling, preferably accentuated by black tips to the hair. Muzzle is blunt. Nose should be black.

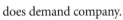

SIZE
Weight is
6.4–8.2 kg
(14–18 lb).

NOVEL COMMUNICATOR
The Pug communicates by grunts, snorts, and snuffles.

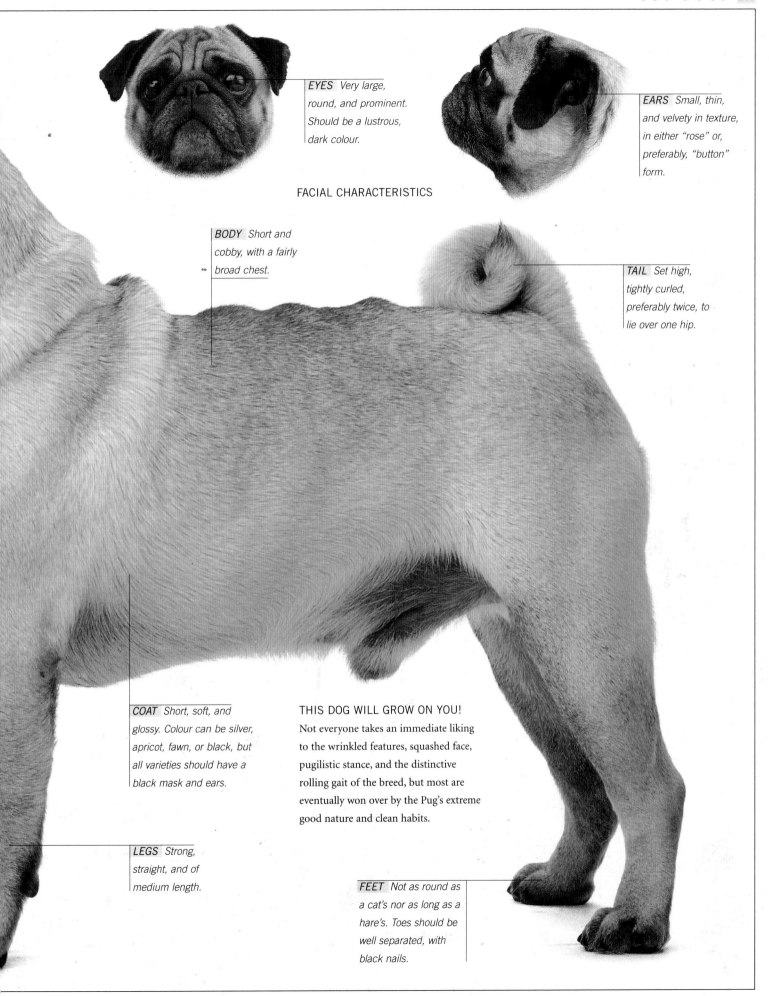

EYES Very large, round, and prominent. Should be a lustrous, dark colour.

EARS Small, thin, and velvety in texture, in either "rose" or, preferably, "button" form.

FACIAL CHARACTERISTICS

BODY Short and cobby, with a fairly broad chest.

TAIL Set high, tightly curled, preferably twice, to lie over one hip.

COAT Short, soft, and glossy. Colour can be silver, apricot, fawn, or black, but all varieties should have a black mask and ears.

THIS DOG WILL GROW ON YOU!
Not everyone takes an immediate liking to the wrinkled features, squashed face, pugilistic stance, and the distinctive rolling gait of the breed, but most are eventually won over by the Pug's extreme good nature and clean habits.

LEGS Strong, straight, and of medium length.

FEET Not as round as a cat's nor as long as a hare's. Toes should be well separated, with black nails.

Australian Silky Terrier

Given the opportunity, it might get into the odd scrap, but the Australian Silky Terrier has never done a scrap of work! Unlike other terriers, this cheerful little dog was not bred to do any particular hunting job, but purely, and most agreeably, to be a companion animal. Nevertheless, its terrier blood shows through in its active, assertive nature, and in the skill it displays killing vermin in its native country.

HISTORY

Sydney was the birthplace of the breed, which was known at one time simply as the Sydney Silky. Australian and Yorkshire Terriers *(see pp.214–15)* were used as part of an intricate crossbreeding programme to produce a dog that combined the best features of both types. The carefully determined result must be counted as a modern success story. Australian Silky Terriers were first shown in Australia in 1907, in Britain in 1930, and were recognized by the American Kennel Club in 1959.

TEMPERAMENT

The Silky is a pretty, lively, and intelligent animal that is quick to warn of the presence of strangers. It makes an ideal watchdog and pet for town-dwellers with small apartments, but it also enjoys country strolls.

BIG-HEARTED BREED
Terrier in spirit, if not in practice, the Silky is an ideal pet for those who want a small companion with a big heart.

BODY *Low-slung, but not too short, with a straight back and the slightest degree of rounding over the loins.*

SHORTHAIRED YORKIE
A kissing cousin to the Yorkshire Terrier, the Australian Silky Terrier has a coat that is extremely similar, although not quite so long.

FEET *Small, round, and compact, like those of a cat.*

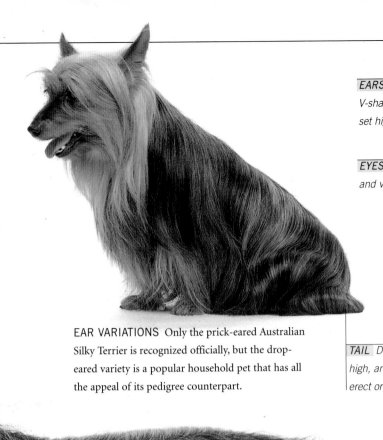

EARS *Pricked, V-shaped, and small; set high on the head.*

EYES *Small, round, and very dark.*

HEAD *Wedge-shaped, fairly long, with a flat skull. Moderate width between ears. Nose is black, and "topknot" can be silver or fawn.*

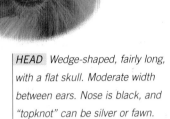

EAR VARIATIONS Only the prick-eared Australian Silky Terrier is recognized officially, but the drop-eared variety is a popular household pet that has all the appeal of its pedigree counterpart.

TAIL *Docked, set high, and carried erect or semi-erect.*

FACIAL CHARACTERISTICS

COAT *Long, fine, glossy, and silky in texture. Colour should be blue and tan. Permitted shades of blue are silver, slate, and pigeon blue.*

LEGS *Short. Hindlegs are muscular at the thigh; forelegs are straight and fine boned.*

SIZE
Dogs 23 cm (9 in) tall; bitches slightly less.

Yorkshire Terrier

Small in stature – closely following the Chihuahua *(see pp.194–5)* as the most diminutive dog of all – the Yorkshire Terrier still looms large in the popularity stakes. Often beribboned and clad in long silky fur, the breed has a "boudoir" appeal that disguises its roguish terrier spirit.

HISTORY

Although the breed is only 100 years old or so, its origins are not entirely certain, probably because the working men of the north of England who developed the Yorkshire Terrier avoided divulging the secret of their success to those who might have cashed in on a lucrative sideline. However, it seems likely that Scotsmen seeking work in the woollen mills of Yorkshire brought with them various types of terrier, including the Skye *(see p.96)* and the now-extinct Clydesdale. These were then crossed with local types, such as the longhaired Leeds Terrier. The Maltese *(see pp.200–1)*, Black-and-Tan, Manchester *(see pp.104–5)*, and Dandie Dinmont *(see pp.96–7)* terriers may also have contributed blood-lines. At first the "Yorkie" was a much bigger animal than the one we see today, but by selectively breeding the smallest individuals, the dog was gradually miniaturized over the years.

TEMPERAMENT

As befits an animal that was once used as a ratter, the Yorkshire Terrier is a spirited, sparkling character that is not intimidated by either larger dogs or intruders into the house. Besides being a good guard dog, the breed makes a particularly loving pet.

HEAD Small and flat, with a muzzle that should not be too long. Nose is black.

LEGS Straight and well covered with hair.

FEET Round, with black nails.

SIZE Weight is up to 3.1 kg (7 lb).

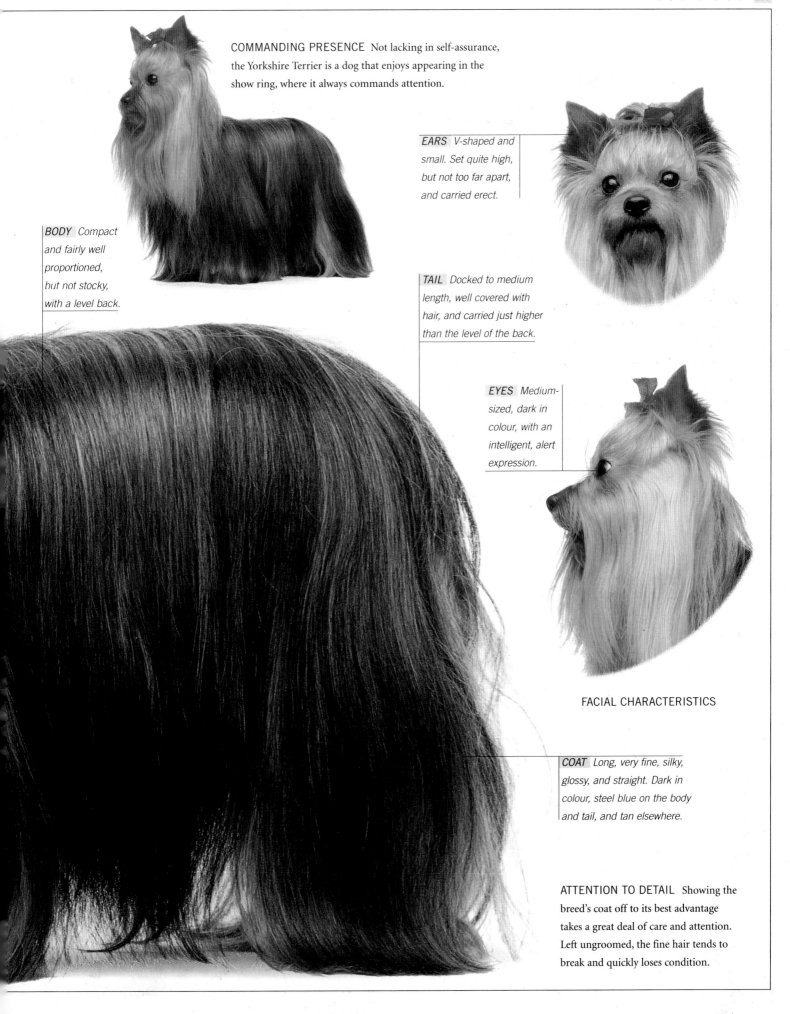

COMMANDING PRESENCE Not lacking in self-assurance, the Yorkshire Terrier is a dog that enjoys appearing in the show ring, where it always commands attention.

EARS V-shaped and small. Set quite high, but not too far apart, and carried erect.

BODY Compact and fairly well proportioned, but not stocky, with a level back.

TAIL Docked to medium length, well covered with hair, and carried just higher than the level of the back.

EYES Medium-sized, dark in colour, with an intelligent, alert expression.

FACIAL CHARACTERISTICS

COAT Long, very fine, silky, glossy, and straight. Dark in colour, steel blue on the body and tail, and tan elsewhere.

ATTENTION TO DETAIL Showing the breed's coat off to its best advantage takes a great deal of care and attention. Left ungroomed, the fine hair tends to break and quickly loses condition.

Mongrels

Nearly all pedigree dogs have been produced originally by mating together different kinds of dogs, and therefore it could be said that they too are mongrels! So, if you are not particularly interested in showing a beautifully coiffured and beribboned canine specimen, and instead you seek companionship, friendship, and loyalty, make your way to a dog's home or humane-society clinic and you will find a dog as good as any in the world.

CHARACTERISTICS

All domestic dogs belong to the species *Canis familiaris*, and mongrels are at least as rich in qualities as the most aristocratic of pedigree dogs. Some might argue that in some cases mongrels are even richer in endearing attributes. Apart from the sheer charm of a "ragamuffin", crossbreeds are endowed with plenty of "hybrid vigour", and are often tougher, better-tempered, less disease-prone, and more adaptable than their pedigree counterparts.

THE TYPICAL MONGREL

If all the pedigree dogs in the world were turned loose to interbreed, the laws of survival of the fittest and natural selection would gradually shape the dog of the future. It would be a happy medium of a dog, without any extremes of physical form or function.

SURVIVAL OF THE FITTEST Most of today's mongrels display moderation in all things. Natural, rather than artificial, selection has ensured that the hardiest, healthiest, and happiest animals survive.

COAT Neither too long nor too short.

EARS Pert and expressive.

BODY Body outline is shapely and well defined. Back is not overstretched. Neck is muscular and of a good length.

LEGS Strong and well proportioned.

FACIAL CHARACTERISTICS

HEAD *Very good bone structure, with a fairly well-developed nose.*

EYES *Bright, with an alert, lively expression.*

TYPES OF MONGREL

In all countries, most pet dogs are mongrels. Humane societies and dogs' homes have more of them than pedigree animals and, if you are looking for a new companion, are the best places you can go.

SHEEPDOG/COLLIE-TYPE CROSSBREED Carrying the intelligence and loyalty of its pedigree relatives, this dog makes a close, loving companion, but one needing plenty of outdoor exercise.

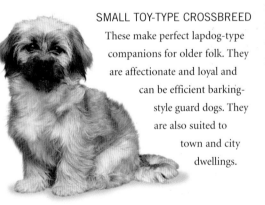

SMALL TOY-TYPE CROSSBREED These make perfect lapdog-type companions for older folk. They are affectionate and loyal and can be efficient barking-style guard dogs. They are also suited to town and city dwellings.

SMALL CROSSBRED TERRIER TYPE A dog like this is ideal both as a town-house companion and for walks in the country. Alert, intelligent, active, and playful, it is also loyal and – quick to bark at intruders – an excellent guard dog.

RETRIEVER-TYPE CROSSBREED This first-rate, loving, family dog is kind and affectionate with children. Because it needs regular walking and running exercise, it is better in the country than in the city centre.

GERMAN SHEPHERD-TYPE CROSSBREED This intelligent, loyal dog makes a superb house guard. It needs lots of exercise so is not suitable for a city flat.

TAIL *Medium length.*

SIZE
All sizes are possible.

Keeping a Dog

Even more than cats, dogs require keeping. There are regular chores to be done, and efforts to be made, if you are to discover the best in your dog. To keep it hale, hearty, and happy through a long life, you must be prepared to provide intelligent care and attention. However, looking after a dog properly need not take too much time, and is enjoyable for both animal and owner. Keeping a dog fit helps keep you fit. Making a dog look good helps keep it healthy. The more time you spend attending to your dog, the more fascinating aspects of *Canis familiaris* are revealed to you.

Dogs can be appreciated and valued on many levels. To some they are the truest of friends, and the best of companions; to others they are skilled workers and assistants, substituting for men or machines. If you become involved in showing or breeding dogs, they can become an enthralling hobby or even a full-time business.

This section covers briefly the main aspects of the care and understanding of the domestic dog, mongrel no less than blue-blood pedigree. Further information is best obtained by talking to breeders and vets, or by reading specialized books on the particular breeds. Whatever kind of dog you have, it will appreciate being looked after – and you are sure to have more fun too!

FRIENDS FOR LIFE The friendship and loyalty of a dog are unconditional, transparent, and enduring. Look after and treat your dog well, and, in return, your canine companion will do its best for you.

Your New Dog

All the care and consideration that goes into picking that dumbest of family pets, the car, needs to be brought into play when planning to acquire a dog. As when buying a vehicle, you need to ask yourself certain questions.

What do I want it to do? How much fuel will it use? What about garaging? Can I afford to have it serviced regularly? Am I capable of driving (exercising) the model I have in mind? And another question has to be asked that does not arise when buying a car: can I make a lifelong commitment (about 12 years on average) to a dog?

WHAT KIND OF DOG?

Try to match your own lifestyle to the physical characteristics, temperament, and particular requirements of the dog. Having done that you must then decide on age, size, and sex, and then whether to go for a mongrel or pedigree dog.

German Shepherds and Borzois are not for apartments on the 16th floor,

Great Danes eat as much meat as a two-year-old lion, and Afghan Hounds demand constant grooming. Think first, think hard, and make an informed choice.

If you do not have the space or the inclination to jog with your dog, or if there is not an abundance of cash around, then think small – a toy or a small breed. Small dogs have the advantage over larger breeds of greater life-expectancy; toys, however, do not generally live quite as long as regular small breeds.

If it is a companion, friend, or watchdog you need, why go for a pedigree anyway? Mongrels are cheap, come in all sizes, give and take as much affection as any blue-blood, are less prone to hereditary disease, and may well have that in-built healthiness that scientists call "hybrid vigour".

PUPPY OR ADULT?

Puppies are great fun particularly if there are children around, but if you want a companion that you can take out with you straight away, a young adult dog may be best. Old people can find an energetic puppy a bit of handful but may be able to give refuge to a homeless older dog. Make

sure that any adult dog you buy is house-trained – a dog that has spent a long time in kennels might not be.

A puppy will need someone to take the place of its mother, to look after it, feed it, house-train it, and generally spend time with it to build a good relationship. So if you are away from home all day, do not even consider getting one.

DOG OR BITCH?

It may not be easy to decide which sex you want. Obviously one of the main drawbacks of bitches, unless you are keen to breed, is their twice-yearly reproductive cycle. During her heat, a bitch is attractive to dogs and may try to escape to go courting. Some people object to the messiness of their vaginal discharge, and some bitches can be prone to phantom pregnancy, which can be worrying. Surgical neutering or the periodic use of contraceptive drugs can also add significantly to the cost of owning a dog.

Some people consider dogs to have a more even temperament than bitches. However, they cannot resist wandering in search of romance if a bitch is on heat in the neighbourhood.

CHOOSING A BED

The traditional wicker basket has many advantages but is difficult to clean. Make sure that your dog does not get into the habit of chewing it, since wicker fragments can be harmful to dogs. Safer alternatives may be plastic or soft-fabric beds. Although the soft fabric is likely to be more comfortable, if your dog has a chewing habit it can make quite a mess!

Plastic basket

Wicker basket with washable cushion

Soft basket

TOYS Play is very important for dogs, especially puppies, and there is a wide range of toys available. Tug o' war is always popular, and the dog-pull allows both animal and owner to get a good grip. The fun-ring can be used in this way too, and also as an object to be thrown and retrieved. Do not use sticks and stones; special toys such as rubber bones, quoits, and large balls are much safer.

COLLARS AND LEADS In Britain it is a legal requirement that your dog wears an identity tag with your name and address on it. A leather collar is usually suitable for everyday wear, with a choke chain often used for larger breeds. There is an argument for avoiding pressure on the neck of a dog when walking, instead using a chest harness or the patented Halti device to which the lead is attached. The lead can be leather, chain-link, or nylon. Retractable leads are particularly good.

Chest harness

Retractable lead

Nylon lead

Leather collar with identity tag

Fixed-noseband head halter

FOOD AND WATER BOWLS Bowls come in three different materials. Heavy earthenware bowls are difficult to knock over but will eventually chip or break. Stainless-steel bowls are the least stable, and plastic bowls are cheap but can get chewed. Special deep bowls for long-eared breeds are also available; these prevent the dog dangling its ears in the food.

GROOMING KIT The basic equipment for grooming is a brush and a comb. Clean and dry these after use and do not let the dog chew them.

Double-sided pin and bristle brush

Wide-toothed comb

Fine-toothed comb

Plastic puppy bowl

Earthenware bowl

Stainless-steel bowl

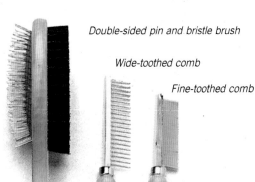

PEDIGREE OR MONGREL?

Pedigrees may well have the shape, proportions, and colour that breeders intend and admire, but they are also heir to some unwelcome hereditary problems that go along with their aristocracy as surely as haemophilia ran through some of the royal houses of Europe.

The long backs of Basset Hounds and Dachshunds are just asking for slipped-disc troubles; German Shepherds can have hereditary hip-joint disease; Irish Red Setters get problems in the retinas of their eyes more frequently than other breeds; the Bulldog is prone to skin disease between its loose folds of facial skin; the higher humidity of the floppy ears of Spaniels can predispose them to canker infection; and there can be whelping difficulties in such flat-nosed breeds as the Pug. All of these complaints, of course, can and do crop up occasionally in mongrels, but not as often.

If you would be happy with a non-pedigree breed, go to a breeder, look for advertisements in the pets' column of a newspaper or magazine, or contact the nearest dogs' home. Avoid pet shops or the sort of puppy farm that churns out animals like a sausage machine; they are so often reservoirs of serious disease. If it is a pedigree you are after, look into the special needs and problems of the breed. Ask local vets about any particular health problems in local strains. Although a vet will not tell you anything about a breeder who happens to be one of his clients without his client's permission, he may well be able to point you in the right direction!

Try to make as many inquiries as you can before going to see a litter of puppies, and take along someone who has experience of that particular breed before confirming the purchase. Remember, it is not likely that you will be given a Crufts champion, no matter what you pay. It is difficult with young puppies for anyone, even an expert, to spot a future star. Why you need your experienced companion is to make sure that you are not palmed off with the runt of the litter, an animal with an imperfect set of teeth, or one that shows faulty congenital features such as white spots on a variety that should be all black. True, the Poodle with one pale blue and one dark brown eye may have the cutest expression and it will still make an attractive robust pet, but you should not be paying the price that a show-worthy individual would fetch.

Ask to see the mother – she should give you an idea of how the puppies will develop. Never ignore the hereditary defects to which some breeds are prone. It is most important that you ask the breeder for written guarantees against any hereditary defects known in the breed.

WHAT TO LOOK FOR

The main thing, assuming that you are not rescuing a homeless animal, is to ensure that the dog is fit. Make an agreement that you can return the puppy to the breeder if it is not healthy. Let the vet examine it as soon as possible (preferably before taking it home to meet the family, just in case...).

EXAMINING A PUPPY

2 Lift the ear flaps to inspect the ear canals, which should be dry, clean, and free from crusty, scaly, or sticky deposits and discharges.

1 A healthy puppy with a good temperament is happy to be picked up. It should not be in pain, and its body should feel firm but relaxed.

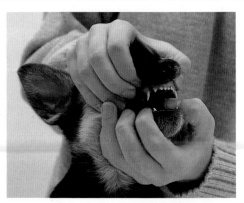

3 Gently part the lips to examine the puppy's tongue, gums, and teeth. The tongue and gums should be pink. The "bite" (relative position of upper and lower front teeth) is important, particularly in pedigree dogs for showing. Consult an expert if in doubt.

PEDIGREE VS MONGREL This pedigree
Dachshund *(left)* may suffer from
slipped discs; a mongrel *(above)*
may be a naturally
healthier proposition.

When selecting a pup look for:
• Lively, fussy behaviour;
• A firm, well-covered body, and no signs
of pain when it is picked up;
• Clean nose, eyes, and ears, with no signs
of discharge – a clear drop of "water" from
the nostrils is okay;
• Pink gums, tongue, and area inside the
eyelids;
• No sign of diarrhoea – look at the
stools, if possible, and make sure
that the area around the anus
and the hair of the legs is not
fouled with loose droppings;
• No spots, sores, or scales in
the coat or on the hairless
part of the stomach;
• No cough.
If the vendor gives an
excuse – such as: "He is
just getting over a bit
of a cold, but it is
nothing", or "Do
not worry about that
tummy rash, you always
get that in Tripehounds" –
prick up your ears. No matter how
eminent the breeder, have the "cold"
or "rash" checked out at once by the
vet. Better still, postpone buying the
puppy until the allegedly trivial ailment
has cleared up.

CRADLE-LIKE SUPPORT This is the correct way
to carry a puppy comfortably.

If the dog is sold as having been
vaccinated, make sure that you receive
a certificate to that effect, signed by a
registered vet. If there is any doubt about
whether the animal has been vaccinated,
have it done again to be sure. Dogs can be
vaccinated against distemper, parvovirus,
leptospirosis, hepatitis, rabies (not in
Britain), and kennel cough.

Of course, if you are taking in a stray
or unwanted animal, things are slightly
different. You may have to deal with an
already sick or infirm individual. But you
will be going into this relationship with
your eyes open, and the vet will be able
to advise you at the outset as to what
problems you may have to face.

4 *The eyes should be clear, bright, and
free from discharges, tears, cloudiness,
or opacity. The dog should be able to keep its
eyes wide open without excessive blinking.
Avoid a puppy that paws at its eyes.*

5 *Run your hand against the grain of the coat
and inspect the skin for sores, scaliness, or
the black dust that betrays the presence of fleas.*

6 *Look under the puppy's tail to ensure that
the anal area is not stained by liquid stools;
this is clear evidence of diarrhoea.*

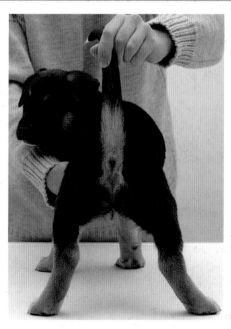

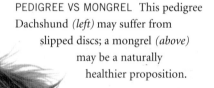

Diet

It would be a mistake to regard the dog family as narrow-minded carnivores. Foxes have a broad taste that ranges through grubs, rodents, snakes, crayfish, mushrooms, acorns, and various sorts of fruit. The jackal tops up its diet with vegetables, fruit, and sugar-cane. The bat-eared fox, or fennec, likes termites, and the Chilean Wild Dog eats shellfish.

NUTRITIONAL NEEDS

Like its wild cousins, the domestic dog needs more than meat in its dish to keep it going. The principal nutritional requirements are:
- Protein for body-building and repair;
- Carbohydrates for energy;
- Fats for energy and good health of skin and hair;
- Vitamins and minerals for certain essential chemical reactions in the body;
- Bulk for trouble-free digestive and bowel action;
- Water for all processes occurring everywhere in the body.

As a rule of thumb we can say that a dog needs the following amounts of kilojoules daily at different periods in its life:
- **Puppy:** 910 kJ per kg (100 calories per lb) of body weight;
- **Adult:** 550 kJ per kg (60 calories per lb) of body weight;
- **Geriatric:** 230 kJ per kg (25 calories per lb) of body weight.

These figures are calculated for moderately active animals.

Apart from age, degree of activity, environment, pregnancy, lactation, and disease, any of which markedly alters an animal's needs, we must never forget that dogs are all individuals and vary in their efficiency at processing foods. It is most important not to overfeed and to reduce the size of meals at the first sign of obesity.

EATING HABITS Dogs are able to eat a wide variety of foods. As long as its nutritional needs are catered for, you can let your pet's taste buds dictate what you feed it.

Dry complete food

Tinned meat and dog-meal

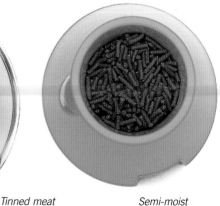

Semi-moist complete food

TYPES OF DOG FOOD Three types of dog food are shown above; also available is a tinned complete food that does not need dog-meal added to it.

due to the absence of an enzyme in their body. This produces diarrhoea and occasionally vomiting but is not serious: simply take milk off the diet.

Cereals

Either as dog-meal or in biscuit form, cereals are an inexpensive source of energy, bulk, minerals, and some vitamins. Cooked rice is an excellent substitute for cereals.

Vegetables

Carrots, cabbage, turnip, and swede are valuable, either cooked or shredded raw, as are cooked potatoes.

Fruit

Dogs make their own vitamin C internally, but moderate quantities of fruit, if they like it, are beneficial from time to time.

Eggs

Whole egg should be fed cooked to avoid the effect of an anti-vitamin B factor present in raw egg-white.

Others

Nuts, edible seeds, and honey are all excellent additions to the diet. And if your dog insists on chewing and swallowing grass and herbs, let it, even if it vomits shortly afterwards. This is perfectly natural behaviour. A word about bones: no, they do not clean the teeth. They can cause problems such as constipation, or obstruction or perforation of the digestive tract. Give only uncooked bones of the broad, marrow-bone type.

SOMETHING FOR EVERYONE Snacks come in many flavours and shapes, so you are sure to find something your dog will enjoy.

FOODS FOR DOGS

Dogs can eat all of the following foods, but, within reason, allowances can be made for your pet's personal taste.

Meat

Meat is low in calcium and rich in phosphorus. An all-lean-meat diet is too low in fat and would be nutritionally unbalanced. Liver should not exceed 5 per cent of the total diet.

Fish

Packed with protein, minerals, and, in some cases, fats, fish is best fed cooked and with the main bones removed.

Cheese and milk products

Products made with cheese and milk are rich in protein, fat, and minerals. Some dogs cannot digest lactose (milk sugar)

HOW MUCH TO FEED?

DOG WEIGHT	TINNED MEAT *	TINNED COMPLETE FOOD	DRY COMPLETE FOOD	SEMI-MOIST COMPLETE FOOD
5 kg (11 lb); Pekingese	225 g (8 oz)	400 g (14 oz)	150 g (5 oz)	170 g (6 oz)
10 kg (22 lb); Bedlington Terrier	370 g (13 oz)	760 g (27 oz)	250 g (9 oz)	285 g (10 oz)
20 kg (44 lb); Springer Spaniel	600 g (21 oz)	1,250 g (44 oz)	400 g (14 oz)	450 g (16 oz)
40 kg (88 lb); German Shepherd	760 g (27 oz)	1,875 g (66 oz)	650 g (23 oz)	760 g (27 oz)

NB: These figures are intended as an approximate guide only. Refer also to manufacturers' instructions on the packaging.

* Dog-meal or biscuits must be added to the tinned meat in the ratio of 1:1 for small breeds, and up to 2:1 for large breeds.

WAYS OF FEEDING

Whether you buy dog food or make it up yourself, your dog must have a nutritionally balanced diet.

Do-it-yourself

The meat, scraps, and biscuit system is still popular, gives variety, and may be economical. The daily intake of meat should be about 30 g per kg (½ oz per lb) of body weight per day for young animals, and 20 g per kg (⅓ oz per lb) for adults. Bear in mind that cooked scraps, including vegetables, may lack vitamins, which are destroyed by heat.

In recent years, a growing number of veterinarians, but still a small minority, have argued persuasively for the so-called Raw Meaty Bones Diet. Noting that wild and zoo carnivores seldom require dental attention, they prefer dogs to be fed on raw, meaty bones with a few table scraps thrown in. They claim that a change to such a regime transforms the health of a pet, with chronic illnesses disappearing along with bad breath, tooth and gum troubles, and even urine burns on the lawn. It is certainly cheaper to feed a dog in this way, and I agree that it will almost always reduce the need for canine dentistry.

Dog food and vegetables

Predictably, of course, the Raw Meaty Bones lobby has been vilified by vested interests in the pet-food manufacturing industry (owners worldwide spend £17 billion annually on pet food) and the veterinary profession!

Commercial foods

Modern dog foods are generally very good, and you cannot go far wrong if you follow the feeding instructions.

Tinned food

There are two types of tinned dog food: the wholly meaty kind that contains very little carbohydrate, and the complete diet that consists of meat, carbohydrates, fat, minerals, and vitamins in correct balance. The first kind is essentially conveniently packed, sterile meat with added vitamins,

Tinned food

and to make a complete diet, dog-meal or biscuits must be added to it in the ratio of 1:1 for small breeds, and up to 2:1 for large breeds.

The complete-diet foods have been produced after careful nutritional research by the big pet-food companies and you do not need to add anything to them to feed your dog properly.

Dry complete food

These pellets or biscuits of dried food contain meat and/or fish products together with carbohydrates, minerals, and vitamins. They are easy to store and the most economical of the convenience foods. They are not to be confused with simple dog-meals or biscuits that are largely cereal in content

AGE AND DIET The nutritional requirements of puppies are different to those of adult dogs. Dogs of all ages need adequate protein, minerals, and vitamins to renew and repair body tissues, but puppies demand relatively more of each in proportion to their body weight in order to grow.

MODERN PET FOODS Diet is a key factor in maintaining the optimum health and wellbeing of the family dog. Scientifically formulated diets of all kinds are now available. Organic pet foods are available, as are special foods for "slimmers", those with weak kidneys, and senior citizens.

and do not provide a complete diet. As ever, a plentiful supply of fresh water is essential.

Semi-moist complete food

This modern, highly processed food makes up a perfectly balanced diet. As value for money it falls between the dry and tinned foods, but it does not store as long as either.

WHICH DIET TO CHOOSE?

All diets have their different advantages. There is no obvious reason why you should not switch from one to the other according to your pet's fads and fancies. If you find that one type is well received by the dog and has no drawbacks, by all means stick to it.

Remember always to prepare food freshly and to serve it in thoroughly cleaned dishes. Clean, fresh water should always be available to the dog.

The best idea is to split the daily requirement into two parts and feed the dog twice. Nutrition is not everything; why not let your dog start the day with a full stomach and go to bed likewise? It is probably best to give the second meal at least an hour before bedtime.

Special diets are now available for dogs with certain types of medical condition. These include ones for pets with chronic kidney problems and, most recently, a product containing New Zealand green-lipped mussel extracts that has been found to relieve many cases of arthritis, the most common cause of joint disease.

Another new development are foods designed to reduce the damage done to genetic material in the dog's body cells and that is linked to the diseases of aging. The damage is inflicted by chemicals called free radicals. Foods containing anti-oxidants such as Vitamins C and E and certain amino acids neutralize these unwelcome

chemicals. In trials it was found that genetic damage was reduced by 26 per cent as compared with dogs on conventional diets. So, very soon choosing the correct diet may lead to a longer life for man's best friend.

TREATS AND CHEWS

There are so many treats and chews available that what you choose should be down to your dog's preference. However, their benefits are different.

TREATS AND BISCUITS Experiment with a wide variety of treats and biscuits to see which ones your dog prefers.

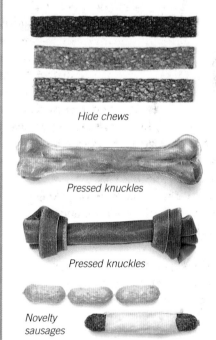

Hide chews

Pressed knuckles

Pressed knuckles

Novelty sausages

MOUTH HYGIENE Dog-chews are better than bones for keeping teeth clean and free from tartar.

Grooming

Grooming is necessary not just to make your dog look good, but also as an important aid to skin health and hygiene, and in order to keep parasites under control.

Grooming enhances your relationship with your dog and, although it takes time, patience, and sometimes a little effort, it should be pleasurable for both groomer and groomed. Start grooming pups from five to six months of age, although wiry-coated breeds can be trimmed lightly around head and tail from about four months. First baths may be given at three months of age or when puppies arrive from kennels.

THE HAIR OF THE DOG

A dog's coat comprises two main kinds of hair, the coarser, primary (or guard) hairs of the outer coat, and the softer, shorter, secondary hairs of the undercoat. The hairs are rooted in skin follicles to which are connected sebaceous glands, which produce oil to give the coat its gloss and some degree of waterproofing and insulation.

The five main types of dog coat are long, silky, smooth, non-shedding curly, and wiry. There are also some oddities, such as the almost hairless Mexican Hairless Dog, and the Hungarian Puli, which has a dense coat twisted into cords.

A coat hair grows to its optimum length, stops growing, and is then pushed out by a newly growing hair and lost, in a process that goes on continuously all over the dog's body. A natural balance of hairs in the three different phases is always maintained.

Most breeds (but not Bedlington Terriers, Poodles, or Kerry Blues) moult to change their coats twice a year, usually in spring and autumn. In moult, a greater loss of hair occurs, under the influence of changes in environmental temperature and length of daylight acting through the dog's hormone-producing glands. Sometimes a dog will moult almost constantly, and this

COMBS AND BRUSHES

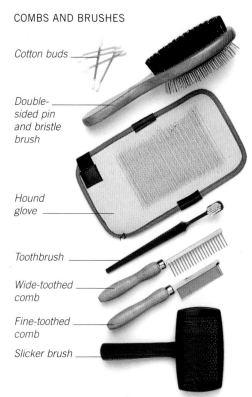

Cotton buds

Double-sided pin and bristle brush

Hound glove

Toothbrush

Wide-toothed comb

Fine-toothed comb

Slicker brush

may be due to its body being deceived by artificial factors, such as central heating and indoor lighting. Diet and hormone irregularities may also be involved.

COAT TYPES

LONG COATS, such as those of Collies, Old English Sheepdogs, Newfoundlands, German Shepherds, and Spitz-type dogs. Brush and comb the coat forwards over the head and shoulders and then comb it back. Brush the flanks following the hair streams. Extra combing is needed when the dog is moulting. Bathing should be done in spring and autumn with dry shampoos during the year if necessary.

SILKY COATS, such as those of Afghan Hounds, Maltese Terriers, Yorkshire Terriers, Lhasa Apsos, spaniels, setters, and Pekingese. These breeds demand a lot of attention. Afghans, spaniels, and setters must be stripped of dead hair and bathed every three months. Yorkshire Terriers, spaniels, and Maltese Terriers require trimming four times a year. Trim excess hair on spaniels' ears and paws to keep them free of mud and grass seeds.

SMOOTH COATS, such as those of Boxers, Whippets, Smooth-haired Dachshunds, Labradors, and Corgis. These are the easiest breeds to groom. A hound glove is all you need for short coats (Whippet, Boxer, and Smooth-haired Dachshund); the others require little more than a comb and a bristle brush. Do not bath these dogs too often. After a bath it takes around six weeks for the coat's natural oil to be replaced.

NON-SHEDDING CURLY COATS, such as those of Bedlington Terriers, Poodles, and Kerry Blues. Although these dogs do not moult, they need a clip and a bath every two months or so. Check the ears frequently, and pluck out excess hair growing in the ear canal (do not use scissors). Clipping of these breeds should first take place at 14 to 15 weeks old.

WIRY COATS, such as those of the Wire-haired Dachshund, Schnauzers, and most terriers. Give these dogs lots of regular combing to avoid matting. Strip and pluck the coat, and then bath every three to four months. An alternative is to machine clip every six to eight weeks. Trim excess hair around the eyes and ears with blunt-ended scissors.

UNUSUAL COATS found on some exotic breeds need specialized attention – consult the breeder or your vet for advice. The coat of the Hungarian Puli (*shown here*) hangs in cord-like strands and should not be combed if the dog is to be shown. Even virtually hairless breeds, such as the Mexican Hairless Dog, require regular gentle brushing and combing.

TRIMMING EQUIPMENT

Blunt-ended scissors ___

Thinning shears ___

Stripping knife ___

Stripping comb ___

Guillotine nail-clippers ___

EQUIPMENT

You must have a brush and comb at least, but a full grooming kit might consist of a pin brush, bristle brush, slicker brush, rubber brush, fine- and wide-toothed metal combs, a hound glove, a carder, blunt-ended scissors, nail-clippers, thinning shears, stripping comb, stripping knife, and a hairdryer. Cotton buds for cleaning excess wax from the ears and a toothbrush for dental care are useful additions to the kit – see the section on Health Care *(pp.238–47)* for how to use them properly.

GROOMING A COCKER SPANIEL

1 *Break up the dog's coat and untangle matted areas using a wide-toothed comb. Spaniels need special attention to the long, silky hair on their ears.*

2 *Use a fine comb under the chin and tail and behind the ears. Carefully tidy up around the eyes and paws and under the tail with blunt-ended scissors.*

3 *Brush as appropriate for the breed. Follow the "hair streams" – lines of hair growth that run from the head down the back and sides to the legs and feet.*

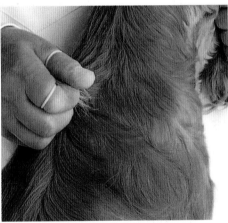

4 *On silky and wiry coats, gently pluck out any dead hairs from the neck and back. Rubber finger cots, as shown here, help to protect the fingers.*

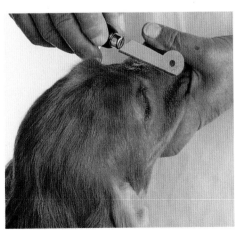

5 *Professional groomers may use a stripping comb or stripping knife, as shown here. They may also thin the coat, if necessary, using thinning shears before giving the dog a bath.*

6 *Bath the dog (see p.230) or use a dry shampoo, as shown here. Rub the powder into the dog's coat one section at a time, and then brush it out. Do the head last.*

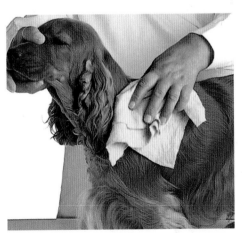

7 *Give a final brush, rub down the coat with a damp chamois leather, and then polish with a piece of silk or velvet. A special spray can be used to give a finishing sparkle for showing.*

Bathing a Dog

When a dog is dirty or smelly it needs bathing, but this should not be done too often. Some dogs, such as Scotties, have a tendency to dandruff and may need a bath once a month. Other breeds may only need bathing once or twice a year. Always groom the dog before bathing, and use special dog or baby shampoo, never household soap.

A dry shampoo is ideal for a quick clean-up if the coat is not badly fouled or smelly. It is a powder that is thoroughly dusted into the coat and then brushed out. Oily coats in particular benefit from the occasional dry shampoo.

1 *Ensure that the water is warm but not hot before lifting the dog into the bath. You may need help to hold the dog still as you pour water liberally over its back and sides. Hold the dog around the muzzle in order to steady it.*

2 *Apply some shampoo along the back and work it well into the coat, moving down over the sides and legs. Wash the head last, taking care to keep shampoo out of the dog's eyes. The dog is most likely to shake when its head gets wet.*

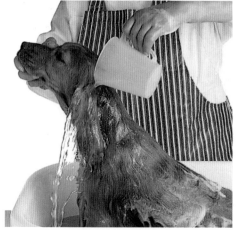

3 *Rinse out the shampoo, starting with the head and working backwards. Use plenty of water to rinse through the coat, and then go over the dog again, squeezing out the excess to leave it as dry as possible.*

4 *Lift the dog out of the bath and stand it on a bath mat. You can either towel-dry it or use a hairdryer. If the dog is not used to hairdryers, it may be frightened, so start from the front, where it can see what you're doing.*

NAIL-CLIPPING

You may prefer to leave clipping of the dog's nails to the vet or a professional groomer, but if you are going to do it yourself, ask your vet to show you how. It is best to use special guillotine-type clippers rather than the human "pliers" design. To avoid causing pain and bleeding, cut at least 2 mm (¹⁄₁₀ in) in front of the pink area (the quick) lying inside the nail. If in doubt, be cautious, and leave more rather than less nail on the toe.

AN EARLY START A puppy's nails should be clipped at two to three weeks of age to avoid them scratching the mother's belly skin with the "kneading" movements the feet make while the puppy suckles. It saves a lot of hard work later on if you accustom the dog to nail-clipping as a puppy.

BATHING KIT

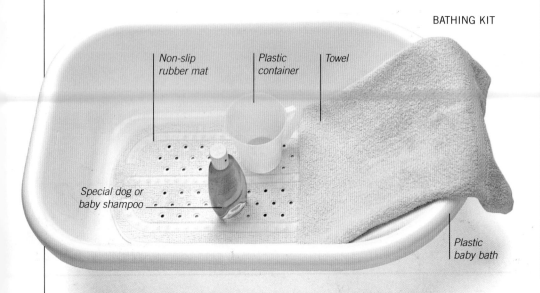

Non-slip rubber mat

Plastic container

Towel

Special dog or baby shampoo

Plastic baby bath

Travelling

The best way to avoid travel sickness is to accustom your dog to travel from puppyhood. Regular car journeys with something pleasant at the end of them, such as a long walk, generally condition the dog to enjoy the ride.

CAR JOURNEYS

Large dogs are best in the back of an estate car behind a dog grille or guard, or even in a cage, if it is big enough. Small dogs can go in special plastic ("voyager") or wicker containers, and cardboard carriers are good for one-off or infrequent journeys. Puppies travel well in an ordinary cardboard box that is well padded and furnished with a hot-water bottle.

If sickness is a problem, ask your vet for travel-sickness pills. Sedatives can interfere with a dog's heat regulation and so are not a good idea. Very nervous and agitated animals can, however, be tranquillized with special drugs available from your vet.

Do not leave a dog alone in a car for a long time, especially in hot weather.

OUT ON THE ROAD Most dogs enjoy car journeys. Cages *(above)* are available, but the safest way to carry a large dog in your vehicle is behind a dog grille *(right)*. Remember to stop on long journeys to allow the dog to walk around a little.

Heatstroke, which is often fatal, can occur surprisingly easily. Adjustable guards that fit inside the open windows provide security while assisting ventilation on warm days, but do not rely on them.

Before starting any journey, give the dog a chance to urinate and defecate. The animal should also have a drink and a snack about two hours before departure. Stop every two or three hours to give the dog an opportunity to have a drink and relieve itself. On very long trips, give a little more food after four or five hours.

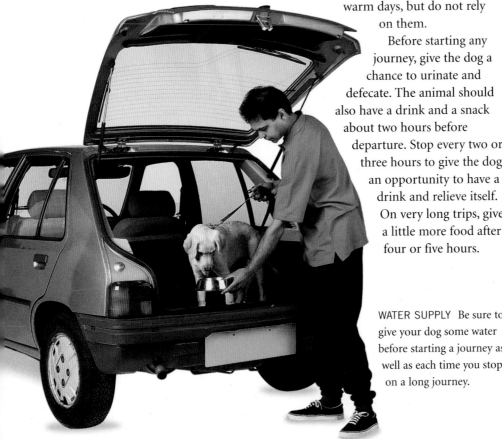

WATER SUPPLY Be sure to give your dog some water before starting a journey as well as each time you stop on a long journey.

AIR TRAVEL

Over longer distances, air travel has advantages, since it is relatively cheap and its speed keeps the period of distress to a minimum. As with other travel, give the dog a small drink and a snack a couple of hours before departure.

All dogs must travel in a container that complies with the regulations laid down by the International Air Transport Association (IATA). Some airlines have their own rules; avoid delays by finding out about such regulations and those of the countries between which the dog will be travelling well before departure.

Other IATA recommendations for travelling by air are:

• Snub-nosed dogs (Boxers, Bulldogs, Pekingese, and Pugs) must be free from respiratory troubles before travelling. Their containers must have open bars from top to bottom at the front end. It is best, if possible, to avoid flying with short-nosed breeds. The dog must not be ill, violent, or in physical distress. Pets should not be sedated for air travel unless specifically recommended by a vet.

• Air travel is not recommended for bitches on heat.

CONTAINER SPECIFICATIONS

Containers for dogs travelling by air must conform to standards laid down by the IATA. Their minimum dimensions must be related to those of the dog, as illustrated (see below).

The container must be large enough to allow the animal to stand freely, turn around, and lie down comfortably. It must, if constructed after 1 October 2000, have a door of welded or cast metal of sufficient thickness to prevent the dog from bending or distorting it. The door hinge and locking pins must engage the container by at least 1.5 cm (¾ in) beyond the horizontal extrusions above and below the door opening where the pins are fitted. The latter requirements do not apply to plastic containers made before October 2000.

The container must be fitted with food and water dishes that can be filled from the outside. The container should be lined with absorbent material. There must be a sufficient number of ventilation openings to provide good air circulation within.

CLEARLY LABELLED The container must display a "This Way Up" sticker as well as an IATA "Live Animals" label. The destination, owner's address, and telephone number must also be included.

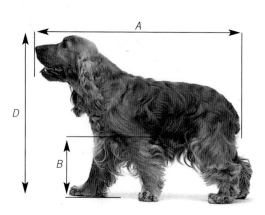

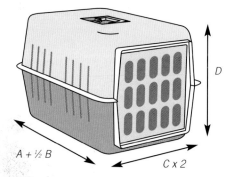

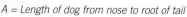

A + ½ B

C x 2

A = Length of dog from nose to root of tail
B = Height from ground to elbow joint
C = Shoulder width
D = Height of dog from ground to top of head

- Nursing bitches and unweaned puppies are not acceptable for carriage.
- Weaned puppies younger than eight weeks should not be transported.
- Puppies may travel well together, although some countries insist that each animal is crated individually.
- A familiar article placed in the container helps to comfort a dog.
- The dog's name must be marked on the outside of the container.

INTERNATIONAL TRAVEL

If you intend to take your dog abroad, you must first find out about any regulations governing the importation of animals into the country of destination. There may be vaccination or quarantine requirements and there will certainly be documentation needed, including veterinary certification in the country of origin. It is your responsibility to obtain all necessary information and documentation from the appropriate embassies, consulates, or government departments well before the date of travel.

In 2000, the Pet Travel Scheme (PETS) was inaugurated in Great Britain allowing pet dogs (and cats) to enter and re-enter the UK without being subjected to a miserable six months in quarantine (see box, opposite). Although this scheme is sometimes referred to as a "pet passport", the animal is not given a one-off travel document similar to that of its owner that lasts ten years. The procedure is rather more complicated, covers one journey at a time, and only works with animals (including returns) from certain eligible countries (see table, opposite).

The Pet Travel Scheme was developed to allow entry of pets from Europe and other approved countries to the UK. Jersey and Guernsey have their own Pet Travel Schemes. The Republic of Ireland is *not* part of the PETS scheme, so dogs have to go into quarantine when entering or re-entering the UK from Ireland. There are no quarantine requirements for the import of dogs into European countries or the United States, but rabies vaccination is often required and the animals must be certified to be in "good health". For more information concerning PETS contact your vet, the local DEFRA office (Department for Environment, Food, and Rural Affairs), or the PETS helpline in the UK on 0870 241 1710.

There is always a risk in taking pets abroad just for a holiday. Parasites and infectious diseases that do not naturally occur in Great Britain can be encountered, sometimes with grave results. Important illnesses such as heartworm and leishmaniasis, unknown in Great Britain, are to be found in many Mediterranean countries, including the Balearic Islands.

THE PET TRAVEL SCHEME (PETS)

The Pet Travel Scheme allows pet owners to take their animals out of the country with them, without having to quarantine them on their return. The scheme operates as follows:

OUTWARD:

1. **Microchipping:** The dog must be implanted with an authorized microchip according to manufacturer's instructions and national guidelines.
2. **Vaccination:** The dog must be vaccinated against rabies. Animals must be over three months old and have already been fitted with a microchip.
3. **Blood testing:** Thirty days after the rabies vaccination, a blood sample must be taken and the owner provided with a declaration of the date of sampling by the vet. This sample is sent to a government-approved lab to check that an adequate level of protection against rabies has been reached.
4. **PETS certificate:** The owner should obtain a PETS certificate, which can only be issued by a government-appointed vet and is valid for travel from six months after the blood sample giving a positive result was taken. This certificate expires on the date the rabies vaccine booster is due. As long as the booster is given by the due date, a new PETS certificate can be issued without the need for another blood sample. There are three licensed rabies vaccines in the UK. Booster vaccines are given annually.
5. **The route:** Only approved routes and transport companies are eligible for the scheme. Owners should speak to the approved carrier to discuss how their pet will travel. Most dogs travelling by air must go as freight cargo; if travelling by sea, they must be contained in a crate or the owner's car in the hold. Pets remain with their owners in their car during a journey through the Channel Tunnel. You are not permitted to bring dogs into the country in any other way, including on private planes or boats.

INWARD (return):

In order to enter the UK under PETS, you will need:

1. **PETS certificate:** This will prove that the pet has been microchipped and vaccinated.
2. **Tick and tapeworm treatment certificate:** This is an official certificate of treatment against ticks and tapeworm (*Echinococcus multilocularis*). This treatment must be administered by a vet 24–48 hours before the return trip to the UK, and owners are given an official certificate from the vet saying this has been done. (It may take a few days for a vet to obtain the necessary certificate, so arrange this well in advance of the inward journey).
3. **Declaration of residency:** Before entry or re-entry into the UK, the owner must sign an official declaration (available in advance of the journey from DEFRA) stating that the animal(s) have not been outside any of the PETS-qualifying countries in the previous six months.

MICROCHIPPING As part of the Pet Travel Scheme it is essential that your dog is microchipped. This is a quick and painless task that your vet will perform. The information on the microchip can be accessed using a special scanner.

PETS ELIGIBLE COUNTRIES

EUROPE:	Germany	Netherlands
	Gibraltar	Norway
Andorra	Greece	Portugal
Austria	Iceland	San Marino
Belgium	Italy	Spain
Cyprus	Liechtenstein	Sweden
Denmark	Luxembourg	Switzerland
Finland	Malta	Vatican
France	Monaco	

FURTHER AFIELD:	Falkland Islands	New Zealand
	Fiji	Reunion
Antigua and	French Polynesia	Singapore
Barbuda	Guadeloupe	St Helena
Ascension Island	Hawaii	St Kitts & Nevis
Australia	Jamaica	St Vincent
Bahrain	Japan	USA
Barbados	Martinique	Vanuatu
Bermuda	Mauritius	Wallis & Futuna
Canada	Montserrat	
Cayman Islands	New Caledonia	

Training

Even if you do not aspire to having a pet with the skills of a guide dog for the blind or a champion sheepdog, you must accept that all dogs, like their owners, require a certain amount of training if they are to be civilized.

HOUSE-TRAINING

First, of course, there is the business of toilet-training a puppy. This should begin as soon as it starts on solid food, at around six weeks old. If you are at home for most of the day and the pup can easily be taken outside, do so when it wakes, after every meal, after every period of activity, when it has not urinated for some time, and, crucially, when it shows signs of wanting to. Do not carry it out – let it follow you to learn the route. At night, put down newspapers by the outside door.

If you live in an apartment or are out for long periods during the day, confine the pup to one room where the floor can be covered with paper. The pup will soon pick one "toilet area" that it prefers. Then remove the rest of the paper. Gradually move the paper toilet until it is by the door. When the weather is fine, move the paper outside, and finally discard it altogether.

Clear up at once any accidental mess the puppy makes, and spray the spot with a

WALKING TO HEEL With the lead held in your left hand, and the dog beside your left leg, start walking straight ahead. When the dog pulls in front, jerk the lead sharply back and say "Heel" firmly. Praise the dog all the time it is in the correct position. The next stage is to practise first right-hand and then left-hand turns. Do not train for long periods without a rest for play and praise.

deodorant aerosol. This prevents it from being attracted back to the same place and "triggered off" by lingering aromas to do the deed again. Be patient – never punish a puppy for slowness in learning or for unfortunate lapses, but make a great fuss of it whenever it performs correctly.

GENERAL TRAINING

If you are interested in specialized dog training as a hobby or as part of your work, there are many training clubs or schemes that you can join. But there are certain desirable things that all owners should teach their dogs to do. The best idea is to join a dog-training club or class, where dogs and owners can all learn together from an expert. You will find that this considerably enhances the relationship between you and your pet.

Begin training when the dog is between three and four months old. The puppy should be accustomed to behaving calmly and obediently when out and about with you. Do not stop for other dogs. Do not let it sniff lampposts. Only gradually introduce it to places with crowds and noisy traffic. Always use pleasant, reassuring, clear tones when talking to the dog.

It should be taught to heel by holding the lead firmly then shortening it so that the animal comes into position with its right shoulder beside your left leg. This is

first practised while you stand still. Then you do it at the walk, going in a straight line and saying "Heel" firmly when you start. Next come right turns, moving away from the dog so that the novice cannot become entangled with your legs, and finally left turns.

After learning to walk and heel correctly, train the dog to sit on command and every time you come to a halt on a walk – for example, at the edge of a kerb before crossing a road. During a walk in quiet surroundings, stop and press the dog gently but firmly into a sitting position with your hand on its back, just in front of the pelvis. As you do this, say "Sit". It will soon get the idea.

SIT Teach the dog to sit when you come to a halt. Holding the lead in one hand, stroke your other hand down the dog's back, and push down on the rump to make it sit. Say "Sit", and praise the dog when it obeys.

WAIT… Using a long lead, get the dog to sit, then command "Wait", and turn and walk away. A few metres away, turn, say "Wait" again, and give the hand signal shown.

SIT AND STAY With the dog sitting, give the command "Stay" and, keeping the lead taut, walk around the dog. If it tries to move, jerk the lead and resettle the dog. Give the command "Sit, stay" with the signal shown, and walk in a wider circle. Over several training sessions you can continue to increase the distance until you are eventually out of sight. Always praise the dog when you return.

Other important techniques you may learn in a dog-training class are how to make the dog stop and lie down on command (which can be a matter of life or death if it is running towards a road), and how to make it defecate on command. If all dog owners taught their charges these two techniques, the anti-dog lobby would have less cause for complaint and much less public support. When training, always keep a dog on the lead until it understands the commands, and never try to train a dog if you are in a bad mood. Do not let the dog get bored by training for too long without a break. Use a firm but gentle tone to give commands, and use the dog's name to gain its attention before giving the command. Remember that if a dog does not obey you, it is almost always because it has not been taught what is required of it. Hitting the dog will not help in any way.

SIT AND STAY

Once the dog will sit on command, introduce the idea of "staying". Walk with it to heel and then make it sit. Holding the lead taut and vertical, command "Stay" and walk around the dog. If it attempts to move, give it a gentle yet firm jerk of the lead. As the dog begins to understand, slacken the lead and walk in a wider circle. Now give the command "Sit, stay" without the lead, again gradually moving further away from the dog. Reinforce the verbal command with a clear visual signal by stretching out one arm towards the animal, palm of the hand outwards. Over successive training sessions you can progress to the next stages, which are to slacken the lead, to let it go altogether, to turn and walk away, and eventually

to go out of sight. Always praise the dog lavishly when you return.

WAIT AND COME

Teaching the dog to "wait and come" is best done using an extendable lead or by adding 10–15 m (10–15 yd) of nylon cord to an ordinary lead. The dog learns to wait the same way it learns to stay. When it sits correctly, command "Wait" and turn and walk away. A few metres away, turn around and call the dog by name, with emphasis on the additional command word "Come".

In all training, bribery with titbits should be used sparingly and not as a rule. Praise and a short session of play is a much better reward for an obedient dog.

END WITH A SIT Shorten the lead as the dog approaches. Bring it to the correct position at your feet by drawing your hands up to waist level and giving the command "Sit".

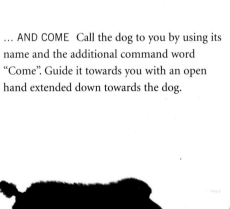

… AND COME Call the dog to you by using its name and the additional command word "Come". Guide it towards you with an open hand extended down towards the dog.

Showing

Showing dogs can be great fun and is a fascinating – though seldom financially rewarding – hobby.

For the serious pedigree breeder, shows are essential to prove the excellence of his or her stock. For the owner of a friendly mongrel, it is less serious, and probably means an enjoyable afternoon competing in the novelty class at a local show.

The first proper dog show was held at Newcastle-upon-Tyne in 1859 and was open only to pointers and setters. Mr Cruft organized his first show in 1886, for terriers only, and his first general show was held in London in 1891. In the US, it all started in 1877 with the prestigious Westminster Dog Show of New York.

Nowadays, as well as a multitude of local, regional, and national shows in countries all over the world, there are obedience shows, as well as sheepdog trials, and field trials for gundogs.

TYPES OF SHOW

Championship: In this type of show, classes are organized on breed lines with further divisions by age and handicap into Puppy, Junior, Novice, Open, and Veteran classes. Dogs and bitches are judged separately in each class. There is a Best of Breed class. The best dog and best bitch of each breed receive a Challenge Certificate. In the next round, the Best of Breed winners from each group (Hounds, Toys, and so on) are judged to find the Best of Group, and finally the Best of Groups are judged to award the accolade of Best in Show.

Open: Similar to Championship shows, but more concise, with Best in Show judged from Best of Breeds.

Exemption: These shows are exempt from the full Kennel Club show rules and are ideal for beginners. They are run in a similar way to Championship shows.

Club: These are organized by breed societies and are ideal for breed enthusiasts as well as beginners in a particular breed.

HANDLING Train your dog to accept handling by strangers; the judge will appreciate it.

TROTTING Practise trotting with your dog at the speed that shows it off to best advantage.

JUST RELAX Competing in a large dog event can be a daunting and nerve-racking experience for both owner and dog – the secret is to relax and enjoy the show.

GROOMING PARTICULARS Some breeds need particular care over their grooming and preparation for a show. This Old English Sheepdog has had its whiskers and fringe tied back to keep them clean and dry.

READY AND WAITING Contestants at a local dog show get their whippets into standing position ready for the judge's tour of inspection.

SHOW PROCEDURE

Before showing, a dog must be thoroughly groomed, but there must be no excess chalk or talc, and no lacquer or hairspray in the coat. No dyes, tints, or bleach can be used to alter the colour of the coat. The set of the dog's teeth must not have been artificially altered. All these things can lead to disqualification.

Make sure that you apply for entry to the show well in advance. You will receive an entry ticket, benching number, and attendance time. Take along the items in the show checklist (see right); a benching chain is needed at some shows to attach the dog's collar to the bench, and the show lead should be a smart one made of leather or nylon.

On arrival, buy a catalogue and go to your numbered bench. Settle your dog on its bed and give it a drink; it is best not to feed it. Check your entry in the catalogue. Calculate how soon you may be called by keeping one eye on the clock and the other on the entrant numbers as they are displayed on the judge's table.

In the ring, you will accompany and handle your dog. It should be accustomed to trotting in a "collected" (disciplined) manner, and also to maintaining a calm but alert stance so that its best points can be displayed. Make sure that your dog is on level ground when standing. Do not fuss over it during the judging.

AMERICAN SHOWS

More than 15,000 competitive shows are held annually in the United States under American Kennel Club (AKC) rule. Events are in three categories: conformation; obedience, tracking, and agility trials; and performance events. The AKC recognizes 150 breeds for registration, and these are divided into seven groups: Sporting, Hound, Working, Terrier, Toy, Non-Sporting, and Herding. There is a further Miscellaneous group based on the uses for which breeds were originally developed.

The American showing and judging system is very similar to that in the UK but, of course, is based on AKC breed standards. Breeds admitted vary from those accepted in the UK. The official standards for breeds in the US can be obtained from the AKC.

SHOW CHECKLIST

- Entry ticket
- Ring clip (to hold your entrant number)
- Grooming kit
- Bed and blanket
- Water (from dog's normal supply, in glass bottle)
  - Food and feeding bowl (for long days)
  - Benching chain and show lead

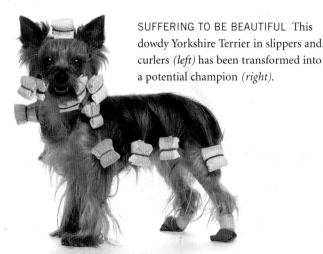

SUFFERING TO BE BEAUTIFUL This dowdy Yorkshire Terrier in slippers and curlers (left) has been transformed into a potential champion (right).

Health Care

An intricate machine needs a skilled mechanic. Do not tinker with your dog. The aim in this section of the book will be to explain some of the common symptoms, and what you should do about them, as well as giving tips on simple, useful first aid.

Seek veterinary help for all but the mildest and briefest conditions. The basic principles behind the more common diseases of dogs will also be outlined, together with the ways in which the vet treats these afflictions.

COMMON AILMENTS

Most common illnesses are easy to treat if they are diagnosed in time. It is important to keep an eye on your dog for signs of unusual behaviour or ill-health and to contact the vet if these persist.

THE MOUTH

Symptoms associated with mouth problems are salivating (slavering), pawing at the mouth, exaggerated chewing motions, signs of tenderness when chewing, and bad breath.

You can help prevent trouble by inspecting your dog's mouth regularly and cleaning the teeth once or twice a week with a soft toothbrush or cotton wool dipped in salt water (or special doggy toothpaste) to prevent the build-up of

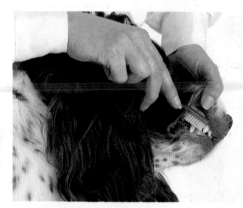

BRUSHING TEETH Avoid the build-up of tartar by cleaning the teeth once a week with a soft toothbrush and special dog toothpaste or a piece of cotton wool dipped in salt water.

troublesome tartar. This is a yellowy-brown, cement-like substance that accumulates on the teeth. It damages the edges of the gums, lets bacteria in to infect the tooth sockets, and thus loosens the teeth. Tartar always causes some gum inflammation and frequently bad breath. Giving your animal dog-chews made out of processed hide can also help to keep tartar down to an acceptable level.

If your pet suddenly displays some of the symptoms described, open its mouth and look for a foreign body stuck between its teeth. With patience, you can usually flick such objects out with a teaspoon handle or similar blunt instrument.

Bright red edging to the gums where they meet the teeth is a sign of gingivitis. Tap each tooth with your finger or a pencil. If there are any signs of looseness or tenderness, wash out the mouth with warm, salty water, and give a tablet of aspirin. There is little else you can do without calling for professional help.

Canine dentistry is easily tackled by the vet. Using tranquillizers or short-acting general anaesthetics, he can remove tartar from teeth with special scrapers or ultrasonic scaling machines. Bad teeth must be taken out to prevent root abscesses and socket infection from causing problems elsewhere in the body, such as blood poisoning, sinusitis, or even kidney disease. Fillings are rarely necessary.

Mouth ulcers, tumours, and tonsillitis also cause some of the symptoms listed above, and these will need veterinary diagnosis and treatment.

THE EYES

Eye problems are indicated by sore, watering, or "mattery" eyes (producing a sticky discharge), and when a blue or white "film" appears over the eye.

If only one eye is involved and the only symptom is watering or sticky discharge, try washing the eye with warm human-type eyewash every few hours. A little antiseptic eye ointment can also be applied inside the lower lid. For safety's sake, keep the tube parallel to the eye's surface at all times.

EYE CARE

1 *If the eye is sore or watering, irrigate it every two to three hours with warm, human-type eyewash or warm water squeezed from a ball of lint.*

2 *When administering eye-drops, steady your hand by resting it on the dog, and always approach from behind and above the eye. Keep the eye-dropper parallel to the surface of the eye, as shown.*

Particularly in young dogs, two mattery eyes may indicate the serious viral disease distemper. Persistent watering of one or both eyes can be due to a slight infolding of the eyelid (entropion) or to blocked tear ducts. A blue or white film over one or both eyes is normally a sign of inflammation of the cornea (keratitis); it is not a cataract but requires immediate veterinary attention. Opacity of the lens (cataract) is a blue or white film much deeper in the eye. It usually occurs in older animals.

If any symptom in or around the eye lasts longer than a day, take the patient to the vet. Inflammations of the eye are treated in a variety of ways. Drugs are used to reduce inflammation, and surgical methods to tackle ulcerated eyes under

WATCH THE NOSE It is true that a wet nose like this is a sign of a healthy dog, but a persistently runny nose can be a sign of trouble.

local anaesthesia. Many problems can be treated surgically nowadays; these include infolding or deformed eyelids, foreign bodies embedded in the eyeball, and even some cataracts.

THE NOSE

Common symptoms of an unhealthy nose are a cracked, sore, dry nose-tip or running, mattery nostrils and the appearance of having the human common cold. The dog with a cold, particularly if both eyes and nose are mattery, may well have distemper.

To relieve the symptoms you can help prevent the nostrils getting caked and clogged up. Bathe them thoroughly with warm water and anoint the nose pad with a little petroleum jelly. If there is the common-cold symptom, you must seek veterinary advice at once.

THE EARS

The symptoms associated with ear problems in dogs are shaking of the head, scratching the ear, a bad smell or discharge from the ear, tilting the head to one side, ballooning of the ear flap, and the dog showing signs of pain or discomfort when the ear is touched.

Where symptoms suddenly appear, an effective and soothing emergency treatment is to pour copious quantities of warmed (not hot) mineral oil into the ear. Do not use so-called canker powders, since these can cause annoying accumulations that act as foreign bodies and worsen the irritation.

See the vet immediately if your dog develops ear trouble. Chronic ear complaints can be very difficult to cure and need early treatment.

Clean your dog's ears often, once a week if it is prone to ear trouble. Using twists of cotton wool moistened in warm olive oil, clean the part of the ear that you can see with a twisting action to remove excess brown ear wax. If it is a breed with hair growing in the ear canal (such as a Poodle or a Kerry Blue), pluck out the hair between your finger and thumb. Do not cut it. (If you are in any doubt, ask your vet to show you how to do this before attempting it yourself.)

Ear irritation may be due to various things that find their way into the ear

canal. Grass seeds, for example, may need professional help to remove them. Small, barely visible, white mange mites that live in dogs' ears cause itching and allow bacteria to set up secondary infections. Sweaty, dirty conditions, particularly in the badly ventilated ears of breeds such as the spaniels, provide an ideal opportunity for germs to multiply. The vet will decide whether mites, bacteria, fungi, or other causes are the main source of inflammation and will prescribe accordingly. Where chronically inflamed ears are badly in need of drainage, plastic surgery is often necessary.

Although tilting of the head may be due simply to severe irritation on one side, it can indicate that the middle ear is involved. Middle-ear disease does not necessarily result from outer-ear infection, but it may arise from trouble in the Eustachian tube that links the middle ear to the throat. It always needs rigorous veterinary attention involving the use of antibiotics, anti-inflammatory drugs, and, in rare cases, deep drainage operations.

The ballooning of an ear flap looks dramatic but is not. It is really a big blood blister caused by a rupture of a blood vessel in the ear flap. It generally follows a bite from another dog or overvigorous scratching of an itchy ear. Surgical treatment is necessary.

EAR CARE

1 *To avoid ear problems, remove excess wax regularly. Use cotton wool or cotton buds moistened with warm olive oil. Clean only the part of the ear that you can see.*

2 *If ear trouble suddenly erupts, contact the vet. A soothing temporary remedy is warm mineral oil poured into the ear. It is easier to use a dropper or syringe rather than a spoon for this.*

3 *Replace the flap and massage gently to work the oil into the depths of the ear. Inspect the ear again; clean any wax that comes to the surface with cotton wool or cotton buds.*

THE CHEST

The signs of chest problems include coughing, wheezing, and laboured breathing. Dogs can suffer from bronchitis, pleurisy, pneumonia, heart disease, and other chest conditions. Coughing and sneezing, the signs of a "head cold", possibly together with mattery eyes, diarrhoea, and listlessness, may indicate distemper. Dogs sometimes do recover from this, though the outlook is grave if there are symptoms such as fits, uncontrollable limb twitching (chorea), or paralysis, which are signs that the nervous system is affected. These may not appear until many weeks after the virus first invades the body and can be, in some cases, the only visible symptoms.

In order to avoid problems, have your dog vaccinated against distemper and other important infectious canine diseases – such as infectious canine hepatitis and canine parvovirus – at the first opportunity, and make sure it gets annual booster doses.

At the first signs of illness contact the vet. Keep the animal warm, give it plenty of fluids, and provide easily digestible and nourishing food. If it is too weak to eat, try spoon-feeding it invalid food, such as meat jelly or glucose and water.

The vet can confirm or deny the presence of distemper or other infectious

RAISING IMMUNITY Vaccination of puppies against distemper is safe and effective, with side-effects being rare. The first shot should be given at six to nine weeks, with a second two to four weeks later, and an annual booster to keep immunity high.

disease if necessary by blood tests. Since it is caused by a virus, distemper is difficult to treat. Antibiotics and other drugs are useful in suppressing secondary bacterial infections. Canine gamma globulin injections are often used both to treat cases of virus disease and to protect susceptible animals that might have been in contact with the disease.

Other types of chest disease can be investigated by the vet using a stethoscope, X-rays, electrocardiographs, and laboratory tests. Heart disease, which is common in elderly dogs, often tends to respond well to drug treatment.

THE STOMACH AND INTESTINES

The most common symptoms of stomach and intestine trouble are vomiting, diarrhoea, constipation, and blood in the droppings. There are many possible causes, and any symptom persisting longer than 12 hours despite sensible first-aid treatment requires veterinary attention.

Vomiting may be due to a mild infection of the stomach (gastritis) or to simple food poisoning. If severe, persistent, or accompanied by other major signs, it can indicate the presence of serious conditions such as distemper, infectious canine hepatitis, parvovirus infection, leptospirosis, heavy worm infestation, or obstruction of the intestine.

Diarrhoea may be nothing more than a mild bowel upset. It may be serious and

GIVING MEDICINE

There are several techniques for giving pills to a dog:
• Gently prise open the mouth by lifting the upper jaw, holding the dog's lips over its teeth to prevent it biting; place the pill as far back on the tongue as possible, then close the mouth and massage the throat to encourage the dog to swallow it.
• Cover the pill in honey, butter, or some other sticky, tasty substance to make it more palatable.
• Cut a slit in a piece of meat and insert the pill before giving it to the dog.
• Crush the pill in flavoured milk and give to the dog as a liquid medicine (see right). (NB: some pills must be given whole; check with your vet.)

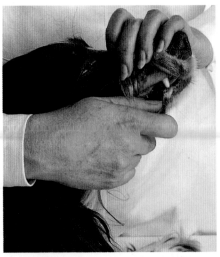

1 To administer liquid medicine, lift the dog's chin up and gently part a pouch at the side of its mouth.

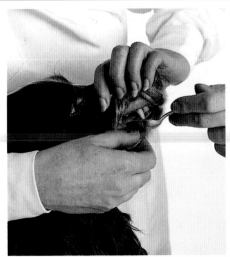

2 Pour the medicine into the pouch. It may be easier to use a dropper, syringe, or bottle, rather than a spoon.

profuse if bacteria or serious viruses are present, as well as in certain types of poisoning and some allergies.

Constipation can be due to age, to a faulty diet that includes too much crunched-up bone (which sets like cement in the bowel), or to obstruction.

Blood in the stools can arise from a variety of minor and major causes: from nothing more than a bone splinter scraping the rectal lining, to the dangerous leptospiral infection.

All you can do in the event of stomach trouble is try to alleviate the symptoms. For vomiting, withhold food and drink for 24 hours, then give nothing but water for the next 24 hours. To treat diarrhoea, give 10–40 ml (2–8 teaspoonfuls) of a human-type kaolin mixture every three hours. In the treatment of diarrhoea, it is important to replace the liquids lost by the body. Cut out solid food, milk, and fatty things. Give small and frequent doses of fluid – best of all are glucose and water or weak bouillon-cube broth. Ice cubes can be supplied for licking. Keep the animal warm and indoors.

Give constipated animals 10–40 ml (2–8 teaspoonfuls) of mineral oil. If an animal is otherwise well but you know or suspect it to be clogged up with something like bone, it is safe to administer one of the small, disposable, ready-loaded, human-type enemas available at the chemist.

Abdominal conditions in general need veterinary attention; if symptoms persist contact the vet no later than the following day. Diseases such as parvovirus infection, infectious canine hepatitis, and leptospirosis require intensive medical treatment with antibiotics, transfusions to replace fluids, vitamins, and minerals, and careful monitoring of progress by blood and urine tests.

Surgical techniques to remove obstructions and foreign bodies and to remedy other stomach complaints are now highly sophisticated. The vet and his team use modern anaesthetics and operate in surgical theatres equipped with most of the hi-tech apparatus of a human hospital.

"BLOAT": GASTRIC DILATION AND TORSION

Bloat is a major emergency caused by a sudden accumulation of gas or fluid in the stomach. The stomach distends and may twist, cutting off inlet and outlet passages and the blood supply to the stomach and spleen. The symptoms of bloat are a sudden swelling of the stomach in the flank, accompanied by severe pain and collapse. The dog will die of shock if a vet does not intervene at once. Contact the vet and get the dog to the surgery as quickly as possible. Bloat occurs typically in larger breeds over two years old that eat dried foods and are allowed to exercise immediately after eating. Possible precautions against bloat are to feed little and often, feed only tinned food, place the food bowl in a raised position to reduce the amount of air taken into the stomach, and to avoid exercising the dog or any vigorous play for two to three hours after a meal.

ANAL GLANDS

Two little glands, one on each side just within the anus, cause a lot of irritation for dogs. Owners complain of their dogs rubbing their bottoms along the floor (known as "scooting") or suddenly chasing their rear ends as if stung by a bee. Worms are often blamed but are rarely the cause.

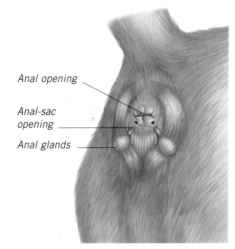

Anal opening

Anal-sac opening

Anal glands

BLOCKED ANAL GLANDS A common cause of irritation to dogs, blocked anal glands should be emptied once you become aware of them.

The anal glands are at the root of the problem, since they tend to get blocked up and impacted. If they become infected, anal abscesses can result. This means antibiotic therapy and, in chronic cases, surgical removal of the glands.

You can avoid problems by ensuring that the dog exercises the glands by producing bulky motions. Add fibre, in the form of vegetables or bran, to the diet. Learn from the vet how to clean out the glands by squeezing them with a pad of cotton wool (see panel, right).

EMPTYING ANAL GLANDS

The dog has two anal glands, located one on each side of the anus. Their purpose is to add a scented fluid to the dog's stools to help them in marking out their territory. Now the dog is domesticated they are no longer needed for survival, but they can cause problems. Swollen glands need to be emptied; they can be felt bulging below the surface of the skin. Ask your vet to show you how to do this before you attempt it yourself. The dog may need to be muzzled and possibly restrained by an assistant. A foul-smelling fluid should be ejected from the anus. If this does not happen, or the glands are very swollen or obviously infected, take the dog to the vet.

1 *Hold the tail up out of the way. Wear rubber gloves and hold a large pad of cotton wool in the palm of your hand to catch the fluid.*

2 *Place your thumb and forefinger in the nine and three o'clock positions as shown, and gently but firmly squeeze together and inwards.*

TAKING THE TEMPERATURE

The best way to take a dog's temperature is to obtain an electronic thermometer and follow the directions that come with it. Failing that, use a conventional thermometer with a stubby bulb.

• Shake the mercury down to 37° C (98.6° F), and lubricate the bulb with mineral oil or petroleum jelly.

• Holding the base of the dog's tail firmly to prevent it sitting down, insert one third of the thermometer's length into the dog's rectum.

• Remove after three minutes, wipe clean, and read the temperature.

Normal temperature in dogs, measured in this way, is around 38.5° C (101.3° F). (NB: if the thermometer should break, do not attempt to remove the broken section from the rectum; contact your vet immediately.)

URINARY SYSTEM

Common signs of urinary problems are difficulty in passing urine, excessive drinking and frequent urination, loss of weight and appetite, and blood in the urine.

As soon as you notice something may be wrong with your dog's waterworks, contact the vet. Inflammation of the bladder (cystitis), stones in the bladder or associated tubes, and kidney disease are all too common and need immediate professional advice. Whatever you do, do not withhold water from an animal with a urinary problem. Do remember to arrange for your dog to be vaccinated against leptospirosis,

and be sure to visit the vet annually for a booster shot.

Cystitis, if diagnosed early, responds well to treatment with antibiotics. A diagnosis of stones in the urinary system can be confirmed by X-ray, and in most cases they can be easily removed by a surgical operation.

Kidney disease needs careful management and supervision of diet. Chronic kidney disease patients can live to a ripe old age if the water, protein, and mineral content of the diet is regulated, bacterial infection controlled, protein loss minimized, and stress of any sort avoided.

GENITALIA

The male has genital problems from time to time (testicle tumours, for example), but the most important and common problems are found in the female; they include persistent heat, heavy bleeding, and vaginal discharge.

Any discharge apart from just prior to whelping or ordinary bleeding while on heat calls for immediate veterinary attention. In non-pregnant bitches the discharge, though looking like pus, is rarely caused by infection. It is usually one of the signs of a hormonal womb inflammation known as pyometra; see the vet at once. He may recommend

medical treatment in the short term, but eventually surgical removal of the womb (hysterectomy) will be advisable. This major operation has a high success rate, but to avoid such emergencies, have the bitch spayed as soon as you decide that you do not want her to have any more puppies.

MAMMARY GLANDS

From time to time turn your bitch over and run your hands along her underside. If you feel any hard lumps in the substance of the breast tissue, within the teats, or just under the skin, see the vet at once. Breast tumours, once established, spread quickly to other parts of the body. Caught early they can be removed surgically.

Inflamed, hard breasts when a bitch is producing milk may indicate the onset of mastitis, which can be treated with anti-inflammatory and anti-bacterial drugs. Sometimes the vet will stop the supply of milk by prescribing hormone tablets.

THE SKIN

There are many kinds of skin disease in dogs. Diagnosis needs examination and often sample analysis by the vet. Common symptoms include thin or bald patches in the coat, scratching, and wet, dry, or crusty sores. Mange, caused by an invisible mite, can cause crusty, hairless sores, and fleas, lice, and ticks can also cause damage to the coat. The presence of just one flea on a dog – terribly difficult to track down – may set up widespread skin irritation as an allergic reaction to the flea's saliva. Dietary faults such as a shortage of certain fats can also produce a poor, unhealthy looking coat.

CHECKING FOR LUMPS Examine your bitch's breasts at least once a month for lumps that may indicate tumours. Tell your vet if you find any swellings larger than 0.5 cm (¼ in) across.

If you see or suspect the presence of any of the skin parasites – mange mites, fleas, ticks, or lice – obtain one of the anti-parasite aerosols, powders, or baths from a pet shop, chemist, or vet. Your vet can also prescribe tablets or "spot-on" preparations that are absorbed through the skin; both are particularly effective against fleas. In the case of mange, there are several types, so let the vet advise on treatment.

Ringworm is a subtle ailment that may need ultraviolet light examination or a fungus culture from a hair specimen. Special drugs given by mouth or applied to the skin are needed, and care must be taken to ensure that humans do not pick up the disease from pets.

With all anti-parasite treatments, make sure you follow the instructions on the label of the preparation being used. With fleas, remember that the flea eggs are to be found not only on the animal's coat but also in its environment. Dog baskets, bedding, carpets, and kennels must be sprayed with anti-parasite aerosol at the same time as the animal is treated.

Skin disease caused by dietary deficiencies is easily avoided by providing balanced meals. Sore, wet "hot spots" that develop suddenly in summer or autumn may be caused by an allergy to plant pollen and other substances. Clip the hair over and around the affected area level with the skin and apply mineral oil liberally. Such cases will require veterinary treatment, perhaps involving antihistamine or corticosteroid creams, injections, or tablets. Though the sores look dramatic, they are quickly cured.

ROUNDWORMS

These can cause looseness of the bowel and upsets, particularly in puppies. They can spread to humans and harm babies severely.

Rid your dog of roundworms by giving one of the modern worming drugs, which are available from the vet or pet shop, at regular three-month intervals throughout its life.

TAPEWORMS

These worms do not usually cause much trouble to dogs, but they can sometimes spread to humans. They spend part of their life-cycle in fleas, which is how they get into dogs.

Avoid tapeworm problems by keeping your dog free of fleas. Tapeworm segments look like grains of boiled rice or off-white bits of flat tape up to 1 cm (½ in) long, and they may move a little. If you see them in the stools or stuck to the hair around the anus, give the dog a dose of one of the modern tapeworm drugs available from the vet or pet shop.

MUZZLING A DOG

Any dog that is frightened or in pain may bite. This muzzling technique allows you to use a length of tape, bandage, or almost any type of material to make the dog safe.

1 *Make a loop in the material and place it over the dog's muzzle.*

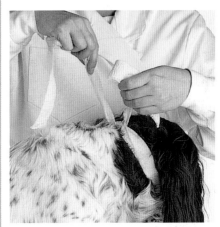

2 *Cross the ends of the material under the dog's chin, and secure in a knot behind the head.*

3 *The dog's jaws are now effectively and painlessly immobilized.*

RESTRAINING A DOG

If there is any danger of the dog biting, it should be muzzled before anyone attempts to treat it *(see panel, right)*. Even when muzzled, the dog will probably need restraining as well, and the correct way to do this varies according to the size of dog:

• A small dog can be grasped firmly by the collar and scruff of the neck.
• A medium-sized dog should be held as at left, with head gripped in the crook of the arm and foreleg raised off the ground.
• Use your body weight to lean on a larger dog, using the same technique; you may also need the help of an assistant to hold the hindquarters.

ACCIDENTS AND EMERGENCIES

An injured, frightened dog may bite. Muzzling is the quickest, easiest way to avoid anyone else getting hurt. After that, get the victim away from danger and into a warm, quiet place indoors. Slip a sheet underneath the dog and carry it as in a hammock or, failing that, by the scruff of the neck. Do not waste time; shock is your principal adversary. Lay the dog comfortably on a blanket and place a warm hot-water bottle next to it. Do not give alcoholic stimulants. Do not give aspirin. You may try to spoon-feed a few teaspoonfuls of warm, sweet tea. Place a thick pad of cotton wool or lint or a folded handkerchief on any areas of heavy bleeding and press firmly – if necessary until the vet arrives. Do not try splinting limbs or experimenting with tourniquets.

It saves time to be doing all this in a car on the way to the vet's surgery, rather than waiting for the vet to come to you.

Bites and wounds

As soon as you detect a wound, clip the hair around its edges down to the skin with scissors. Bathe the area thoroughly in a strong (saturated) solution of Epsom salts (magnesium sulphate) in warm water. Apply some antiseptic cream or powder to any minor injury that does not appear to need professional attention. With a bite, however, a long-acting shot of antibiotic from the vet is a prudent measure. Minor wounds should be left open to the air, without any dressing.

Cut paw pads are troublesome but not serious. They heal slowly and are often not stitchable. Cover the paw with a child's cotton sock after cleaning the cut and applying antiseptic ointment. Do not tie on a waterproof dressing such as a plastic bag, and never fix a foot dressing with a rubber band. The dressing must allow air through, and should be held by a strip of adhesive tape or by a few turns of narrow bandage.

MOVING AN INJURED DOG

1 *After an accident, the first priority is to move the dog away from immediate danger. Use a flat piece of board, if possible, as a stretcher or, failing that, a towel, blanket, or coat. Get other people to assist you to help support the dog and to avoid bending its spine, and take care to be as gentle as possible.*

2 *The dog will receive treatment more quickly if you notify the vet and take the dog to the surgery yourself, rather than calling out the vet. When lifting the dog into a vehicle, make sure someone gets in first to steady the stretcher, and avoid jolting the dog or bending its spine.*

NATURAL REFLEXES

When an accident occurs, or during serious illness, a dog may be found in an unconscious state. Certain nervous reflexes can be significant indicators of life and, if present, may be mentioned when telephoning the vet in an emergency. However, absence of a reaction does NOT conclusively indicate that the animal has died.

1 *Gently touching the corner of the dog's eye will elicit a blink response.*

2 *Shining a bright light close to the eye, ideally from a pen torch, will cause the pupil of the eye to contract.*

3 *Pinching the skin or webbing between the toes of a hindleg will stimulate a reflex flexion and withdrawal of the limb.*

A VETERINARY EXAMINATION

The vet will visually, and by handling, appraise the dog's condition, weight, and demeanour and will check for points of tenderness or pain. He or she may also:

• Look in the outer ears for evidence of disease.

• Inspect other special areas such as feet, anus, genitalia, and stomach skin.

• Take the temperature anally.

• Feel the dog's abdomen to assess the size, position, and condition of certain major internal organs.

• Visually examine eyes, nose, and mouth, pulling the eyelid down to check the colour of the eye membrane, and opening the mouth to inspect the teeth, gums, tongue, and throat.

• Examine the heart and lungs using a stethoscope and also perhaps by tapping the chest wall with the fingertips.

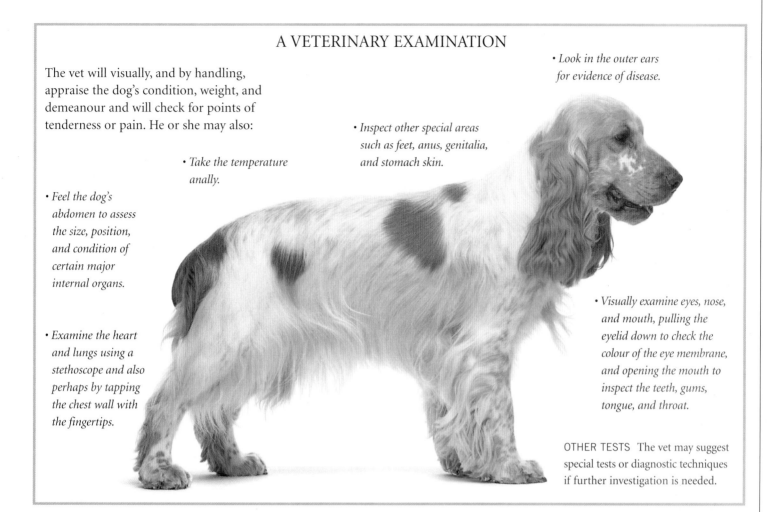

OTHER TESTS The vet may suggest special tests or diagnostic techniques if further investigation is needed.

THE OLD DOG

Like their owners, dogs are living longer nowadays, but few pass 17 (equivalent to 84 human years). The oldest dog on record was an Australian Cattle Dog that died in 1939 at just over 29 years old. In 2002, a Collie in Somerset, England, fed on a vegan diet, celebrated her 27th birthday. Bigger breeds of dog tend not to live as long as small ones; Great Danes and Wolfhounds have a life-expectancy of 10 to 11 years, while Fox Terriers and Miniature Pinschers average 13 to 14 years. Special consideration needs to be given to the care of dogs when they enter their teens. As the years pass, they become heir to many of the age-related problems that also affect human senior citizens.

AVOIDING OBESITY Owners should reduce their dog's food intake at the first sign of obesity. Overfeeding seriously reduces a dog's life-expectancy.

SIGNS TO WATCH FOR

Overweight animals will not live as long as they might. Obesity leads to heart trouble, liver inefficiency, and diabetes. It is wise when contemplating the slimming of an extremely overweight animal to consult the vet first. He may recommend a special obesity diet.

Some older dogs lose weight. A common cause is failing kidneys that "leak" body protein away into the urine. You will need veterinary advice in caring for such a dog, but special diets are available.

The kidneys are often among the first organs in the dog's body to show the effects of old age. If leptospirosis

vaccination was properly carried out when the animal was young and has been boosted regularly throughout its life, the chances of chronic infectious nephritis, once a common dog killer, are remote.

True rheumatism is uncommon in animals, but arthritis frequently occurs in various forms. As with humans there is no absolute cure, but much can be done to relieve pain, keep the joints moving, and reduce lameness. At the first signs of "bad running", let the vet examine your dog. A whole range of anti-arthritic therapy, from corticosteroids to acupuncture to anti-inflammatory chemicals, is now being used to tackle the problem in dogs. As with humans, regular doses of cod liver oil, fish oil, chondroitin, and glucosamine can be highly beneficial in many cases of chronic canine joint ailments.

I mentioned in the Diet section *(see pp.224–7)* the new New Zealand green-lipped mussel dog food that might also be worth trying. Certainly, obese dogs with joint complaints will be greatly helped by being put on a slimming diet. If you need to do that, talk to the veterinary nurse in your local practice.

Aging of the brain of dogs can lead to the gradual onset of signs, frequently

EXTRA VITAMIN INTAKE Multivitamin supplements can be beneficial for old dogs; these are available in tablet and powder form *(see left)* and as liquids.

quite subtle, of mental deterioration – canine dementia. Research suggests that one in four dogs over eight years of age suffer from it. Owners may begin to notice irritability, lack of enthusiasm, forgetfulness, and episodes of apparent confusion. Previously treated by tranquillizers or euthanized, such canine old-timers are now beginning to benefit from progress in the treatment of human Alzheimer's disease. A major advance has been the use of a compound called selegiline hydrochloride – this is a non-addictive medication that is alleviating the mental symptoms of an increasing number of old dogs.

The new anti-oxidant foods mentioned earlier in this book *(see p.227)* can also play an important role in the prevention and, hopefully, treatment of dementia. Chronic heart disease in dogs comes on gradually. Signs may include a general slowing down and loss of energy, a chronic cough, or fast and laboured breathing. The

vet can examine the animal's heart and circulation in a number of ways, certainly by stethoscope and, if required, by electrocardiograph. A wide range of effective drugs, and even, in appropriate cases, the fitting of pacemakers, can be used to alleviate any problems.

With any onset of deafness, the most important thing is the owner taking steps to protect the dog in circumstances where it might unwittingly walk into danger or be unpleasantly surprised; all it takes is for you to be aware of the fading faculty and show consideration.

Failing sight in the dog can be due to a variety of conditions. Veterinary examination will determine the cause, and in some cases treatment to improve vision can be given. In many cases of cataract blindness, for example, an operation to extract the degenerated lens is well worth considering.

With all elderly dogs, a regular – say, annual – check-up at the

CARING FOR AN ELDERLY DOG

Through regular checks and paying attention, you can avoid illness, pain, and discomfort in your dog's old age. By doing the following things, none of which are time-consuming or difficult, you will spot some troubles early and prevent others from occurring. It's just looking, smelling, and feeling!

1 *Check the ears for accumulations of greasy material or sticky liquid. Wipe out the ear with cotton wool and a little olive oil. See your vet if there is a bad smell or the dog resents having the ear handled.*

2 *Look at the eyes. Are the lids free of discharge and crusty accumulations? Keep them clean with cotton wool dipped in warm water. Look out for changes in the appearance or transparency of the eyes.*

vet's is eminently sensible. Daily doses of multivitamins and trace elements in later life are also, in my experience, highly worthwhile.

Smells

Old dogs may become somewhat odorous. The commonest source is the mouth. Do not waste your money on deodorant tablets that contain chlorophyll; these are only a temporary cure. Instead, take the dog to the vet, who can check the mouth and clean up the gums and teeth.

Other sources of smell in old animals are ears and bottoms. Look out for canker, particularly in breeds with floppy ears, such as spaniels. When a dog is getting forgetful as to how to pass a motion neatly, see that its rear end is kept free of long hair that might become soiled.

A general deterioration in the coat of the elderly dog, with the production of more scurf and grease, may be the cause of the characteristic "old dog" smell. In that case, bath the dog every couple of weeks in a human-type shampoo that contains selenium.

Bowels

In later years, the bowels may become sluggish, unpredictable, or loose. Make sure that you provide plenty of bulk in the diet: fibrous vegetables and wholemeal bread, for example. Do not give much liver, and do not give bones.

EUTHANASIA

When the time comes, you may be lucky enough to have your pet die quietly in its sleep. If not, as a responsible, loving owner, you must be prepared to give it a dignified end. You should discuss euthanasia with your vet when an animal is in pain that cannot be easily relieved or when it is incapacitated or in any way prevented from leading a normal life.

The best method of euthanasia is by overdosage of one of the anaesthetic chemicals, usually barbiturates, given by your vet. This is a peaceful end; once the dog is unconscious, its pain and infirmities are blotted out forever.

All the above applies equally to even the youngest puppy. Never, ever drown a pup – it is sheer cruelty.

"DOGGY" SMELLS Old dogs are not bound to be smelly. Regular inspection and basic attention by the owner will eliminate sources of bad odour.

3 *Inspect the mouth and gums, as well as the teeth. Clean the teeth regularly with the dog's own toothbrush and dog toothpaste or salt and water. See your vet if there is a bad smell or if the gums have lost their normal salmon-pink colour.*

4 *Run your hands over the animal's body. See your vet if you find any unusual bumps or lumps anywhere. Do the leg joints bend freely and easily without any "crunching" sensations or evidence of pain or discomfort? If not, take the dog to the vet.*

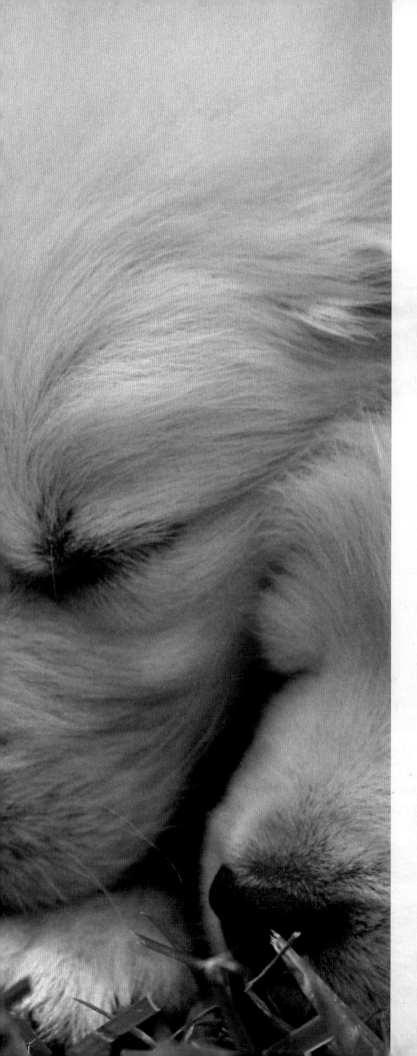

Reproduction

One of the greatest pleasures for some dog-lovers is to have their bitch give birth to a litter of puppies. The next section offers the basics on the subject of dog reproduction.

The canid family as a whole are seasonal breeders and generally have one litter a year following a pregnancy period that ranges from seven weeks in the bat-eared fox, or fennec, to nine weeks in the domestic dog, and up to 11 weeks in the African Wild Dog. The largest litter of puppies so far recorded in a domesticated dog is 23. This has been achieved by an American Foxhound (1944), a St Bernard (1975), and a Great Dane (1987). At least in the case of the American Foxhound, it is known that all the litter survived and grew to maturity.

Domestic dogs differ from wild dogs in that the females usually come into heat twice a year. They are also generally promiscuous, although there is evidence that the Beagle shows a degree of mate preference. Wolves, jackals, and coyotes, on the other hand, show both strong mate preference and fidelity, and they rarely indulge in promiscuity under normal free-living conditions.

It was by manipulation of the reproductive processes of the dog, and with the benefit of pregnancy and maturation periods that are not very long compared to some other mammals, that man engineered the development of the wide variety of dog breeds we see today.

PUPPY LOVE Watching the steady growth and development of a litter is utterly fascinating and enjoyable, but having puppies means plenty of work – not only for the bitch herself, but equally for the dogs' owner.

Sex and Heredity

Breeding for showing depends on the workings of the fundamental mechanisms of heredity. Living bodies are composed of cells, and within each cell lies a nucleus.

The nucleus contains, among other things, a number of structures called chromosomes. These resemble microscopic strings of beads, the beads being called genes. Each gene on a chromosome string carries details of the design, size, or function of some particular part of the body, printed in the form of a remarkable chemical called DNA.

Physical characteristics, such as eye colour, ear shape, and coat length, are determined by genes.

THE CHROMOSOME BLUEPRINT

The genes are arranged in a certain order along the length of the chromosomes, which together form a blueprint of the total make-up of an individual creature. The chromosomes are arranged in pairs in the nucleus. Each cell nucleus contains the same set of chromosome blueprints, so that, whether it be a cell from the liver, a tooth, or a paw pad, it has within it a complete plan of the whole body. Domestic dogs carry 78 chromosomes arranged in pairs of 39, compared with pairs of 19 chromosomes in the cat and pairs of 23 in the human.

When dog cells multiply by splitting into two, the 78 chromosomes produce 78 identical copies of themselves by dividing lengthways. Thus the genetic information is passed on from generation to generation.

Of the 39 pairs of chromosomes in a cell nucleus, 38 are virtually identical pairs, but one may differ slightly. This is the pair that determines the sex of the individual. Females carry a pair of XX chromosomes, while males carry one X and one Y chromosome. The reproductive germ cells of the body – the eggs in the female and the

MATING The best time to mate is generally on the tenth day of the bitch's heat period, and again on the 12th day, although this varies from bitch to bitch. Things go better if at least one of the mating pair has some experience.

1 *Let the dogs get acquainted if they are strangers. Here the bitch is playfully nipping the dog's legs to indicate her interest in mating.*

2 *After some exploratory sniffing and licking by the dog, the bitch signals her readiness to mate by standing with her tail held to one side.*

5 *If the bitch is not steadied by her owner, she may damage the dog with her struggles. This is the correct position for the tie, back to back.*

6 *After about 20 minutes, on average, the tie is broken, the dogs part, and both retire to lick themselves clean.*

spermatozoa in the male – are unique among all the cells of the body in having only one set of chromosomes (39) instead of pairs. This means that when they fuse together at the moment of conception, standard chromosome pairs are formed, each pair consisting of one chromosome from the male and one from the female. All the sex chromosomes of a female are X, whereas the sex chromosomes of a male can be X or Y. Thus the sex of a puppy is dependent on whether an X or Y sperm is the first to penetrate the egg of the female.

The fertilized egg contains the genes of both mother and father in equal amounts but arranged in a slightly different order along the chromosome string. It is this new arrangement that gives each fertilized egg its individuality and makes the puppy that grows from it unique.

MUTATIONS

Occasionally, outside factors can alter the fundamental characters of genes within a cell nucleus. Atomic radiation, X-rays, and certain chemicals can do this, and the changes they cause in the body that develops from the cell are called mutations. This is why sex organs have to be specially protected against, for example, excessive ionizing radiation. Sometimes, though very rarely, a gene mutation occurs apparently spontaneously. These events lie at the very core of the evolutionary process, and they result in the sudden emergence of new breeds, colours, and types of dog.

Apart from mutations, non-genetic, non-hereditary processes can influence development of the embryo after its conception. Cells arrange themselves in the growing tissues in a slightly imprecise fashion, and this type of congenital but non-hereditary variability results in modifications such as the unpredictable distribution of white patches on a particolour or pied coat. Again, certain chemicals and forms of radiation may affect the arrangement of growing cells in the embryo, and this is why pregnant bitches should only be given medicines under the supervision of a vet.

3 *The dog mounts the bitch, clasping her around the loins with his forelegs. He makes thrusting motions and releases his semen within a minute.*

4 *After ejaculation of the semen, the dog's penis expands to lodge itself in the vagina. This is the "tie", and the bitch may try to escape.*

7 *After a thorough clean-up, the dogs may join each other to play together or just rest peacefully.*

Pregnancy and Birth

The bitch usually becomes sexually mature somewhere between eight and 12 months old. It may be as early as six months in some cases, or be delayed until 18 months. If a bitch has not had her first heat period by 20 months old, consult a vet.

COMING INTO HEAT

A heat is generally 18 to 21 days long, although the bitch will only accept the dog and conceive during a few days around the middle of the heat period. The first stage of heat is indicated by puffiness of the lips of the vulva. Soon bleeding begins (this is not equivalent to the menstrual period in human females). While she is bleeding, which may last from four to 14 days (ten days on average), the bitch is highly attractive to dogs but will not accept their advances.

Following this stage, the bleeding diminishes or ceases altogether, the vulva attains maximum enlargement, and the bitch will accept the dog. This is the fertile period and it lasts from five to 12 days, with sexual desire at its height during the first two or three days. This is the time to let mating take place if you are planning to have puppies. Mating should be repeated two days later to increase the chance of a successful fertilization. If a bitch conceives, the heat period tends to end sooner than otherwise.

In the domestic dog, heat normally occurs twice a year, except in Basenjis, which, like wild dogs, wolves, and foxes, have only one sexual cycle per year. Most bitches have a spring heat in January–March, with the autumn heat in August–September. Exceptions

frequently occur, however, and some bitches may have longer or shorter intervals between heats.

Hormones, given by mouth or injection, can be used to halt a heat, to postpone it, or to suppress the sexual cycle altogether. Be guided by your vet's advice if you are considering using hormones in this way on your bitch.

PREGNANCY

The length of pregnancy is, on average, 63 days. Swelling of the abdomen becomes more noticeable from the fifth week onwards, though if only one or two pups are being carried or the bitch is plump anyway, this sign of approaching maternity may be difficult to spot.

The breasts enlarge and the teats become larger and pinker from about the 35th day of pregnancy. A watery secretion can be drawn from the teats three or four days before the pups are born. In bitches that have had several litters, enlargement of the breasts may not begin until the last week of pregnancy, and true milk can often be produced as early as five or six days before the start of labour. During a bitch's pregnancy you should feed her extra quantities of high-quality food, add multivitamins and calcium supplements to the diet as recommended by your vet, and exercise her gently right up to the end. The bitch should be given anti-roundworm tablets three times: at the very beginning of pregnancy, ten days before whelping, and ten days after whelping.

Get things ready for the arrival of the puppies. The whelping and nursing mum will need a quiet, clean refuge, such as a

4 *The puppy is born, covered in the membrane of the water sac.*

3 *The water sac containing the foetus appears at the vulva. This puppy is arriving rear end first; just visible is its tail and one of its paws.*

2 *The bitch strains when the foetus enters the pelvis; the puppy will soon be born.*

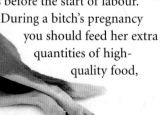

1 *During the first stage of labour, the bitch sleeps peacefully.*

5 *The bitch strips off the membrane and bites through the umbilical cord.*

6 *By licking the puppy clean, the mother stimulates it to take its first few breaths.*

7 *The bitch rests between births and supervises her puppies suckling.*

box, basket, or kennel, with lots of old newspapers on hand for disposable bedding. If you are new at the game, have a chat with a reliable breeder or your vet before the big day.

WHELPING

If you are certain of the date of the last possible mating, do not worry if your bitch goes over the prescribed 63 days by a few days, provided that she is eating and is generally well, has no coloured discharge from the vulva, and has not been seen to strain on any occasion other than when passing a motion. But if any of these rules are broken and pups have not appeared within two hours, consult your vet immediately.

When birth is imminent, the bitch becomes restless, may go off her food, pants fitfully, and prepares her bed. This means that she wanders about, sometimes chooses a site quite different from the one you had planned, paws fretfully at the bedding, and turns round and round in circles before lying down, only to be up again in a short while. This state of pre-labour usually lasts about 12 hours, but it can be much briefer or continue for a day or two, sometimes with intervals of normal behaviour. If there is no straining, no coloured discharge from the vulva, and the bitch is otherwise well in herself, all is in order. Labour proper can be regarded as beginning either when you see the first strain by the bitch or when a coloured (often bottle-green) discharge appears. Count from now. Within one hour the first pup should be born. A water sac appears first and is sometimes ruptured by the licking of the bitch. Then follows the puppy, wrapped partly or entirely in the membrane of the water sac. Puppies are often born back feet first; this is not a breech birth and is nothing to get alarmed about.

Once delivered, the puppy remains attached to the afterbirth by a cord until the mother severs it with her teeth. If this does not occur, and particularly if the puppy's face is covered by membrane, you can help. Clear the membrane away from the nostrils and face and break the umbilical cord. Do not use scissors. Pull the cord apart between the fingers of your two hands. Make the break about 4 cm (1½ in) from the navel. Return the puppy to the mother without delay.

Between the birth of each successive pup the bitch may rest for minutes or for hours. The intervals tend to get shorter as labour progresses, but may well be irregular.

EMERGENCIES

The maximum time limit for the birth of any one pup, counting from the first strain, is two hours. Remember that this is two hours from the beginning of labour for that pup, not from the beginning of whelping. After the two hours is up, with the pup still undelivered, contact the vet. The total time for whelping an average litter of four to eight pups is up to six hours.

The afterbirths will be expelled after each pup, or irregularly in clumps at intervals, or at the end of whelping. Prevent the bitch eating them, which is a natural instinct; burn or otherwise dispose of them.

Most bitches have no trouble giving birth; where problems do arise the vet may help the animal manually, use drugs, or advise a Caesarean operation. The latter is done under general anaesthetic and is recommended in most cases where labour has lasted longer than 12 hours. A Caesarean operation does not rule out future breeding and normal labour in subsequent whelpings.

You should only assist in labour when a puppy is half in and half out of the vulva and progressing slowly. First, make sure that your hands are scrubbed clean. Then grasp the baby firmly and pull smoothly and gently, with a slight screwing action, at the same time pushing against the bitch's body. Try to pull along with the natural strainings of the bitch.

8 *A newborn puppy only minutes old.*

Maternal Behaviour

Bitches make good mothers, and you can generally leave the care of the pups to them. You should be there to supervise, however, and to assist in case anything goes wrong.

The bitch's biological role can lead to problems even when she is not carrying or caring for pups. The responsible owner should know about these and how best to cope with them.

FALSE PREGNANCY

It is quite common for a bitch that has not been mated to show signs of pregnancy. Eight or nine weeks after her heat, she will exhibit the restlessness, bed-making, and fullness of the breasts that occur in truly pregnant bitches. Milk may run from the teats, and an old slipper or child's toy may be carefully guarded and tended in the place she has selected as her nursery.

The bitch is not consciously or unconsciously wanting to have puppies when this happens. It will not result in ovary or womb disease. It may or may not occur after each heat.

The cause is the ovary, which, having shed eggs during the heat period, carelessly assumes that fertilization must have ensued as night follows day. It therefore produces the hormones that prepare the body for the arrival of the phantom puppies. Treatment is easy. You can either let the phenomenon run its full course (only a couple of weeks or so) or contact your vet. He may well prescribe a contraceptive injection or pills, which have the additional function of suppressing false pregnancies.

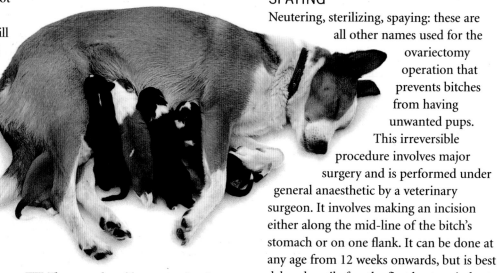

1 *These one-day-old pups are already expert at suckling, and, although deaf and blind, each finds its way to a nipple.*

2 *After the meal, the bitch licks the puppies' faces and genital areas and cleans up any mess they make.*

SPAYING

Neutering, sterilizing, spaying: these are all other names used for the ovariectomy operation that prevents bitches from having unwanted pups. This irreversible procedure involves major surgery and is performed under general anaesthetic by a veterinary surgeon. It involves making an incision either along the mid-line of the bitch's stomach or on one flank. It can be done at any age from 12 weeks onwards, but is best delayed until after the first heat period.

Spayed bitches are less prone to troublesome false pregnancies, and if the

PATERNAL BEHAVIOUR

It is rare for puppies to meet their fathers. In theory, both dogs should behave as strangers and establish their respectively subordinate and dominant positions in the canine hierarchy.

FATHER AND PUP Here a four-week-old pup meets its father, who at first sniffs it with no more than a vague interest

3 *The bitch and puppies relax after the meal and get some sleep.*

4 *The puppies are now 26 days old* (below) *and the bitch finds it easier to feed them standing up. She now needs about three times her normal amount of food.*

CARE OF NEWBORN PUPS

You must provide the mother with a comfortable nursing box, daily changes of bedding, and extra high-quality food. It is almost impossible to overfeed a nursing bitch, and her nutritional requirements peak at about three times normal. She will have been eating more than usual in the last weeks of pregnancy, and her appetite will drop off sharply as the puppies are weaned.

Newborn puppies from a healthy litter find their way to their mother's teats soon after being born. The milk the mother produces in the first day or two (colostrum) provides a puppy with enough antibodies to protect it against most diseases for its first six to ten weeks. It is therefore important that all puppies in the litter suckle properly for the first few weeks at least.

If the bitch does not feed her pups for some reason or appears to have a shortage of milk, consult your vet. In many cases, a simple injection of pituitary hormone can produce an immediate flow.

operation is performed before they are two years old, their chances of breast cancer are also reduced. Some do get fatter after spaying, but probably because their owners overindulge and underexercise them.

Spaying is the surest method of preventing unwanted pups. It also has the major benefit of preventing pyometra, the common and serious disease of bitches that occurs in middle and old age.

Although not a cheap operation, spaying is an important once-and-for-all contribution to the well-being and longevity of your pet – if you are sure you will never breed from her. If in doubt, use the contraceptive injection or pills for a while. Spaying can be done later when you decide, or when the bitch has had a litter or two of puppies.

PUPPY LOVE Gradually the father progresses to circling the pup in a playful manner, and even licks its head in a tentative attempt at grooming.

PLAYTIME! The father is finally overwhelmed by other members of the litter and abandons himself to play.

Puppy Development

At seven days the puppy can still only sleep and suckle.

At 14 days the puppy's eyes are opening and it may be able to hear.

At three weeks old the puppy can focus its eyes and move around.

Puppies are born both blind and deaf. Their eyes open when they are ten to 14 days old, but it takes them another week to focus properly. The ear canals open at around 13 to 17 days.

For the first week of their life, puppies do virtually nothing but sleep and suckle. They become steadily more active and at three weeks old will be exploring their whelping box. But right up to the age of three months, puppies will alternate bursts of boisterous activity with periods of deep sleep.

KEEPING PUPPIES WARM

The outside world is cold compared with the constant 38.5° C (101.3° F) of the bitch's womb. The puppy arrives in the world wet and prone to chills. It may not show any signs for up to 48 hours, by which time a serious and possibly lethal infection may have established itself.

Until they are seven to ten days old puppies are unable to regulate their body temperature. You must therefore provide extra heat in the form of room heaters, hot-water bottles, heating pads, or infrared lamps for at least the first two weeks, even if the puppies are in the whelping box. You will need to keep them warm even longer than that if they are orphan, rejected, or hand-reared puppies.

The room temperature should be kept at around 30–33° C (86–91° F), although puppies can tolerate slight variations on this for short periods. Alternatively, you can keep the room temperature at a minimum of 20° C (68° F) and provide supplementary heat for the bitch's box. Every two weeks you can drop the room temperature by 3° C (5° F) until it returns to normal. Take care not to burn puppies with any supplementary heat source. Direct heat can damage their delicate skin.

SPECIMEN MENU FOR PUPPIES OF 6–12 WEEKS

BREAKFAST
Bowl of puppy meal, baby cereal, or breakfast cereal with milk.
LUNCH
Cooked mince, chopped tinned dog food, semi-moist complete food, or dry complete food.
TEA
As for lunch, plus one drop of human-type multivitamin syrup.
SUPPER
As for lunch, plus puppy meal or cereal with milk.

At 12 weeks old, drop either lunch or tea, but continue the multivitamin syrup. At six months old, feed twice a day.

MOTHERING SKILLS Bitches are very good mothers and cater to most of their litter's needs, but humans can help the growing puppies in a number of ways.

At 30 days the puppy begins to play with its littermates.

At six weeks the puppy has all its milk teeth and is ready for weaning.

Puppies should not be separated from mothers until they are eight weeks old.

HEALTHY OR SICK?

You can tell healthy puppies because they are warm and dry to the touch and their skin has an elastic quality. They wriggle when you pick them up and, though tiny, they have a muscular, spring-like feel. The sound of a healthy litter is a gentle murmuring, with enthusiastic squeaks at feeding time. Weak puppies are limp to the touch and their skin does not spring back into place when you pick up and release a fold. They crawl around restlessly, emitting thin, plaintive wails. Eventually they give up and lie passively in a corner – often well away from the mother. Their bodies are quick to chill. Watch also for puppies that are not getting enough milk, because a puppy that misses several feeds becomes too week to suckle. It will probably have to be removed from the litter and reared by hand. Ask your vet for advice on this and any other pup health problem you may encounter.

SOCIALIZATION Between six and 12 weeks old, puppies learn the social skills necessary for survival.

• Most breeds (but not all) should have the dewclaws at the "wrist" and the "ankle" removed by a vet at five to seven days old.
• Tail-docking should be done at the same time, but only if the breed standards demand it and you intend to show the dog. Docking is becoming less common in dogs kept as pets.
• At two to three weeks old it may be necessary to trim the puppies' claws to prevent them scratching the bitch's belly skin.
• Puppies begin teething at three to five weeks and should receive their first worming dose, as prescribed by the vet, at this stage. This should be repeated every two to three weeks up to 16 weeks old.
• As soon as puppies have teeth, they should be gradually introduced to solid foods such as puppy meal or cereal with milk. Do not rush changes to the diet.
• The first vaccination against serious dog diseases should be given at around six to eight weeks, with

a second dose two to four weeks later. Keep puppies away from other dogs and public places until two weeks after the first shot.
• At six weeks, puppies should begin the weaning process in earnest, and this should be completed by ten weeks old.
• In the fourth month the growth of the puppy's permanent teeth may give rise to "teething troubles" similar to those suffered by human babies.
• At six months old, give another dose of worming medicine, and repeat this at 12 months old.

KEEPING WARM These 18-day-old puppies are huddled together for warmth.

Raising and Fostering

In some cases, such as when a puppy is weak or a bitch does not have enough milk, you may have to consider artificial rearing. If the puppy or puppies are healthy and the problem lies in the milk supply, fostering on another lactating bitch is sometimes possible.

Artificial rearing of puppies is much more than simply buying a bottle and teats and making up some formula milk. You have certain other maternal functions to perform by proxy, although in some cases it is possible to return the babies to their mother between feeds. However, certain highly strung bitches will reject their puppies totally once a human takes over the feeding. Others will clean and nibble the puppies in such a frenzy, so keen are they to rid their offspring of your scent, that they may actually cause harm. But many bitches do seem to relish their human friends becoming involved in the nursing process and do not mind a bit not having to breast-feed.

Whatever the attitude of the bitch, it is important to handle puppies that are kept with their mothers as little as possible, and to do so after washing your hands with an unperfumed soap and then stroking the bitch with both hands so that her scent masks your own to some extent. Premature puppies and puppies of bitches that are at first reluctant to "let down" milk are best kept with their mother and only removed for feeding. Their presence will usually stimulate an increase in the milk flow.

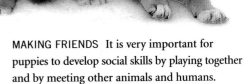

HAND-REARING With a little care, puppies raised apart from their mother can develop quite normally.

BOTTLE-FEEDING PUPPIES

If artificial feeding is indicated, do try to let the puppy have at least a few drops of the first milk (colostrum) from the bitch, if necessary by gently milking her teats. This milk provides the puppy with precious antibodies.

Get a special pet-feeding bottle or premature-baby bottle from a pet shop or the vet. Between feeds, clean and sterilize the bottle and teats in boiling water or disinfectant solution.

Feed newborn pups at two-hourly intervals at first and then three-hourly. The amount given depends on appetite. Hold the puppy gently but firmly around its chest and guide the teat into its

WEIGHT WATCH Check that the puppies are putting on weight by weighing them regularly.

MAKING FRIENDS It is very important for puppies to develop social skills by playing together and by meeting other animals and humans.

mouth. Let the legs move freely so that they can make their natural kneading or "paddling" action while feeding.

The food itself is made up in a similar fashion to that for a human baby, usually by adding warm water to one of the standard bitch milk powders. Follow the preparation instructions on the product label. If in doubt as to which brand to use for your puppies, ask your vet. Again, as with human babies, some pups thrive better on one brand than another. Make up a fresh supply of the artificial milk every day and keep it in the refrigerator. Feed it at blood heat, around 38° C (100° F).

An alternative method is to make up your own substitute milk using easily obtained ingredients. The formula is as follows:
• 800 ml (28 fl oz) whole milk
• 200 ml (7 fl oz) single cream
• 1 egg yolk
• 6 g (1 teaspoonful) sterilized bone flour

TOY TIME A good variety of toys helps the puppy develop its physical skills.

BOTTLE-FEEDING A PUPPY

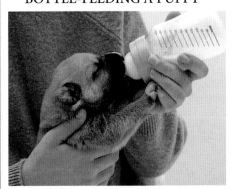

1 *Leave the feet free to make the natural "paddling" movements.*

2 *Rub the genitals with a warm, damp cloth to stimulate defecation.*

3 *After each feed, clean the puppy's fur with another damp cloth.*

- 4 g (1 teaspoonful) citric acid powder
- 2–3 baby (human) vitamin drops.

Weak puppies may need a lighter feed. For the first few feeds give them cow's milk, diluted with one third the volume of water and with 10 g (2½ teaspoonfuls) of glucose added per 500 ml (17 fl oz). In order to compensate partially for the missing colostrum, add two drops of a paediatric vitamin mixture per 500 ml (17 fl oz).

Heat the mixture to around 38° C (100° F) and feed at least every two hours. (Very weak puppies may take tiny amounts as often as half-hourly until they improve.)

A puppy that will not or cannot feed will quickly fade and die. Give it two hours to recover from the birth and meanwhile try to drip a little milk into its mouth. If this fails, consult the vet, who may start tube-feeding. Forcing milk into a puppy is dangerous – a few drops of milk going accidentally down the windpipe can cause a rapidly fatal pneumonia.

CLEANING UP

After each feed you must do what the natural mother would do by licking – clean the puppy. This has the additional function of stimulating normal bowel and bladder action. Clean the face with a warm, damp cloth and then use it gently to massage the tummy and anus. Afterwards apply a little petroleum jelly around the anus.

Sometimes artificial diets cause constipation. You can try to alleviate this by putting a drop of mineral oil into the feed or directly into the mouth, and also by lubricating the anus by means of a stubby-bulb thermometer dipped into petroleum jelly and gently introduced into the rectum – no more than 1 cm (½ in) deep.

If a puppy develops diarrhoea, try diluting the artificial feed to half-strength. Should diarrhoea persist for 24 hours, contact the vet.

MOTHERLY LOVE This maiden bitch was quite happy to provide warmth and cleaning and grooming services to these orphaned four-week-old fox cubs.

Official Breed List

The following are the names and groups of the Kennel Club of Great Britain's breed registry.

HOUND GROUP
Afghan Hound
Basenji
Basset Bleu de Gascogne
Basset Fauve de Bretagne
Basset Griffon Vendéen (Grand)
Basset Griffon Vendéen (Petit)
Basset Hound
Bavarian Mountain Hound
Beagle
Bloodhound
Borzoi
Dachshund (Longhaired)
Dachshund (Miniature Longhaired)
Dachshund (Smooth-haired)
Dachshund (Miniature Smooth-haired)
Dachshund (Wire-haired)
Dachshund (Miniature Wire-haired)
Deerhound
Norwegian Elkhound
Finnish Spitz
Foxhound
Grand Bleu de Gascogne
Greyhound
Hamiltonstovare
Ibizan Hound
Irish Wolfhound
Norwegian Lundehund
Otterhound
Pharaoh Hound
Rhodesian Ridgeback
Saluki
Segugio Italiano
Sloughi
Whippet

WORKING GROUP
Alaskan Malamute
Beauceron
Bernese Mountain Dog
Bouvier des Flandres
Boxer
Bull Mastiff
Canadian Eskimo Dog
Dobermann
Dogue de Bordeaux
German Pinscher
Greenland Dog
Giant Schnauzer
Great Dane
Hovawart
Leonberger
Mastiff
Neapolitan Mastiff
Newfoundland
Portuguese Water Dog
Rottweiler
Russian Black Terrier
St Bernard
Siberian Husky
Tibetan Mastiff

TERRIER GROUP
Airedale Terrier
Australian Terrier
Bedlington Terrier
Border Terrier
Bull Terrier
Bull Terrier (Miniature)
Cairn Terrier
Cesky Terrier
Dandie Dinmont Terrier
Fox Terrier (Smooth)
Fox Terrier (Wire)
Glen of Imaal Terrier
Irish Terrier
Kerry Blue Terrier
Lakeland Terrier
Manchester Terrier
Norfolk Terrier
Norwich Terrier
Parson Russell Terrier
Scottish Terrier
Sealyham Terrier
Skye Terrier
Soft-coated Wheaten Terrier
Staffordshire Bull Terrier
Welsh Terrier
West Highland White Terrier

GUNDOG GROUP
Bracco Italiano
Brittany
English Setter
German Longhaired Pointer
German Shorthaired Pointer
German Wire-haired Pointer
Gordon Setter
Hungarian Vizsla
Hungarian Wire-haired Vizsla
Irish Red-and-White Setter
Irish Setter
Italian Spinone
Kooikerhondje
Lagotto Romagnolo
Large Munsterlander
Nova Scotia Duck-Tolling Retriever
Pointer
Retriever (Chesapeake Bay)
Retriever (Curly Coated)
Retriever (Flat-coated)
Retriever (Golden)
Retriever (Labrador)
Spaniel (American Cocker)
Spaniel (Clumber)
Spaniel (Cocker)
Spaniel (English Springer)
Spaniel (Field)
Spaniel (Irish Water)
Spaniel (Sussex)
Spaniel (Welsh Springer)
Spanish Water Dog
Weimaraner

PASTORAL GROUP
Anatolian Shepherd Dog
Australian Cattle Dog
Australian Shepherd
Bearded Collie
Belgian Shepherd Dog (Groenendael)
Belgian Shepherd Dog (Malinois)
Belgian Shepherd Dog (Laekenois)
Belgian Shepherd Dog (Tervueren)
Bergamasco
Border Collie
Briard
Collie (Rough)
Collie (Smooth)
Estrela Mountain Dog
Finnish Lapphund
German Shepherd Dog (Alsatian)
Hungarian Kuvasz
Hungarian Puli
Komondor
Lancashire Heeler
Maremma Sheepdog
Norwegian Buhund
Old English Sheepdog
Polish Lowland Sheepdog
Pyrenean Mountain Dog
Pyrenean Sheepdog
Samoyed
Shetland Sheepdog
Swedish Lapphund
Swedish Vallhund
Welsh Corgi (Cardigan)
Welsh Corgi (Pembroke)

UTILITY GROUP
Akita
Boston Terrier
Bulldog
Canaan Dog
Chow Chow
Dalmatian
French Bulldog
German Spitz (Klein)
German Spitz (Mittel)
Japanese Shiba Inu
Japanese Spitz
Keeshond
Lhasa Apso
Mexican Hairless
Miniature Schnauzer
Poodle (Miniature)
Poodle (Standard)
Poodle (Toy)
Schipperke
Schnauzer
Shar Pei
Shih Tzu
Tibetan Spaniel
Tibetan Terrier

TOY GROUP
Affenpinscher
Australian Silky Terrier
Bichon Frise
Bolognese
Cavalier King Charles Spaniel
Chihuahua (Long-coat)
Chihuahua (Smooth-coat)
Chinese Crested
Coton de Tulear
English Toy Terrier (Black and Tan)
Griffon Bruxellois
Havanese
Italian Greyhound
Japanese Chin
King Charles Spaniel
Lowchen (Little Lion Dog)
Maltese
Miniature Pinscher
Papillon
Pekingese
Pomeranian
Pug
Yorkshire Terrier

Index

Acknowledgments

Author's acknowledgments

Many, many thanks are due to my editors at Dorling Kindersley – Deirdre Headon and Simon Tuite – and to the rest of the staff at DK who have been working on this revised edition. Also to my researchers and typists – Christine, Liz, Nicola, and Penny – and my colleagues in the International Zoo Veterinary Group, to my sister-in-law Niki Levy, and my family, who, one and all, have doggedly given me support and invaluable assistance.

Publisher's acknowledgments

Dorling Kindersley would like to thank: Nick Harris for support and guidance; Jillian Somerscales and Jane Mason for editorial assistance; Sandra Schneider and Lester Cheeseman for design help; Margaret Little for typing the manuscript; Ella Skene for the index, Anne Lyons for picture research; Debbie Harris for printing and initializing the disks; those dedicated dog handlers, Karen Tanner, John Fisher, and Vivienne Braddon; Gerry and Cathy of Intellectual Animals; Hazel Taylor for handling, rearing, and helping the puppies to happen; and Teresa E Slowick, of the Kennel Club of Great Britain, for all her expert advice.

Packager's acknowledgments

Sands Publishing Solutions would like to thank: Hilary Bird for revising the index; David Roberts at DK Cartography for sourcing the map on pp.8–9.

Picture credits

The publisher would like to thank the following for their kind permission to reproduce their photographs:
(Abbreviations key: t=top, b=bottom, r=right, l=left, c=centre)

2: Corbis/Lawrence Manning. 4: Getty Images/Johnny Johnson. 6: Corbis. 8: anticlockwise round map: Bernard Gerard/Hutchison Library; Syndication International; Stephen J Krasemann/Bruce Coleman. 9: clockwise round map: Henry Ausloos/NHPA; Stephen J Krasemann/NHPA; Jen & Des Bartlett/Bruce Coleman; Steve Krongard/Image Bank/Getty Images. 10: JP Ferrero/Ardea (bl), Jane Burton (t); Zefa (br). 11: Jane Burton (t); Getty Images/Peter M Miller/Image Bank (bl); Norbert Rosing/Bruce Coleman (br). 14: Jane Burton. 15: Jane Burton (t); Animals Unlimited/Paddy Cutts (br); Getty Images/Sobel/Klonsky/Image Bank (bl). 16: Corbis (tl),/Dale C Spartas (br), Paul A Souders (tr); Getty Images/GK & Vikki Hart/The Image Bank (bl). 17: Corbis/Robert Dowling (br), Yann Arthus-Bertrand (tr), (bl); Getty Images/Gary Randall/Taxi (tl). 18: Corbis/Daniel Aubry (c). 19: Corbis/Mike King (tr), Yann Arthus-Bertrand (cr). 30: DK Picture Library/Tracy Morgan (c), (b). 31: DK Picture Library/Tracy Morgan (c), (l), (t). 36: Animal Photography/Sally Ann Thompson (t). 40: DK Picture Library/Tracy Morgan (b). 41: DK Picture Library/Tracy Morgan (tr), (cr). 42: OSF/Animals Animals/Robert Piercy (tr). 54: Corbis/Dale C Spartas (c). 55: Corbis/Dale C Spartas (tr), (cr.). 56: Animal Photography/Sally Ann Thompson. 57: Animal Photography/Sally Ann Thompson (b). 58: Animal Photography/Cabon/Vloo (bl). 59: Animal Photography (b). 61: Animal Photography/Sally Ann Thompson (br). 62: Animal Photography/ R Wilbie (bl). 63: Animal Photography/Sally Ann Thompson (cr). 64: Animal Photography/R Wilbie (bl). 65: Animals Unlimited/Paddy Cutts (br). 66: Animal Photography/Sally Ann Thompson (l). 67: Animals Unlimited/Paddy Cutts (tl). 68: Corbis/Robert Dowling (bl). 70: DK Picture Library/Tracy Morgan (c), (bl). 71: DK Picture Library/Tracy Morgan (tc), (tr). 72: DK Picture Library/Tracy Morgan (bl) Warren Photographic/Jane Burton (t). 73: Warren Photographic/Jane Burton (b), (l). 74: DK Picture Library/Tracy Morgan (c), (b). 75: DK Picture Library/Tracy Morgan (cr), (br). 77: DK Picture Library/Tracy Morgan (tl), (tr), (c). 80: DK Picture Library: (bl). 82: Corbis/Philip James Cowren. 83: Corbis (tr); Robert Dowling (cr). 86: DK Picture Library/(bl), Tracy Morgan (c). 87: DK Picture Library: Jerry Young (tr), Tracy Morgan (tl). 93: Animal Photography/Sally Ann Thompson (tl), (br). 96: Animal Photography/Sally Ann Thompson (b). 98: Animal Photography/Sally Ann Thompson (b). 106: Animal Photography/Sally Ann Thompson (bl). 114: Corbis/Robert Dowling. 115: Ardea London Ltd/John Daniels (tr); Corbis/Renee Lynn (cr). 121: animal Photography/R Wilbie (br). 127: Zefa (tr). 130: Animal Photography/Sally Ann Thompson (tr). 134: Zefa/DJ Fisher (c). 135: Bruce Coleman/Hans Reinhard (tl). 140: Corbis/Larry Williams. 141: Corbis/Robert Dowling (tr,) (cr). 146: Animal Photography/Sally Ann Thompson (b). 147: (br). 149: NHPA/Gerard Lasz (cr). 152: Animal Photography/Sally Ann Thompson (c). 154: NHPA/Gerard Lasz (c). 156: DK Picture Library/Tracy Morgan, (b), 159: Animal Photography/Sally Ann Thompson (cr). 163: Animal Photography/Sally Ann Thompson (cr). 168: Corbis/Martin Harvey; Gallo Images. 169: Corbis/Charles Philip (cr); Peter Steiner (tr). 172: Animal Photography/Sally Ann Thompson (c). 173: Zefa/M Schneider (t). 174: Animal Photography/Sally Ann Thompson (bl) . 175: Animal Photography/Sally Ann Thompson (cr). 177: Ardea/J Ferrero (cr). 179: Corbis/John Howard (tr) NHPA/Yves Lanceau (cr). 190: Corbis/Robert Dowling. 191: Corbis/Robert Dowling (tr), Yann Arthus-Bertrand (cr). 195: Animal Photography/Sally Ann Thompson (br). 196: Animal Photography/Sally Ann Thompson (bl). 203: Bruce Coleman/Hans Reinhard (cr). 217: Animals Unlimited (c); Ardea London Ltd/Johan de Meester (bc), (br); RSPCA/Angela Hampton (tc); Warren Photographic/Jane Burton (tr). 218: Corbis/Tom Stewart. 220: Stephen Oliver all except (t). 221: Stephen Oliver. 222: Jane Burton except (t). 223: Jane Burton. 224: DK Picture Library/Tracy Morgan (c); Stephen Oliver (b). 225: Stephen Oliver (c). 226: DK Picture Library (tr), (cl). 227: Corbis/Tom Stewart (tl). 228: Stephen Oliver (tr). 229: Stephen Oliver (tl). 230: Stephen Oliver (bl). 231: Jan Baldwin (t). 232: Warren Photographic/Jane Burton (t). 233: Warren Photographic/Jane Burton (t). 234: DK Picture Library/Tim Ridley (tl). 235: DK Picture Library/Tracy Morgan (br). 236: Animal Photography/Sally Ann Thompson (cr); Animals Unlimted (cl). Getty Images/L Fried/Image Bank (bl). 237: Animals Unlimited/Paddy Cutts (t). 245: Stephen Oliver (b). 246: DK Picture Library (bl), (br). 247: DK Picture Library (bl), (br), (t). 248: Corbis/Jim Zuckerman.

All other images © Dorling Kindersley.
For further information see: www.dkimages.com

Studio Dogs

pp.20–21
Afghan Hound
Amudarya Shafi
owned by Linda Llewelyn

pp.22–3
Basenjis
Zizunga Beguiling Whim
Zizunga Satin Doll
owned by Mrs Irene Terry

pp.24–5
Grand Basset Griffon Vendéen
Ambassador at Dehra
owned by Mr Frost
Spinone
Kevardhu Fyn
owned by Mrs Andrea Bullock

pp.26–7
Basset Hound
Kentley Blind Date
owned by Mrs Humphries

pp.28–9
Beagle
Rivenlea Gangster
owned by Angela Haddy

pp.33–3
Bloodhounds
Nineveh's Miracle of Brighton
owned by Mrs Ickeringill

Nineveh's Mimosa of Chasedown
owned by Mr and Mrs D Richards

pp.34–5
Borzoi
Vronsky Zapata
owned by Rosemarie Downes

pp.36–7
Smooth-haired Dachshunds
Yatesbury Big Bang
Yatesbury Evening Star
owned by Mrs Pam Sydney
Miniature Longhaired Dachshunds
Southcliff Starsky
Starsky of Springbok
owned by Mr Alan Sharman

pp.38–9
Elkhounds
Llychlyn Morgan
Kestos Adheryn
owned by Mr R Lee

pp.42–3
Foxhounds
The Berks and Bucks Draghounds

pp.44–5
Greyhound
Singing the Blues of Solstrand
owned by Mrs Dagmar Kenis
Segugio Italiano
Ira's Girl of Chahala
owned by Jenny Startup

Italian Greyhound
Philtre Foulla
owned by Mrs Carter

pp.46–7
Irish Wolfhounds
Finneagle Frederick
Finneagle Forever True
owned by Alexandra Bennett

pp.48–9
Rhodesian Ridgebacks
Bruet the Gentleman
Bruet the Countryman
owned by Peter and Cilla Edwards

pp.50–51
Salukis
Al Caliphs Damn Flight
Al Caliphs Joel
owned by Mr Tom Fryer

pp.52–3
Whippets
Hammonds Sebastian
Norwell Barley at Hammonds
owned by Angela Randall

pp.56–7
German Shorthaired Pointer
Jennaline Kentish Krumpet
owned by Jenny Jennings

pp.58–9
Bracco Italiano

Lory
owned by Jonathan and Liz Shaw

pp.60–61
Golden Retrievers
Melfricka Wassailer of Saintcloud
Alphinbrook Lodestar of Saintcloud
Sequantus Valkyr of Saintcloud
owned by Shirley Skinner

pp.62–3
Labrador Retriever
Donacre High Climber
owned by Mr, Mrs, and Ms Heyward

pp.64–5
Irish Setter
Caskeys Jezamy owned by Mrs Heron

pp.66–7
Cocker Spaniels
Donlawn Partners Choice of Bidston
Misty of Bidston
owned by Mrs Hillary Bidston

pp.68–9
American Cocker Spaniel
Ashweald Shoo Shoo Baby
owned by Carol Jarvis

pp.78–9
Hungarian Vizslas
Russet Mantle Quiver
Russet Mantle October
owned by G Gottlieb

pp.80–81
Weimaraner
Wilhelm Maximillian
owned by Ms B von Dwingezo-Luïten

pp.84–5
Airedale Terrier
Bradus Quicksilver
owned by Mrs Wild
Welsh Terrier
Kadabra Go To Work Onan Ogg
owned by Mrs Edge

pp.88–9
Bedlington Terrier
Dalip Limited Edition
owned by Mr Kitchen

pp.90–91
Border Terriers
Moonline Dedication
Thoraldby Tolomeo
Halstow First Lady
owned by Mrs Moonie

pp.92–3
Bull Terrier
Kerby's Tipple
owned by Mrs Youatt

pp.94–5
Cairn Terrier
Deneland Super Trooper
owned by Mrs Towers

pp.96–7
Dandie Dinmont Terrier
Josal Jester of Margham
owned by Margaret Hamilton

pp.98–9
Wire Fox Terrier
Flyntwyre Flyntlock
owned by Hazel Bradford

pp.100–1
Jack Russell Terriers
Ryemill Fudge
Ryemill Mighty Mouse
owned by Mrs Edge

pp.102–3
Kerry Blue Terrier
Deedilly Didilly Dee of Downsview
owned by Mrs Campbell

pp.104–5
Manchester Terriers
Plutarch the Wise of Tyburn
L de Lavis-Trafford
owned by Mr Crawley

pp.106–7
Norwich Terrier
Elve the Sorcerer
owned by Michael Crawley

pp.108–9
Sealyham Terrier
Stephelcher Snow Wizard
owned by Mr Stephen Woodcock and
   Mr Richard Belcher

pp.110–11
Soft-coated Wheaten Terrier
Berkley Brockbuster
owned by Lesley and Neil Smith

pp.112–13
West Highland White Terrier
Cedarfell Movie Star
owned by Karen Tanner
Scottish Terriers
Anniversary of Kennelgarth
Cherry Brandy of Clemegarn
owned by Mrs Hills

pp.116–17
Japanese Akita
Overhills Cherokee Lite Fut
owned by Meg Purnell-Carpenter

pp.118–19
Boston Terrier
Chilka Kirsty
owned by Mr and Mrs Barker

pp.120–21
Bulldog
Mipoochi Delilah
owned by Mrs Leah Edwards

pp.122–3
Chow Chow
Benchow the Chinaman
owned by Mrs M Bennett

pp.124–5
Dalmatian
Elaridge Endeavour
owned by Mrs Stokes

pp.126–7
Keeshond
Neradmik Jupiter
owned by Mrs Sharp-Bale

pp.128–9
Lhasa Apsos
Chobrang Misha
Chobrang Le-Shi
owned by Irene Chamberlain

pp.130–31
Toy Poodle
Philora Silver Warlord
owned by Sandra Martin
Miniature Poodle
Glayuar Galactica
owned by June Clark

pp.132–3
Schipperke
Keyna's Artful Rogue
owned by Ms C Hart

pp.134–5
Miniature Schnauzer
Courtaud Carefree Casey
owned by Mr and Mrs S Court

pp.136–7
Shar Pei
Bao Shou-Shi of Jentiki
owned by Jenny Baker

pp.138–9
Shih Tzu
Magique Magpie of Chelhama
owned by Mrs Goodwin

pp.142–3
Alaskan Malamute
Highnoons Nansamund
owned by Mr and Mrs Croly

pp.144–5
Bernese Mountain Dog
Sir Stanley from Meadowpark
owned by G and B Rayson

pp.146–7
Bouvier des Flandres
Mr Bo Jangles at Aiulys
owned by Sue Garner

pp.148–9
Boxer
Bitza Shout and Roar
owned by Mr and Mrs A Varney

pp.150–51
Bullmastiffs
Dajean Loganberry
Dajean Rocky Won
owned by Ms S Wood

pp.152–3
Dobermann
Sallate's Ferris
owned by Mr and Mrs Bevan

pp.154–5
Great Dane

Daneton Kiri of Maricol
owned by Colin and Marie Stevens

pp.158–9
Mastiffs
Tresylyan Bitter Sweet
Brookview Lucy Lastic of Tresylyan
owned by Mr and Mrs K Taylor
Neapolitan Mastiff
Kwintra Imra
owned by Mr John Turner and Dr Jean Clark

pp.160–1
Newfoundland
Seebar von Drachenfels of Yaffles
owned by Rosemary Miller

pp.162–3
Rottweiler
Potterspride Pure 'n' Free
owned by Violet Slade

pp.164–5
St Bernard
Groveacre Sophie's Choice
owned by Mr and Mrs Garey

pp.166–7
Siberian Huskies
Leejo's Tumak Musinka
Snowolf's Brecon
owned by Mr Ray Ball

pp.170–71
Australian Cattle Dogs
Formakin Kulta
Formakin Minky
owned by Mr John Holmes

pp.172–3
Belgian Shepherd Dogs
Heritiere du Pays des Flandres of Questenberg
Questenberg Oklahoma Kid
owned by Karen Watson

pp.174–5
Bearded Collie
Desborough Dulcinea of Snowmead
owned by Mrs Waldren

pp.176–7
Rough Collie
Leighvale Oliver Twist
owned by Les and Viv Norris

pp.178–9
German Shepherd Dogs
Charvorne Dielander
Charvorne Lolita
owned by Mr and Mrs P Charteris

pp.180–81
Old English Sheepdog
Kalaju Resident Rascal
owned by June Wilkinson

pp.182–3
Pyrenean Mountain Dog
Clarance Brynhafod Barkin-Side
owned by Mr and Mrs S Clark

pp.184–5
Samoyeds
Krishe Khloe of Nikara
Nikara Special Edition
owned by Mrs Val Freer

pp.186–7
Shetland Sheepdogs
Willow Tarn Telstar
Willow Tarn Trueman
Willow Tarn Tokaji
Trinket of Willow Tarn
owned by Mrs Rosalind Crossley

pp.188–9
Pembroke Welsh Corgi
Kaytop Dice of Rossacre
Cardigan Welsh Corgi
Deavitte Blue Fox of Rossacre
owned by Mrs Alli Boughton

pp.192–3
Bichon Frise
Kynismar Heaven Sent
owned by Mrs Myra Atkins

pp.194–5
Long-coated Chihuahua
Natimuk Wilf
owned by Dr Geoffrey Curr

pp.196–7
King Charles Spaniels
Simannie Corny's Pride and Joy
owned by Barry and Sheila Byers
Grenajay Julie's Boy of Curtana
owned by Mrs Julia Huggins

pp.198–9
Japanese Chins
Sangria Eclipse
Sangria Imperial Dragon
owned by Mr Bryan Bond and
   Mr George Farmer

pp.200–1
Maltese
Caramalta Sweet Melody of Ellwin
owned by M Lewin

pp.202–3
Miniature Pinscher
Tygorsaf Tendertrap for Torilea
owned by Mrs P Powers

pp.204–5
Papillons
Ju John, Miss Ash at Ringlands
Ringlands Stella Star
owned by Mrs Norula

pp.206–7
Pekingese
Chophoy Have a Nice Day
Chophoy Pittsburgh Stealer
owned by Mrs S Stag

pp.208–9
Pomeranian
Taurusdale Intan Merah
owned by Mr Kee

pp.210–11
Pugs
Puggleberry Pippa
Puggleberry Pingpong
owned by Mr and Mrs Hicks

pp.212–13
Australian Silky Terrier
Marshdae Tumberlong
owned by Ms Anne Marshall

pp.214–15
Yorkshire Terrier
Bananas du Domaine de Monderlay at Gaysteps
owned by Mrs Anne Fisher

pp.216–17
Mongrels
Nipper
owned by Mrs Westrope
Barney
owned by Mrs Burke
Tizzy
owned by Mrs Gardener